I Would Like to Travel the World

Guy Gaucher

I Would Like to Travel the World

Thérèse of Lisieux: Miracle-Worker, Doctor, and Missionary

Translated by James Henri McMurtrie

SOPHIA INSTITUTE PRESS
Manchester, New Hampshire

Original edition: *"Je voudrais parcourir la terre . . ." Therese de Lisieux thaumaturge, docteur et missionnaire* (Paris: Éditions du Cerf, 2003).

Cover design by Updatefordesign Studio.

Cover photo of St. Thérèse at age fifteen courtesy of the Archives of the Carmel of Lisieux.

Sophia Institute Press
Box 5284, Manchester, NH 03108
1-800-888-9344
www.SophiaInstitute.com

paperback ISBN 978-1-64413-848-9

ebook ISBN 978-1-64413-849-6

Library of Congress Control Number: 2023934574

First printing

Saints hardly ever age. They never get stuck in time. They continue to be witnesses of the Church's youth. They never become people of the past — men and women of "yesterday." On the contrary, they are always men and women of the "future" — men and women of the evangelical future of man and the Church — witnesses "of the future world."

— St. John Paul II, Lisieux, June 2, 1980

The narrow slit of a loophole is enough to witness the sun across the thickest wall of the darkest dungeon. Thus, the furtive encounter of a saint in this world that is now deaf and opaque is enough to bear witness to God.

— Fr. Henri de Lubac

Finally, what did St. Thérèse of Lisieux of the Child Jesus do? *Nothing!* Nothing, except for the most mundane and insignificant things. But she was a real and total presence — a presence that was so radically given to Jesus Christ that she became a presence to the whole world.

— Maurice Zundel

Contents

Thanks

Thanks . . .

To the team that worked on the critical edition of the texts and words of St. Thérèse of Lisieux (*Nouvelle Édition du Centenaire*) for more than twenty years:

- Sr. Cécile of the Immaculata, from the Carmel of Lisieux
- Sr. Geneviève, a Dominican from Clairefontaine (d. May 10, 1980)
- Jeannette and Jacques Lonchampt
- Fr. Bernard Bro, a Dominican, who was the director of Editions du Cerf at that time

For Thérèse's becoming a Doctor of the Church:

- in memory of Fr. Gustave Desbuquois (1869–1959), a Jesuit who was the editor of *L'Action Populaire* and was the first to work toward Thérèse's being proclaimed a Doctor of the Church
- to all those who worked for that proclamation in various ways, only one hundred years after Thérèse's death

For the relics' world trips:

- to Fr. Raymond Zambelli, rector of Lisieux's pilgrimage from 1992 to 2001, who generated these travels
- to Sr. Cassien, from the Congregation of the Immaculate Heart of Mary
- to Fr. Bachir
- to Sr. Monique-Marie of the Holy Face from the Community of the Beatitudes, who have been particularly active in Lisieux for these trips in the five continents

To the thousands of volunteers who worked in twenty-seven countries to receive the relics, and especially:

- to Fr. Conrad de Meester, O.C.D., for Belgium
- to Fr. Giuseppe Scarpellini, for Italy
- to Cardinal Lucas Moreira Neves (d. 2002), for Brazil
- to Fr. Timmermans, from the Emmanuel Community, for the Netherlands
- to Srs. Tamara and Christelle, from the Community of the Beatitudes, for Russia and Kazakhstan
- to Msgr. Patrick Ahern, retired auxiliary bishop of New York
- to Fr. Donald Kinney, O.C.D.
- to Alexandra Plettenberg-Serban and Frances Renda, for the United States
- to Msgr. Ramon Arguëlles, for the Philippines, Taiwan, and Hong Kong
- to Fr. J. Linus Ryan, O.C., for Ireland
- to Messrs. Jacques Gauthier, Gérald Baril, and Jacques Binet, for Canada
- to Honoré and Maeva Reid, for French Polynesia
- to the Mariamite fathers and the Carmelites, for Libya
- to Msgr. Jean Sleiman, the Latin archbishop of Baghdad, for Iraq

But above all, to the Carmelites in Lisieux, who opened their archives to allow for the Centenary Edition and who lent their sister's relics to the entire world.

And finally, thanks to a secret and fervent communion with the millions of friends of Thérèse who came to pray to her to understand Jesus' merciful love better.

"Everything is a grace."[1]

[1] June 5, 4 in *St. Thérèse of Lisieux: Her Last Conversations,* ed. John Clarke (Washington, D.C.: ICS Publications, 1977), 57.

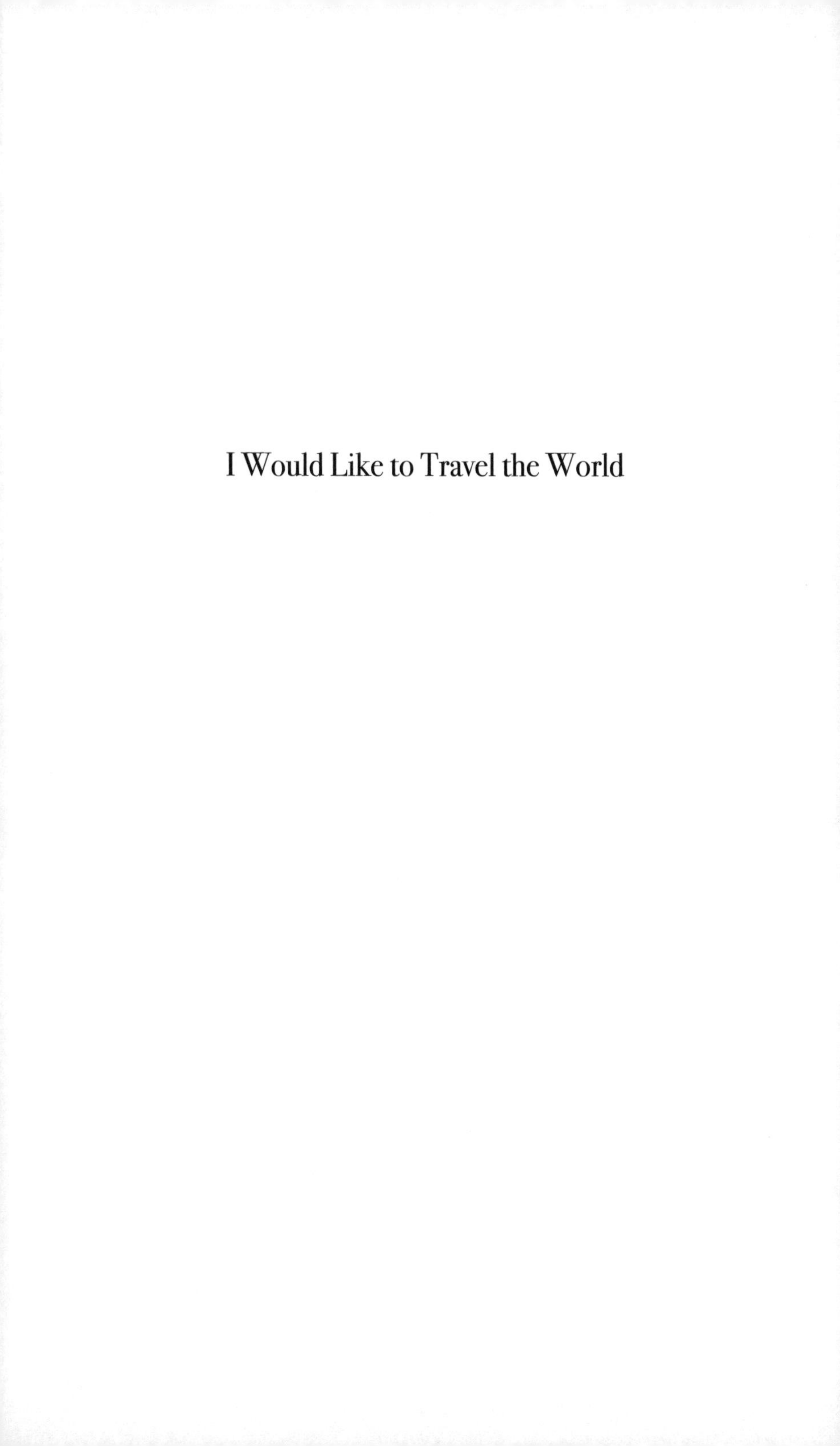

I Would Like to Travel the World

Introduction

It was the friendly pressure of an editor I worked with for more than thirty years that urged me to write this book — as it was for *La Passion de Thérèse de Lisieux* (*The Passion of Thérèse of Lisieux*) (1972), *Histoire d'une vie* (*The Story of a Life*) (1982), *Jean et Thérèse* (*John and Thérèse*) (1996), and *"L'Histoire d'une âme"* (*Story of a Soul*) by Thérèse of Lisieux (2000).

This time, I didn't resist much, for it seemed to me that I had to witness what I had seen and experienced for fifteen years as the auxiliary bishop of Bayeux and Lisieux. All that had only one ultimate purpose: to praise the mercies of the Lord that came through the intervention of a young woman. Her brief life was like a shooting star that streaked across the dark night of the nineteenth century with a lasting illumination that was written in Heaven.[2] She started "to run as a giant"[3] on December 25, 1886, and her life culminated in the universal glory of her canonization in 1925. God "made me understand that my own

[2] St. Thérèse of Lisieux, Manuscript A, 18r, in *Story of a Soul: The Autobiography of Thérèse of Lisieux*, trans. John Clarke (Washington, D.C.: ICS Publications, 1977), 43.

[3] Manuscript A, 44v, in *Story of a Soul*, 97.

glory would not be evident to the eyes of mortals, that it would consist in becoming a great *saint*."[4]

I'm writing these lines in my office, while a fiery sun, which isn't so common in Normandy, is making the landscape vibrate. Through the window on the right, I see a wall of the Carmel of Lisieux and two magnificent cedars. About a dozen yards from there, that life of twenty-four years and four months ended on September 30, 1897, around seven o'clock in the evening. This occurred after nine years that St. Thérèse spent on this acre that is surrounded by high walls made out of red bricks.

The basilica stands out against the blue sky through the window on the left. Within this space between the Carmel and the basilica, no more than a kilometer, emerged in a hidden silence a spiritual destiny that influenced five continents.

My gaze can go from one to the other — from the Carmel to the basilica — and sum up what this existence was:

> One weak spark, O mystery of life,
> is enough to light a huge fire.
> That I want, O my God,
> To carry your Fire far and wide,
> Remember.[5]

Through these pages, I hope to bear witness to Thérèse's story as an auxiliary bishop. I received a missionary letter of February 18, 1989, from the bishop of Bayeux and Lisieux, Msgr. Pierre Pican, successor to Msgr. Jean Badré (d. September 17, 2001), asking me to "promote St. Thérèse of the Child Jesus' spiritual mission."[6]

4 Manuscript A, 32r, in *Story of a Soul,* 72.

5 St. Thérèse of Lisieux, Poem 24:17.

6 "Church of Bayeux," *Semaine religieuse,* March 12, 1989, 139–140.

For me, everything had started by chance when my provincial, Fr. Bernard Delalande, had asked me in 1969 if I would agree to work "a little" on the edition that he was preparing of St. Thérèse's *Last Conversations*. Since the death in 1961 of Fr. François de Sainte-Marie, the editor of the *Autobiographical Manuscripts* (1956), Fr. Bernard led the team that worked on this project. By naively and joyfully accepting this proposition, I didn't know that I was getting involved in an adventure that would end in 1992 with the publication of the *Nouvelle Édition du Centenaire* in eight volumes — that is to say, 6,200 pages. It was the fruit of the work of a persevering team that defied winds and floods.[7]

These daily visits with Thérèse's texts (manuscripts, correspondence, poetry, plays, and prayers) and the testimonies in the processes and elsewhere prepared me for many years, without my knowing it, for pastoral encounters with thousands of pilgrims in Lisieux and with friends of Thérèse throughout the world from all backgrounds, languages, and cultures. Thérèse is a universal sister who crosses all geographical, psychological, and religious boundaries.

These pages are the fruit of a duty to bear witness but are also the echo of a thanksgiving and an untiring amazement. Once we have overcome any obstacles that have prevented us, and might still prevent us, from reading Thérèse's writing ("It doesn't suit me," "it's a mushy style," "the nineteenth century repels me," etc.), we will never read a fragment of a manuscript, letter, or poem without finding something new in it — the inexhaustible Thérèse! Likewise, we don't tire of hearing the testimony of a pilgrim about a conversion, a healing, or an indestructible friendship with the young Carmelite. I heard this so many times in Lisieux, New York, Manila, Rimini, and Irkutsk: "Thérèse is my sister. She is part of my life."

7 Paris, Éditions du Cerf — DDB, 1992.

In 1938, Cardinal Pacelli, before becoming Pius XII, said that Thérèse was "the most famous miracle-worker of modern times."[8] Therefore, we must not be astonished that she has friends everywhere.

There was another, more precise paragraph in my mission statement that was much more difficult and restrictive: "It will be up to you to take over the case of St. Thérèse's becoming a Doctor of the Church, which was opened in the 1930s."

Thérèse, a Doctor of the Church? This was a goal that I had no doubt would be attained one day, but in 1989, it seemed to me to be very far away. I wondered, above all, how to go about it. The second part of this book will talk about how, eight years later, on October 19, 1997, on World Mission Sunday, Pope John Paul II proclaimed St. Thérèse of Lisieux a Doctor of the Church in St. Peter's Square, in the presence of her relics, in front of sixty thousand pilgrims.

Sometimes, after returning from meetings with the Congregation for the Causes of Saints — following the example of Fr. Gustave Desbuquois[9] — I told myself that I wouldn't see Thérèse proclaimed a Doctor. No matter, I told myself; she'll be a Doctor someday. That's all that counted.

Beyond all the good reasons for its achievement (and, as we will see, there were a lot of them), I became certain about it because of Thérèse's famous text from September 1896: "I feel called to be ... a Doctor.... Ah! In spite of my littleness, I would like to enlighten souls as did the Prophets and Doctors."[10] I rationalized in this way: since the Lord had always fulfilled Thérèse's desires,[11] He could only respond to

[8] Speech to the French Seminary in Rome, March 23, 1938, in *Vie thérésienne*, no. 93 (January 1984): 31.

[9] We will get back to this Jesuit priest, who was the first to ask Pius XI to have Thérèse proclaimed a Doctor, in 1932.

[10] Manuscript B, 2v-3r, in *Story of a Soul*, 192.

[11] She had always found compelling this text in St. John of the Cross: "The more You want to give, the more You make people want."

this one — to be a Doctor — as well. She wanted it, so she formulated it. She would be one.

In the same way, her desire had been fulfilled beyond all expectations. For God granted it very abundantly — via Pius XI's proclamation on December 14, 1927, when he made her the Patroness of the Missions.

What we don't get tired of admiring is the way the Lord fulfilled this child — a mature and strong woman — beyond all her desires. Thérèse always kept her promises. She continues to and will continue to keep them.

The third part of this book responds to Thérèse's missionary desire, which was already clearly formulated in this September 1896 text:

> I have the vocation of the Apostle. I would like to travel over the whole earth to preach Your Name and to plant Your glorious Cross on infidel soil. But O my Beloved, one mission alone would not be sufficient for me. I would want to preach the Gospel on all the five continents simultaneously and even to the most remote isles. I would be a missionary, not for a few years only but from the beginning of creation until the consummation of the ages.[12]

This desire would evolve even faster when her death was about to occur. Thérèse was only twenty-four years old. "The greatest desire of all — the desire to continue to do good after her death — to spend her heaven doing good on earth until the end of the world."[13]

[12] Manuscript B, 3r, in *Story of a* Soul, 192–193.

[13] St. Thérèse of Lisieux, *Yellow Notebook,* July 17, 102. See Conrad de Meester, "Thérèse de Lisieux et son désir de 'faire du bien' après sa mort" [Thérèse of Lisieux and her desire to "do good" after her death], *Teresianum* 49 (1998): 3–50.

This wish to go into the world to evangelize — indissolubly *loving Jesus and making Him loved*[14] — was first realized in France from 1945 to 1947, after the end of the Second World War. Thérèse's reliquary had traveled across France. It went from Paris to the smallest villages.[15] But who would suspect that fifty years later, Thérèse would leave her Carmel again — to tour the world this time?

In fact, since 1994, Thérèse's travels have not ceased and have taken her, while I'm writing, to the twenty-seventh country she has visited — Mauritius Island — before reaching Italy again and then traveling to Malta, Spain, and Benin. Has there been a saint in two thousand years of Christianity who has undertaken such a trip to five continents, attracted millions of people, provoked a spontaneous evangelization, and brought out, in front of astonished pastors, crowds of people — many of whom usually don't bother with churches?

The third part of this work is necessarily in progress since this unique phenomenon is continuing. Nobody knows when it will end. It's still too early to draw any general conclusions from it. But already, after nine years, we can stress some features and ask questions about what is called the "popular devotion."

This three-part division corresponds to the stages of Thérèse's posthumous life, in which I seem to see three phases. Each one doesn't annul the preceding one but integrates it and surpasses it to raise it to a higher level.

[14] Letter 96 to Céline and Letter 114 to Sr. Agnes of Jesus, in *Letters of St. Thérèse of Lisieux*, vol. 1, *1877–1890*, trans. John Clarke (Washington, D.C.: ICS Publications, 1982), 587, 662. Letter 201 to Fr. Roulland in *Letters of St. Thérèse of Lisieux*, vol. 2, *1890–1897*, trans. John Clarke (Washington, D.C.: ICS Publications, 1988), 1013.

[15] On May 3, 1944, Pius XIII had proclaimed St. Thérèse France's secondary patroness. The number of those who gathered around her relics in Paris (February 27–March 8, 1945) reached a million people.

The first period seems to me to cover the years from 1898 — when *Story of a Soul* appeared — to 1925, the date of the triumphal canonization of St. Thérèse of the Child Jesus and the Holy Face by Pope Pius XI in Rome. These are the years that go from the discovery of the young Carmelite in Lisieux to the worldwide "storm of glory" that was essentially motivated by this "shower of roses" (miracles of all sorts) that has been falling on the five continents.

Barely thirteen years after her obscure death in a small unknown Carmel, the Church opened an informational process in anticipation of her beatification. *Story of a Soul* was translated into many languages.[16] Thérèse jostled the habits of Roman congregations. Popes Pius X, Benedict XV, and Pius XI favored having the process held, and finished in 1917, despite the difficulties of the First World War.

On April 29, 1923, Pius XI beatified Sr. Thérèse, and barely two years after that, he canonized her in Rome on May 17, 1925, with five hundred thousand people in attendance. This was an exceptional event. The devotion to "the world's cherished child," as Pope Pius XI called her, spread like a landslide. The "little miracle-working saint" had conquered the world.

From 1925 to 1997, a second period opened on another aspect of her personality and holiness. Devotion to St. Thérèse certainly continued and was becoming unified. Pilgrimages to Lisieux were organized under the determined and prophetic impetus of Msgr. Germain, the first rector of the Basilica of St. Thérèse of Lisieux.[17] Chapels, churches,

[16] I have listed fifty-four — a number that isn't exhaustive — in *L'Histoire d'une âme de Thérèse de Lisieux* [*Saint Thérèse of Lisieux: Story of a Life*] (Paris: Éditions du Cerf, 2000), 171.

[17] See François Delteil, *Mgr. Germain, l'homme providential d'une grande cause* [Msgr. Germain, the providential man of a great cause], Ed. des Annales de Lisieux, 1967.

basilicas, and cathedrals that were dedicated to St. Thérèse of Lisieux would emerge on the five continents.[18]

The editions of *Story of a Soul* increased, and the translations continued in different languages and dialects.[19]

But, as of 1925, a new way of approaching Thérèse appeared. People gradually discovered that she had a message for the Church and the world. Of course, the popes had emphasized this aspect of the saint's writings in their documents for her beatification and canonization. Pius XI, in particular, had declared her to be a "Word of God for the world."[20]

They had highlighted the fruitfulness of her "little doctrine" of "confidence and love."

The first book of theology that was dedicated to St. Thérèse appeared in 1925. It was the work of a Dominican — Fr. Hyacinthe Petitot (1880–1934).[21] He showed the strength and solidity of what the young Carmelite said and did. He didn't hesitate to compare her thinking to St. Thomas Aquinas's train of thought. Many other theologians and spiritual leaders followed him — Fr. Marie-Eugène of the Child Jesus, Fr. Philipon, Fr. Réginald Garrigou-Lagrange, Fr. André Combes, Hans Urs von Balthasar, and others.

Theresian literature would rapidly expand, for better or for worse. The religious iconography of her time didn't serve her and even did her a disservice as it transformed her — deformed her — into a pious, mushy, syrupy nun.

[18] There were about 2,000 of them until 1953.

[19] See my book, which has already been cited — pp. 167-170.

[20] *Vie thérésienne,* I. c., 279.

[21] *Sainte Thérèse de Lisieux, une renaissance spirituelle* [St. Thérèse of Lisieux, a spiritual renewal], Ed. De la Revue des Jeunes (1925): 282. See Conrad De Meester, "Le dominicain Hyacinthe Petitot et sainte Thérèse de Lisieux" in *Thérèse et ses théologiens* [Thérèse and her theologians] (Saint Paul–Éditions du Carmel, 1998), 67–81.

As of 1932, during a theological convention for the inauguration of the crypt of the Basilica in Lisieux (which wasn't yet built), Fr. Gustave Desbuquois spoke of Thérèse's possibly becoming a Doctor. This hope became a reality in 1997 after a lively history of sixty years. For this, it was necessary to examine Thérèse's original texts and to have, as Pius XII had ordered, the *Autobiographical Manuscripts* published in 1956 and later the critical edition of all her works. This work wasn't completed until 1992. Thérèse wouldn't been granted the title of Doctor without that critical edition.

Finally, a third period opened in 1994, and we cannot see when it will end. Thérèse, the miracle-worker and Doctor, is also a tireless missionary, as she was in her life on earth. She wanted to be one after her death, and she was one by the power of the Holy Spirit, who doesn't allow Himself to be confined in any enclosure. Since 1994 and, in particular, since December 13, 1997, the date of her traversing the Atlantic Ocean to crisscross Brazil for one year, she undertook a new stage of her spiritual action. It was to reach the "most remote isles," to visit friends who would never come see her in Lisieux and to travel thousands of kilometers in a Boeing 747, in a military plane, in a helicopter, in a police car or a firetruck, on a cruise ship or a steamer, on horseback, or in a sled pulled by dogs. Such is her current mission "to plant the glorious Cross of Jesus over the whole earth."[22]

This is a formidable epic that is occurring before our very eyes and whose fruits we can't foresee in the near future. What does it matter? The "secrets of the king" (see Tob. 12:7) can remain hidden. Sometimes, some of the feast's crumbs come to us. What matters is that this epic exists and continues to exist for the benefit of those who are experiencing these moments of grace.

[22] Thérèse of Lisieux, Manuscript B, 3r, in *Story of a Soul,* 192.

Our story and testimony will unfold according to these three stages: Thérèse the miracle-worker, Thérèse the Doctor, and Thérèse the missionary.

May Thérèse guide and enlighten our journey, as she has always done, with her charisms as a novice mistress, which are inspired by the Holy Spirit.

Part 1

Thérèse the Miracle-Worker

I really count on not remaining inactive in heaven.

— Letter 254 to Fr. Roulland[23]

Cardinal Pacelli — the future Pius XII — declared in 1938 that Thérèse was "the greatest miracle-worker of modern times."

Nobody can object to this statement, as it is obvious. Thérèse has chosen no one group to "do good [to] on earth." All ages have been involved — from little children to the elderly. All social backgrounds have been affected — well beyond Catholics: Protestants, the Orthodox, Jews, Muslims, agnostics, and even atheists.

The Carmel of Lisieux had received letters talking about miracles (healings, apparitions, and conversions) since 1899 and had started to publish some of these testimonies in the *Story of a Soul*'s successive editions. The book was first published on October 21, 1898.[24]

[23] *Letters of St. Thérèse,* vol. 2, 1142.

[24] We have told this story in the *L'Histoire d'une âme* [*Story of a Soul*] by Thérèse of Lisieux (Paris: Editions du Cerf, 2000).

We find some accounts of the "favors" starting from the 1907 edition. This movement would accelerate as *Story of a Soul* spread. (The first English translation dates from 1901.)

As of 1901, the Carmel of Lisieux published a volume called *Pluie de roses* (A shower of roses), which talks about 125 miracles and favors.

That same year, only thirteen years after Sr. Thérèse's death, a diocesan beatification process, called an Ordinary Process, opened, for which Pope Pius X was responsible. Mother Agnès of Jesus (Pauline Martin, sister of Thérèse) brought no fewer than thirty-three miraculous occurrences to the tribunal. It would retain three of them.

The First World War would provide many testimonies of soldiers who were protected or helped by the young Carmelite of Lisieux. A special volume of *Pluie de roses* was dedicated in 1920. Another one appeared in 1923 and was dedicated to missionary countries.

We noted an escalation of miracles throughout the world with the beatification (April 29, 1923) and canonization (May 17, 1925) of St. Thérèse of the Child Jesus and the Holy Face by Pope Pius XI.

The last volume of *Pluie de roses* was published in 1926. Then the periodical *Annales de sainte Thérèse*, which was founded in 1925, sporadically talked about miracles that were reported on the five continents. This has continued until now. The periodical *Thérèse de Lisieux* took over in 1992.

We can count 3,252 accounts of these favors on the five continents in the seven volumes of *Pluie de roses* that stretched from 1910 to 1926 (3,400 pages total).[25]

[25] See Antoinette Guise's master's thesis, "Les miracles de soeur Thérèse de l'Enfant-Jésus entre 1898 et 1926. Genèse d'un culte" [The miracles of Thérèse of the Child Jesus between 1898 and 1926: the origin of a devotion], under the direction of Mr. Claude Langlois, École pratique des hautes études, 2000.

The publication was interrupted after the canonization of 1925, but that doesn't mean that the saint's posthumous action stopped. Quite the contrary. The more Thérèse made herself known in the world, the more she touched people who prayed to her and received her graces. This has continued into the twenty-first century. There's no reason why St. Thérèse of Lisieux wouldn't continue to keep her promises.

It appears to me now, after twelve years of pastoral work in Lisieux and meeting thousands of people in France and in the thirteen countries where Thérèse has led me, that the written and spoken testimonies are only a little visible part — like the tip of an iceberg — of the reality of these favors.

I wouldn't say we have kept only a tenth of them — to take the image of the iceberg — but the real number is surely higher than that of the "cases" that are talked about in *Pluie de roses*.

I want my experience to be a proof. How many times, after the four hundred or so conferences that I've given since 1987, and during hundreds of retreats, sessions, and symposiums, was I approached by someone who wanted to confide in me that he had been healed by Thérèse of Lisieux in his childhood? I would then ask the person if he had communicated that blessing to the Carmel of Lisieux. The answer was very often negative. We keep this to ourselves. It's too intimate. But suddenly, after decades, we talk about them on this occasion. We don't know why.

I have often experienced this scene: During a meal, I talk about St. Thérèse and her action in the world. After leaving the table, one of the guests, a respectable man, takes me aside and takes out his wallet, from which he removes a small, completely damaged image of Thérèse or a little crumpled relic and tells me: "When I was very little, I was healed by St. Thérèse." This man, who might be a lawyer or an industrialist, wasn't a pillar of the Church. But the link between him and the little sister remained indestructible. Of course, I've also had this experience with very ordinary and simple people, such as a ninety-six-year-old monk who wasn't a priest. He had worked as an agricultural laborer since he was seven. He had entered the monastery when he was twenty-five, thanks to Thérèse, and he showed me a faded relic that never left him.

I recall a man who had done some counterintelligence work in Southeast Asia and had been saved from dying during birth. His mother had dedicated him to Thérèse when the birth promised to be very dangerous. This adventurer, who had experienced situations that were worthy of a James Bond–style film, had kept a small image of Thérèse throughout his life.

We're going to offer some characteristics of these "showers of roses," which were published by the Carmel of Lisieux, to illustrate the diversity of Thérèse's interventions.

In the face of the planetary size of this storm of benefits, we have evidently wondered — by trying to "understand," as it were — why this young, hidden, unknown Carmelite had posthumously become one of the greatest miracle-workers in the history of Christianity.

Her writings, words, and promises have helped us understand this. If they don't completely clarify the conclusive and mysterious reasons for such an adventure, they nevertheless shed some light.

Let's listen to Sr. Thérèse in the last months of her short life. She knew she was going to die soon, and she asked herself if the mission of "making Jesus loved" and praying "for sinners" would stop now since she had lived for such a short time — hardly more than twenty years.

Whereas an elderly saint, having lived a long life in the service of God and men, yearns for happiness and heavenly rest, Thérèse didn't wish to rest. When she announced her upcoming death to her spiritual brothers, she forbade herself from wanting to leave the fight to take refuge in rest — even if it was heavenly rest, which she had so much hoped for:

> I really count on not remaining inactive in heaven. My desire is to work still for the Church and for souls. I am asking God for this and I am certain He will answer me. Are not the angels continually occupied with us without their ever ceasing to see the divine Face and to lose themselves in the Ocean of Love without shores? Why would Jesus not allow me to imitate them?[26]

When Thérèse faced her death, she estimated that this was the greatest desire she could have. She always relied on St. John of the Cross's statement: "The more You want to give, the more You make people desire."[27] She often cited this sentence, one of the pillars of her *bold confidence*.[28]

Therefore, if she hoped to continue and even accentuate the mission of making Jesus loved on earth, it's because this desire lived in her. "God would not have given me the desire of doing good on earth after my death, if He didn't will to realize it; He would rather have given me the desire to rest in Him."[29]

Thérèse was used to praying for this intention. She prayed the Novena of Grace to St. Francis Xavier from March 4 to March 12, 1897,

[26] Letter 254, to Father Roulland, in China, in *Letters of St. Thérèse*, vol. 2, 1142.

[27] Letter to Mother Eléonor of St. Gabriel on July 8, 1589. See maxim 45: "The more God wants to give us, the more He increases our desires to the point of emptying the soul in order to fill it with His goods." *Maximes et avis spirituels de Notre Bienheureux Père Saint Jean de la Croix* [Spiritual maxims and thoughts of our Blessed Father St. John of the Cross] (Houdin, 1895). Thérèse used this book. It was very dear to her.

[28] For example: Letter 201 to Fr. Roulland, in *Letters of St. Thérèse*, vol. 2, 1013; St. Thérèse of Lisieux, Manuscript C, 31r, in *Story of a Soul*, 66; Letter 253 to Fr. Bellière, in *Letters of St. Thérèse*, vol. 2, 1139; St. Thérèse of Lisieux, *Yellow Notebook*, July 13, 15 and July 16, 2.

[29] St. Thérèse of Lisieux, *Yellow Notebook*, July 18, 1, 102.

in order to enable her "to spend heaven doing good upon earth."[30] Although the novena to St. Joseph was often taken for granted and therefore forgotten, Sr. Thérèse didn't hesitate to make her request through St. Joseph's intercession. Here is what her sister Marie of the Sacred Heart reported on March 19, 1897, his feast day:

> I recall that I was in her Hermitage on the Feast of St. Joseph. She [Thérèse] came. She was very sick. I told her it would have been better for her to go directly to her cell than to make this detour. She told me: "I'm coming to ask St. Joseph to obtain God's blessing of spending my heaven doing good on earth." I answered her: "You don't need to ask St. Joseph for that," but she said: "Oh! But yes" with a gesture that meant: I need him to support my request. She had also asked St. Francis Xavier for it via the Novena of Grace (March 4–12).[31]

Not only did Thérèse pray, but she also reflected. What struck her was the situation of the angels, who were very present in her time and thought. She reasoned in this way: since the angels, who celebrate the heavenly liturgy, have missions on the earth,[32] why couldn't Thérèse do as they did?

She continued her letter to Fr. Roulland:

> Brother, you see that if I am leaving the field of battle already, it is not with the selfish desire of taking my rest. The thought of eternal beatitude hardly thrills my heart.... What attracts me to the homeland of heaven is the Lord's call, the hope of loving

[30] Thérèse of Lisieux, *Yellow Notebook*, July 17, 102.

[31] Sr. Marie of the Incarnation's Notebook, p. 134: conversation recorded on July 10, 1934; St. Thérèse of Lisieux, *General Correspondence* II, 966, note K.

[32] The term *Angelos* means "sent."

him finally as I have so much desired to love Him, and the thought that I shall be able to make Him loved by a multitude of souls who will bless Him eternally.[33]

When she composed the play *St. Stanislas Kosta*[34] that she had performed on February 8, 1897, for Sr. Saint Stanislaus's fifty years of religious profession, eight months separated Thérèse from her death. She confided to Sr. Mary of the Trinity:

What pleased me in composing this play is that I expressed my certitude that after death, we can still work on earth for the salvation of souls. St. Stanislas, who died so young, served me admirably to say my thoughts and aspirations on this subject.[35]

Here's what St. Stanislas said to the Virgin Mary in Thérèse's play:

Oh! How happy I am.... Sweet Queen of Heaven, I ask you, when I'll be near you in the Homeland, allow me to return to the earth in order to protect holy souls — souls whose long career here below will complete mine. Thus, I'll be able to present an abundant harvest of merits to the Lord through them.[36]

Finally, on July 17, 1897, Mother Agnès noted this in the infirmary, where Thérèse had been since July 8:

Saturday, at 2:00 a.m., she coughed up blood.

"I feel that I'm about to enter into my rest. But I feel especially that my mission is about to begin, my mission of making God loved as I loved Him, of giving my little way to souls. If

33 Letter 254 to Fr. Roulland.

34 *Récréations pieuses* 8.

35 Ordinary Process 469–470. See *Nouvelle Edition du Centenaire, Pious Recreations*, 268.

36 See *Nouvelle Edition du Centenaire, Pious Recreations*, 410 and 397.

> God answers my desires, my heaven will be spent on earth until the end of the world. Yes, I want to spend my heaven in doing good on earth. This isn't impossible, since from the bosom of the beatific vision, the angels watch over us.
>
> "I can't make heaven a feast of rejoicing; I can't rest as long as there are souls to be saved. But when the angel will have said: 'Time is no more!' then I will take my rest; I'll be able to rejoice, because the number of the elect will be complete and because all will have entered into joy and repose. My heart beats with joy at this thought."[37]

All that we have just cited about this desire to "do good" after her death[38] could have seemed like the delusion of a young feverish Carmelite — the frenzy of a heated mind.

But the facts are there. As soon as she died, Thérèse kept her promise — with astonishing generosity. The Carmel of Lisieux collected as many of the countless testimonies that came from all over the world as it could.

This immense universal action isn't a past event. Today, in the twenty-first century, in the third millennium, Thérèse is still at work to make Jesus, the Holy Trinity, and merciful Love loved. Her "shower of roses" hasn't stopped.

This isn't about indefinitely drawing out the accounts of these important favors that are Thérèse's responses to the call of those who implore her intercession. Some examples will suffice to testify that the "mercies of God" aren't stopping in the twenty-first century.

37 We'll notice the parallelism with the July 14 letter to Fr. Roulland that we have cited (Letter 254).

38 See Fr. Conrad de Meester, "Thérèse de Lisieux et son désir."

"Raphaël Was Born . . . Perfectly Normal"

Raphaël Cavan's dual healing is remarkable in itself, but it attracts more attention because his mother, who is reporting these facts, is a doctor.

Here is her testimony:[39]

I became pregnant in December 1996. . . . At the four-month ultrasound, I was shocked when the doctor, who knew that I was a doctor, insisted that I get an amniocentesis since, according to him, many signs indicated that the baby could have Down syndrome. He added that if his diagnosis was confirmed, it was time to terminate the pregnancy.

Upset by this announcement, I sought a second opinion at another medical center, where the radiologist questioned the earlier results and reassured me that the signs from the previous ultrasound didn't appear on this one.

My obstetrician, however, wanted to do an amniocentesis because of the risk that he mentioned. I refused to have this done, for I knew all too well that it could cause a miscarriage. My husband and I wanted to keep the baby no matter what.

[39] It was published in *Thérèse de Lisieux,* no. 819 (February 2002): 22–23.

At that time, Thérèse's relics were at the Carmel in Créteil. My mother took me there. A few days earlier, after the first ultrasound, she had gone to Lisieux, where she prayed intensely. She ... entrusted us to St. Thérèse's protection by confiding my pregnancy and my baby to her.

I was deeply moved in the presence of St. Thérèse's relics, and I started to pray a lot for perseverance, as my pregnancy became psychologically difficult toward the end. I was quite scared. But I tried to remain confident.

When the birth occurred, I had a liver problem that could have caused serious consequences for the baby. But Raphaël was born with eyes as blue as the sky and the beautiful face of an angel. The one we had been calling Thérèse's child was perfectly normal and well formed — to the first radiologist's great surprise! Thank you, Thérèse!

Later, Raphaël had a lot of health problems since he was very small. He had to be hospitalized for asthmatic bronchitis and was very often sick — perhaps because of this difficult pregnancy.

The hardest part came in September and October 2000, when Raphaël developed a digestive infection, as he often did. This time, however, the usual treatment had no effect, and his condition worsened in a few hours, so he had to be hospitalized. At the hospital, Raphaël was mistakenly treated for a serious digestive infection, even though there was no sign of it. His persistent stomachaches were attributed to his anxiety, and he left the hospital supposedly healed of this problem.

Nevertheless, his stomachaches persisted, and the fever resumed a few days later, which required him to be hospitalized again. The next morning, a test was ordered because of his alarming condition. But Raphaël was too weak to undergo the test, and the radiologist didn't want to do it.

That's when Thérèse started to intervene. My mother, who knew we were worried about this test, phoned Lisieux and spoke with one of the sisters in the Carmel, who went to the church to slip a picture of Raphaël under Thérèse's shrine and to pray.

Despite the intensity of Raphaël's fever, I was gradually able to make him drink the preparatory fluid for the test. Only God and Thérèse knew how I managed. The test was administered, and it showed an infection of both kidneys. There had been a diagnostic error during the first hospitalization.

Thanks to the test, a treatment was administered, and it started to lower the fever. My battle wasn't won yet, however, for, because of the initial misdiagnosis of the infection, I continued to experience doubt and anxiety. When Raphaël weakened soon after, I looked in vain for a priest to anoint him. But Raphaël felt better that evening.

Each time Raphaël took a turn for the worse during that hospital stay, I prayed to God and Thérèse to protect him and give him the strength to fight, and my prayers were answered. Moreover, I received another unexpected outpouring of grace. Sr. Z, who had had surgery, was (by chance?) in the room right above Raphaël's. When she learned that Raphaël was nearby and in poor health, she also prayed to God and Thérèse.

One month later, a malformation of Raphaël's urinary system was discovered. This required surgery (a repositioning of the two ureters on the bladder). Fortunately, Raphaël was treated in a children's nephrology department, and thanks to God and Thérèse, he lost only a third of his right kidney's function.

Raphaël was operated on in Trousseau Hospital in February 2001, and the subsequent tests showed a complete healing of his malformation. He asked that we pray during all the high points of his hospitalizations. He also asked me to pray the day before the renal scintigraphy that was supposed to show his kidneys' condition.

Today, he's doing well and, even though we still worry about him, he's being very well taken care of medically. He's going to make his First

Communion in Lisieux, and perhaps the four of us will be receiving this sacrament because we need it.

Here's Thérèse's last wink. Thérèse appeared in Honfleur via her relics during our August vacation in Normandy. We could thank her up close, and it was a real joy to know that she was so near to us — as much in our pain and anxiety as in our joy and calm. Thank you, Thérèse. Thank you. Thank you.

"Your Husband Survived by a Miracle"

Mrs. H. wrote this letter on September 9, 1999:

I've taken care of my husband for forty-eight years. He suffers from manic depression. Moreover, in 1989, he was stricken with Alzheimer's disease. He was hospitalized in a palliative care unit on October 15, 1997. He no longer spoke or recognized me. He had lost sixty-six pounds. He looked like a skeleton. He had a catheter, a gastric tube, and an incision in his stomach for the tube. I went to see him each day from 11:30 a.m. to 8:30 p.m., and I fed him with a tube to relieve the nurses' work.

One day, when I arrived, I said to the doctor, "Oh! My husband isn't doing well." He responded: "Yes, we're no longer counting the days but the hours."

"My God, please don't abandon me," I said, and I left to call my three children.... I ran into the supermarket to pick up supplies for their visit, and when I went to load the groceries into the trunk of my car, I found on the ground a little square of paper . Intrigued, I picked it up and saw that it was a third-class relic that read: "St. Thérèse of the Child Jesus of Lisieux." I immediately thought that the person who lost the square would be sad. I was unable to return it, so I put it in my wallet. When I got home, I looked at it and said to myself: "Why me?" That night, I thought about that square. What did it mean?

The next day, while visiting my husband, I said to myself: "What if I put this square that touched St. Thérèse's relics on his forehead?" Then questions rushed into my head, and I hesitated. Finally, I spoke to Thérèse and asked her to relieve my husband's suffering — not to cure it. I put the cloth on his forehead. He immediately jumped and opened his eyes. I was afraid because up to this point, he had been unresponsive. I put the square away without telling anyone about it. When our children arrived, he recognized all of them. The doctor said: "I don't understand. He was very sick, and then bingo! He's doing better. Usually it happens that things seem to go well and then suddenly worsen."

But as the months went by, his health didn't get any better. One day, I arrived and was prevented from going into his room. "Your husband has an infection." I insisted on seeing him. "It's blood poisoning. This time, it's over."

I put on gloves and a white coat and gave him fluids through the tube. This time, I was sure it was over. Suddenly, I thought of St. Thérèse. I entrusted my husband to her again and told her: "You know the pain I'm in. I'm not asking you for my husband to be healed, which is impossible. Only God knows how much longer he has to live. I'm asking you to prevent him from suffering, please." I rested the square on my husband's forehead again. The same thing happened. He jumped and looked at me in a funny way. I was afraid again, but I continued to apply the square and traced several crosses with it on his forehead as I explained to him that I was praying to St. Thérèse for him.

He was very agitated. The nurse who came by thought his agitation was strange. I gave him the last three syringes of water in the gastric tube at 8:30 p.m., as I did every day, and I stroked his cheek with my gloved hand. (I wasn't permitted to kiss him.) I told myself that he might not be here tomorrow. He gazed at me very intensely, which he usually didn't do.

I talked to the nurse about this as I went by the office. She looked at me compassionately and said: "Yes, there's often this kind of reaction at the end."

I didn't sleep that night and spent it at the foot of my bed with St. Thérèse. When I saw my husband the next day, I thought he looked calm. He looked at me. I was concerned. I searched for the syringe on the table to feed him, as on the other days. I didn't find it and said out loud: "What did they do with the syringe today?"

Then, my husband said: "The syringe fell."

"What — the doctor removed it?"

"No, it fell all by itself."

I looked at him incredulously and thought I'd find a bandage [over the hole for his gastric tube]. But there wasn't any. The hole was well sealed, clean, and neat.

Suddenly, I said: "You're talking!"

"Yes, and I'm eating."

"What?"

"Yes, I ate my breakfast this morning."

I went to see the nurse and asked her: "Did you remove my husband's tube?"

"No, he must have removed it by himself."

"But you didn't put a bandage on him?"

"No, there was no need for one. We don't understand it, but the result is there. He's doing better."

I fed my husband with a fork at noon, and he ate everything.

I asked to bring him back home a week later.

"But you're unaware that he's not walking and is unable to leave," the doctor said to me.

"Nonetheless, he's eating well, he talks, and he has regained all of his memory."

"Yes, something has happened," he said to me.

Two days later, the doctor said: "Your husband is leaving this afternoon."

For four days, I found myself alone with a very sick man without any help. Later, an aide came three times a week to wash him, along with a physical therapist. They thought he was doing too well to need extra help.

Three months later, my husband was walking and gardening. The establishment's doctor summoned us for some tests.

My husband said, "No, that's enough."

"You be quiet," the doctor said to him. "You have nothing to say. You've already survived by a miracle."

When we went for the tests, the nurses, who recognized me, gazed wide-eyed at my husband and said: "I'm dreaming! This is Mr. H.?"

"Yes, since he came home, he has been fine. He doesn't have the strength he did before, but that's normal. He's seventy years old. The resistance isn't the same, but he's healed, thanks to St. Thérèse."

Our personal physician is an atheist, but she also said that my husband survived through a miracle.

"Thanks a million, St. Thérèse."

"I Was Driving Drunk on a Country Road"

In 1991, I had been a punk, an alcoholic, an atheist, and a secularist for thirteen years. I actively opposed the Catholic Church as much as I could because I thought religions were a big fraud.... I bore a grudge against the Catholic Church especially, for the area where I lived was deeply Catholic. I fought against this "opium of the people" — thinking I was doing something beneficial.

One early evening at the end of December 1991, I went into a leftist bar in Morlaix. On the way, I had wandered into a church, where I had taken a magazine titled *Thérèse de Lisieux*. I don't know why I did that.

In the bar, there were about a dozen customers, including a Muslim, and the two owners. A fire was burning in the fireplace. One of the owners saw me but refused to serve me, and he went upstairs to clear the tables. I threw the magazine on the fire and stayed to talk with the customers. After about fifteen minutes, everyone turned around and stared at the fireplace. The whole magazine had burned except for a picture of Thérèse and the cross (from July 1896), which was floating horizontally above the flames. The picture was intact! There were ten sober witnesses of this! I was so scared that I immediately sobered up.

Everyone was paralyzed by this inexplicable phenomenon. Someone said: "I'm not going to stay here all night!" I extended a hand toward the picture, removed it from the flames, and put it on the counter. For half an hour, it had floated horizontally above the blue and white sparks that sprang up from all sides of the fire! This was unexplainable!

I put the picture back in the flames, facedown this time, and the picture instantly burned!

I went to see some physics and chemistry teachers to ask them if this phenomenon had an explanation. They replied: "None!" The picture should have burned like the rest of the magazine.

So I returned to my life of drinking and messing around.

Seven months later, on July 5, 1992, at 2:00 a.m., I was driving drunk on a country road about four and a half miles from Morlaix on a bike without a light. A completely new Peugeot 205 GTI hit me head on and just missed crashing against a wall. The car's passengers were unharmed, and I had only a broken leg. This was the second miracle.

I was hospitalized and operated on three times in six months. My leg didn't want to mend. I had a calcium deficiency. (Alcohol isn't a food item.)

The surgeon told me: "You're going to lose your leg. You lost some calcium."

I asked him what I had to do. "Nothing. You only need to pray to your God."

I was an atheist. I didn't believe in God.

After a few days, I started to fear losing my leg. I was only forty-six years old. So I half-heartedly made two vows: if my leg was healed, I'd stop drinking alcohol and go to Lisieux. Against the odds, my leg started to absorb enough calcium to be completely healed! This didn't, of course, occur in two weeks; it took several months. I'm walking very well now and limping only a little. Thank you, Thérèse! This was the third miracle.

I tried to keep my promises. The most urgent one was to stop drinking alcohol. I sought admission to the Centre de postcure Croix Bleue in Lorient. I was told on the phone: "Fill out an application. You'll come when there's room." I waited.

Someone called me around May 15, 1993, to say there would be room available on May 18. I stopped drinking alcohol on May 17, 1993, since I couldn't be drunk at the facility. As an atheist, I didn't know it at the time, but May 17 was the anniversary of Thérèse's canonization. The date was a coincidence! It was more than a coincidence; it was the fourth miracle.

I've gone to Lisieux six times since then. I rediscovered the Faith during a friend's burial on June 6, 1995!

Not bad, right? There were four miracles for a man like me! I was a renegade, a pariah, and an outcast before little Thérèse reached out to me. I've abstained from alcohol for four years. I strive to respect the law of God and man as best I can.

Shortly before my conversion, I discovered in Lisieux that God is love. He created man in His image, and He loves each of us like little children, no matter what we do!

Thérèse reached out to me. It was, if you will, the hand that saved me when I saw myself in Hell's flames. The captain of the ship that the sailor Thérèse was on was, of course, God our Father, with Jesus, His Son.

I, Georges, who survived by a miracle, can testify that Thérèse's doctrine will open the twenty-first century up to love!

— Georges Guégen
May 29, 1997

A Healing on the Day Thérèse Became a Doctor of the Church

Here are a few lines about a healing that occurred in Córdoba on the day that Thérèse of the Child Jesus became a Doctor of the Church, October 19, 1997. We can communicate this to you firsthand since the beneficiary came here and told us himself how everything had taken place.

On that afternoon, our mother superior received a phone message from a man who had asked her urgently to call him back. The man had been hospitalized in the room next to the room of one of our sisters who had to undergo surgery.

His name was Raphaël M. Pérez, and he was about seventy years old. He and his wife had grown children and some grandchildren. Our mother told us that Raphaël and his wife were very devout. We had met them in the Jesuit church in Córdoba. When Raphaël could no longer go to church because of his illness, his wife received permission to bring him Communion, and she did this very reverently.

Raphaël had undergone thirteen heart operations. He also had a stroke, which led to paralysis on his right side. He partially recovered after a while, but after two more strokes, he could no longer talk or walk. He bore it all bravely, however.

He was in this condition on October 18. His wife told him that it was okay for him to complain a bit when they were by themselves; he didn't have to smile all the time. He responded by pointing to Heaven, as if to signify to her that he was happy about everything God was sending him. How could he have complained?

In the morning, they all watched on television the ceremony in which St. Thérèse was proclaimed a Doctor of the Church. Raphaël told us that he had never asked God for health but only for the strength to suffer. During the procession of St. Thérèse's reliquary, Raphaël felt compelled to say: "Lord, not for me, but for my loved ones who are suffering so much, You can heal me, through St. Thérèse's intercession, if You want to."

When his wife returned from Mass that day, she had brought him Communion. When he received the holy Host, he repeated this to the Lord: "Lord, You can heal me through St. Thérèse's intercession if You want to." He then felt a jolt, and he shivered from head to foot. He got up and shouted for his wife, who had left the room.

Startled, his wife told her son: "Your father's calling me."

The son replied, "But that's impossible for him!"

Both of them came running and found Raphaël standing in the middle of the room. Imagine their surprise and joy when he told them what had happened! They called their other children, who rushed over to see him, and they called us. You can imagine the impression it made on us!

Some time later, Raphaël, his wife, and his son-in-law came to the monastery to offer his cane as a gift to the Virgin Mary. This was marvelous. It had a golden ring, and there was a marble rose on the knob. (It must have been a command baton). Raphaël's son-in-law, a parishioner from Córdoba, told us that he was astonished when he arrived for dinner and saw his father-in-law talking and walking! The seasoned doctors told him there was no natural explanation.

— The Carmelites from St.-Calixte Monastery, Córdoba, Spain

"God, If You Exist . . ."

My father, who died in an accident when I was a few months old, wanted me to be baptized when I was very small. But then my mother remarried, and I grew up in an environment that was completely atheistic.

I had always been very interested in religion, however. My drunken stepfather beat me as a child. I didn't understand why he did this. I searched for meaning in my life, but I didn't know where I fit in. I spent years drinking and getting high on different drugs; some of them were hard. I got off to a very bad start in life! I had completely withdrawn. I thought I detested the people who had so often disappointed me. I rejected them and wouldn't talk to anyone. I stayed inside for entire days to anesthetize myself.

I felt as if I had never received any love. My mother didn't show her feelings. I'd never felt her affection. I thought: "Does love really exist? Then show it to me!"

I'd become a real mess. I had created a shell to protect myself since I was a child. Nobody knew my real personality. I couldn't take it anymore. I looked everywhere for a way out, but I couldn't find it. I often tried committing suicide and thought I would go crazy. Then one day, a therapist said something to me that made me think: "Don't you think it's time for you to shape your personality?" I wanted to get off drugs, but I didn't know how to do it. I felt imprisoned in a cold, dark place.

Then, last summer, a friend convinced me to take a trip with him to Paray-le-Monial. Let's be honest. I went there to meet people (I had gradually opened myself up to the outside world) — and girls in particular! The first night, my friend and I ate with a gentleman who told me at the end of the meal: "You're going to experience some miracles." I mocked him a little bit: "Miracles? They've never been for me!"

It was a wonderful vacation. I spent a lot of time observing things. We visited the city on the first day. I felt uneasy going into the churches. I had never even made the Sign of the Cross.

August 16 arrived — the day of my true birth. We decided to go to the vigil. I was lost in my thoughts. Suddenly, I heard the priest say: "If you have a prayer request, write it on a little sheet of paper, and deposit it at the foot of St. Thérèse's visiting relics." I played the game. I wrote: "God, if You exist, may You enlighten my heart." I went forward, put the paper near the relics, made the first Sign of the Cross I had ever made, and started to walk away.

Suddenly I felt as if I had been struck by lightning. I experienced an immense love that overwhelmed me. I thought my heart was going to explode. I thought: "God loves me madly despite everything I've done!" My heart ached. I felt a sweet and strong pain. It was indescribable. I cried and was unable to stop. Even a few hours before that, I would never have imagined myself crying in front of people!

I was certain that I had arrived safe and sound. I was with my family. All my fear and anxiety flew away in an instant. I received the most beautiful gift that anyone could give me — an infinite love!

Yet I started to doubt. I thought, "It's too beautiful to be real." My heart had opened up. I had become attentive to the teachings of the Church, and everything seemed to make sense. I started talking to God. Nonetheless, I was still resisting: "You're not going to believe that," I said to myself. During another vigil, I seemed to hear: "Do you still need proof?" I heard myself say: "No, Lord," and an immense joy overwhelmed me.

Despite that, I continued to resist. I considered going to Confession, but I was too afraid to make the move. A friend helped me to pray and prayed for me. I finally decided to meet with a priest. I told him everything. That was like a complete release.

Those who knew me before this day didn't recognize me. They had never seen such a smile on my face. I actually learned how to smile! I gradually started to speak with others and love them from the depth of my heart.

I decided to stop taking drugs. God had done so much for me. It was my turn to prove to Him that I loved Him!

I love life today. I have plenty of projects. I want to live completely for God. I'm rediscovering the simplest things — the singing of birds, the beauty of nature, which awakens in the spring . . . It's as if I'm being inwardly transformed — like a flower that's blooming!

But faith is a daily struggle. It's never won in advance.

One day, my weakness discouraged me. I had received so much and was incapable of making an effort for God! A priest told me, "Listen! When you have a broken arm, you need a cast to get your arm back in shape. Well, it's the same thing for you. Accept that God is reeducating you, is filling your emptiness and straightening what is curved." So, I'm going through some highs and lows, but I am learning to be confident day after day and to rely on God, who is my Father — everyone's Father! I meditate a lot on surrendering to God, and I try to do so day by day. I rediscovered my childish heart, and my being is coming together a bit at a time.

— Cédric, twenty-five years old[40]

[40] *Il est vivant,* Spécial Thérèse edition.

"Thérèse Came"

I had just helped myself to a mug of steaming coffee when three-year-old Eliott entered the room and upset the mug, and the coffee spilled on him.

He screamed. I rushed him the hospital, where he was diagnosed with second-degree burns on his stomach and torso. The doctor told me that he'd need to receive treatments at the hospital every two days for the next six weeks.

Eliott didn't complain. He just hurt during the treatments.

Ten days after the accident, when I woke Eliot up, he told me: "My bandages are bothering me."

I replied, "Do you have a stomachache?"

"Oh no," Eliott replied, "Thérèse is on my stomach."

I admit that I was moved, and my little boy's faith touched me.

At noon, he came to me and said, "I'd like to see Our Lady of Mount Carmel." We had often talked about Mary in our family and prayed to her, but we hadn't talked about Our Lady of Mount Carmel. I was very surprised that Eliott, who was only three, was talking about her. He added: "She's carrying Jesus in her arms, and He's sleeping." I promised him that after his treatment at the hospital that day, we'd go to the Carmel.

At the hospital, the nurse removed his bandages and compresses. After only ten days, there was no trace of pus, and his skin was completely pink. The nurse seemed astonished (and I was delighted).

We ran to the Carmel to thank Mary and Thérèse of the Child Jesus and the Holy Face.

A priest advised us to ask Eliott what had happened.

Eliott told us, "Thérèse came. She put her hands on my stomach, and everything left."

I don't know anything more than this.

We went to Mass on the following Sunday, and I said to Eliott, "We can thank Jesus for the healing."

"No," he said, "not Jesus but Thérèse."

Eliott's patron saint is Eli, and he always wears the medals of Our Lady of Mount Carmel and Thérèse on him since his Baptism two years ago.

— Testimony of his mother, Mireille B.

"Thérèse Accompanied Me Every Day"

I was an agnostic. When I was forty-seven years old in 1985, I experienced depression and anxiety that had no physical cause.

While traveling, I visited Solesmes Abbey with my wife, who was a believer but not a regular churchgoer. My eyes were attracted to St. Thérèse's picture on the cover of *Story of a Soul,* and I immediately had a strong impression that she had something crucial to tell me. So I bought the book, without knowing anything about Thérèse, since I confused her with Teresa of Ávila. I browsed through the first pages and quickly closed the book. I was disappointed and even annoyed by the writing style, which I thought was too mushy.

A few months after this episode, in January 1986, I attended Mass in Saint-Benoît-sur-Loire. I experienced a sudden conversion there. I cried a lot and was very joyful, which disrupted my life and my family's life. I picked up Thérèse's memoirs right after that and learned quite a bit about God's mercy.

My wife and I, thanks to Thérèse, have experienced profound spiritual healings. Our desire for God was so strong that we lived in a community for two years. Since then, we have kept a very powerful connection with the community, as well as with the Benedictine Saint-Benoît Abbey. We provide a ministry of compassion and listening in the church. St. Thérèse has never stopped guiding us, and we entrust everything to her.

Since then, Thérèse has accompanied me every day, and I've received many graces through her intercession. Thérèse's words "I want to spend my heaven doing good on earth" have truly been a reality for me.

"Glory to God!"

— Doctor O. B., March 14, 1999

Healing from Throat Cancer

I visited Lisieux in July 1997 when I was afflicted with throat cancer. I took part in a healing session and felt that St. Thérèse was there and that I would be healed.

Now, three years later, my condition has slowly but surely improved. The pain in my throat and my head seem to have disappeared, and I can only bear witness today and talk about all my gratitude to St. Thérèse for having restored my health.

— A seventy-three-year-old Vendean
with a glad thank-you, L.P.

She Saw Thérèse Smiling at Her

Dr. Nikos is a young surgeon — one of St. Thérèse's devotees. We sisters offered him some pictures of little Thérèse and gave him a relic for his wedding. He prays to Thérèse every day and was healed of a serious case of meningitis through her intercession about two years ago.

Recently, one of his colleagues had a malignant cancer. Dr. Nikos brought her one of Thérèse's icons (which came from the Carmel), and she put it on the night table. At one point, the patient saw Thérèse smile and approach her. She got scared and turned her head. This phenomenon reoccurred. Dr. Nikos called us right away. He was very moved and asked us to pray for this young woman's healing, since Thérèse had manifested "something." Subsequent tests were all good, according to a recent sample. The nursing staff was astonished! The young woman's first name is Stavroula (derived from *Stavros,* "Cross").

— Carmel of Athens, January 7, 2002

"I Owe Her So Much"

The only time I went to Lisieux was with my parents and my sister when I was about twelve. Although I felt compelled to be a believer then, I retained this sentence of Thérèse, which moved me: "I will spend my heaven doing good on earth." But as time went by, and I fell away from the Church, I forgot this beautiful little sentence. But I didn't forget Thérèse.

She who loves to look for sinners came to retrieve me last year from the edge of the abyss. It's a beautiful story of a soul's conversion and salvation. I owe her so much and love her like a little sister.

I have so many very funny stories to tell about the graces she has flooded me with, and she continues to do so.

I live far away from Lisieux, but I'll certainly go back there someday to greet this adorable saint.

In the meantime, there's something that would make me very glad. I'd like to possess something of hers — a piece of cloth or a veil that belonged to her (if there are any left), for example.

I'd be extremely happy to wear it on my heart as a token of all the gratitude and love that I have for her.

— M.C., January 4, 2001

In a Complete Coma

On March 3, 1972, Nogent-le-Roi's firefighters took me to the hospital in Dreux after I fell off a horse. I had lost consciousness, and my scalp was bleeding profusely.

Two days later, I was still unconscious. My condition had worsened, and an ambulance drove me urgently to the ophthalmological unit at the Hôtel-Dieu in Paris. I had a large exophthalmos: my right eye was swollen for no apparent reason. But the eye problem was incidental. I had hardly arrived when the ambulance left again for the Pitié-Salpêtrière Hospital. This was to remove an extradural temporo basal blood clot on my right side. I was in a coma and wasn't aware of any of this.

There was a lesser aggravation. The appearance of a hemiplegia on the right side required another surgery on March 15. The exophthalmos was still very large and had required that my eye be sewn shut.

I gradually recovered after this surgery. There were more and more substantial moments of clarity. My right eye made me suffer a lot. One night (around March 20 or 21), I saw a lovely young woman, radiant and smiling, coming near my bed. I should say, a young girl. But I was twenty-three years old at that time, and she seemed older than I. She wore a white dress and carried something in an "apron" that was raised toward her waist. She came close to the right side of my bed and leaned toward me. She showed me two or three rose petals (from a rose that was very pale — almost white) that she took from her "apron" and then put them on my eye. She didn't leave any trace of them, but from then on, I felt very blessed, and I'm no longer hurting at all.

She spoke to me in a gentle voice. (But it was a normal voice. It didn't seem to me that she was whispering): "I am Thérèse of Lisieux. There. I must leave already. You know, I'm very much in demand right now. I have a lot to do."[41] That was, in essence, what she told me.

I felt quite peaceful after she left. She had come from the right side of my bed, and she left again, not by vanishing but by walking away calmly and confidently.

When the nurse came to clean my eye the next morning, I said to her: "I'm no longer hurting because —" without ending my sentence. A second time, I added: "Someone came to heal me last night." She nodded her head. Maybe she thought I was hallucinating.

Since I was doing better, a nurse brought me a pile of letters that I had received. The first letter she opened was from my older sister Astrid. The first line of her letter said: "I prayed to St. Thérèse a lot." I understood that if she had mentioned another saint, I'd have seen that saint. Since then, I've deeply believed in prayer. . . .

Although I had received a religious education, I had moved away from God. It wasn't aggressive or rebellious — far from that! But I was an advertising copywriter. I no longer had time to go to church. I had a lot of friends and was intoxicated by this exciting and alluring fake world of advertising!

I had several revelations after my accident. The first was the very real benefit of prayer. Another was that St. Thérèse truly is spending

[41] Note that 1973 is the year of the centenary of Thérèse's birth and the occasion of feasts in her honor around the whole world. — Ed.

her Heaven doing good on earth, according to her own words. There was also the revelation that God doesn't abandon His own. This accident came precisely at the right moment — when I was turning away from Him.

I've been very lucky since then.

Of course, I have continued to be handicapped. I have balance problems; without support, I can't go down a stairway or even a sidewalk if it's too high. But I'm an active mother. I was very happy to marry a former classmate, who teaches the classics. We are delighted to have two adorable daughters.

I got a bachelor's degree in modern languages (1982) and a master's degree (1983) with distinction at the Sorbonne.

I'm a diligent parishioner. I very happily attend Sunday Mass and devote a lot of time to prayer.

I thank the Lord and His faithful St. Thérèse for all this! I even go so far as to thank them for the very positive "shock" of my accident.

— Nadine C., Paris, May 17, 1994

"My Cousin Opened Her Eyes"

I'm writing in gratitude to St. Thérèse of the Child Jesus for the special favor I received through her intercession. My cousin Mary Jane from California was in critical condition in the ICU with pneumonia. She was seventy-five years old and was in a coma with respiratory assistance. The doctors had informed her family that she wouldn't live. I wanted to do something to help Mary Jane, so I sent her a relic of St. Thérèse and prayed for her healing.

When the relic arrived in California, my cousin's family attached it to her wrist and prayed to St. Thérèse. After a few hours, my cousin opened her eyes and spoke to my family. The doctors were stunned and couldn't explain the change in her condition. My cousin left the hospital after a few days. She's now recovering at home.

We felt that the healing was due to St. Thérèse's intercession. We are very thankful to the Lord for this favor.

— Sr. F. M. G., O.S.B., Arkansas, June 27, 1999

"He Is Saved!"

I was at the bedside of a dying child — my eleven-year-old nephew. He was afflicted with a lethal peritonitis, and there were no antibiotics for it at the time. He had returned from the operating room in a coma, and the doctor didn't know whether he would survive. I myself was barely out of my teens. My nephew's exhausted parents had asked me to stay with him for a few moments, and I was alone with him. His death rattle, in the silence of that sterile white clinic room, had plunged me into inexpressible anguish. It seemed to me that death was hovering over. Suddenly, the child had a deep death rattle and started to vomit some black substance. Thinking that he was about to die, I screamed inside myself, as you might scream when despair lays you low. To whom was I screaming — Thérèse?

Yes, to you, Thérèse. Why? Undoubtedly because my mother had given me your medal, and I wore it despite my timidity, my skepticism, my rationalizing, and the fashions and tastes of that time. I called to you in the deepest part of my being with a mixture of despair and hope. In order for me to survive, Heaven had to intervene — this Heaven that I only timidly believed in. It had to overcome this affliction and restore what death was trying to destroy in the natural order. This child whom I loved couldn't die at my side, in the face of my powerlessness. I asked this grace from you, Thérèse. It was done in a flash of unconscious faith. You heard me.

In the seconds that followed, while I was rushing toward the call bell, I clearly and surprisingly perceived the sounds of an opening door, light footsteps, and the rustling of a dress. Then the door of the room really opened, and the nurse entered. She rushed toward the child to catch the vomit that was still escaping from his mouth, and she asked me to help her lift him. We were on each side of his bed and looking intently at his dark face, which already looked lifeless. *I shouted at you in my heart, Thérèse.*

Suddenly, the vomiting stopped. The child jerked. Then his face relaxed and regained its natural color. He opened his eyes and smiled at me when he saw me at his side. Then he began to speak: "If you want some coffee, I think there's some in the thermos on the table." The nurse and I were completely amazed. We were speechless and looked at each other as if we were in a dream. The child, who was pink and smiling, didn't stop talking.

The door opened again — in front of the doctor this time. He was accompanied by the parents. The same astonishment struck all three of them. We were like statues and just stared at each other, in turn, in a deafening silence. Then the doctor finally articulated: "Well, he's saved."

The word *miracle* wasn't pronounced by anyone at any time. My nephew's parents didn't have a strong faith and weren't ready to believe — even in such circumstances — in a supernatural phenomenon. The doctor, who was visibly bewildered, confined himself to a simple assessment: the operation had succeeded.

I felt overwhelmed by perplexity. I wasn't familiar with miracles. I had never paid attention to them until then. I had no reaction. I never mentioned my attempt to pray, and I withdrew as if nothing had happened, leaving my sister and her husband alone in their joy.

So, there was our first meeting, Thérèse.

— Geneviève Baïlac (2000)[42]

[42] This child's healing dates back to 1947. But it was the start of a very strong connection between Thérèse and Geneviève Baïlac.

Three Cancers

When I was nineteen, I was found to have breast cancer. This was forty-two days after the birth of my first child. Therefore, I had to undergo cancer treatments while trying to take care of my newborn, a precious gift of God. I firmly believe that that gift of God and my desire to raise my little daughter saved my life.

Four years later, I gave birth to a son, another heavenly gift. Shortly after that, I was diagnosed with uterine cancer. When my son was six and my daughter was nine, my husband abandoned me. I had to undergo more horrible treatment and decided that I needed a good job. I enlisted in the army to serve my country and to build a good life for my children and me. The treatments lasted a few years. At that time, I returned to the Catholic Church, and I thought my health problems were behind me. There wasn't a trace of anything for eleven years. Life went on. I was especially attentive to St. Thérèse of Lisieux. I had read many books about her. She always had a special place in my prayer.

In 1996, I was found to have colon cancer. My prayers increased, and my children and all my friends prayed for me. I asked St. Thérèse of Lisieux to pray for me, and six months later, I was ready for the operation. But there was nothing. My doctor asked me if I had done anything in the meantime.

I asked him, "What do you mean, Doctor?"

He replied: "Jane, there's no cancer."

I started to cry and looked at the ceiling, thanking God and St. Thérèse of Lisieux. I really think that if I had not asked my friends and my family to pray to St. Thérèse, I wouldn't have made it.

— February 10, 2003

"This Saint Who Opened Up My Heart"

My two-year-old son, Thomas, had been diagnosed with terminal cancer (neuroblastoma). A lady suggested that I entrust him to a saint named Thérèse of Lisieux. I had not heard of her. In October, this saint's relics drew a lot of people to St. Joseph's Oratory in Montreal. The hospital where Thomas had chemotherapy was nearby. My wife went to the oratory in the morning. I went in the afternoon, but I didn't get in line to see the relics. So I sat down and tried to pray, wondering what I would say. I must have dozed off. I was at peace. After a while, I literally felt the coolness of rose petals. It was very gentle. But it still frightened me.

The following week, some police officers stopped me to verify my vehicle. After the officer told me everything was in order, I realized, to my surprise, that there was a church called St. Thérèse de Lisieux in that neighborhood. Moreover, the saint's relics were being displayed there.

Finally, I was alone in the hospital's anteroom on the evening of December 12 when I saw what seemed like a great light source in the middle of the room. The most surprising thing was that it didn't create any light. On the contrary, the objects seemed, in turn, to radiate this milky cream lighting. I wondered why the light source didn't move when I got up. At the same time, I received answers to the doubts that I had been expressing.

In short, nine days after this event, my son left the hospital, never to return, except for routine tests.

Today, I'm trying to know this saint who opened up my heart. From now on, nothing will be the same, and nothing in the world will make me doubt the existence of God, in His simplest expression as well as in all His splendor.[43]

— Franck, Canada

[43] *Thérèse de Lisieux,* no. 832 (April 2003): 26.

A Stunning Face

In my thirties, I led an easy, comfortable life as a stewardess. Although I had a Christian education, I didn't feel concerned about religion, but I thirsted for spirituality. Deep down, however, I felt empty at times.

One day, I was drawn to a book cover in a store window. There was an amazing face on the cover. Without stopping, I thought: "That look! That girl understood something. There was something dwelling in her soul that made her stand out from other people." I was dumbstruck. I stopped and turned back to look at those eyes and that radiance again. I stood there for a few moments. Then I felt as if I were being pushed to go in and buy the book, so I did. I was sure I had bought a treasure. I then continued on my way to the airport to catch a flight.

After the flight, I went to the hotel where the crew usually stayed. We made a good team, and we often met at a bar or at the pool or explored the area together. But that day, I shut myself in my room to discover my treasure. Several people called me on the phone to try to lure me to the pool instead, but nothing could be done.

"No, no, don't wait for me, I'm reading something fascinating!"

"All right. Do you want to pass it along to me afterward? What is it?"

"It's the life of St. Thérèse of Lisieux," I replied.

The person I was speaking to was silent for a moment. "All right. See you later."

But after reading *Story of a Soul,* I didn't want any "later." I was fascinated. St. Thérèse's look hadn't gripped me for nothing. I found in it the answers to many questions I had had, as well as a reason for being. Thus, St. Thérèse led me to Jesus. In fact, after I closed that precious book, I had only one desire: to know Jesus, to whom Thérèse had attracted me. "How will I know Him better than through the Gospel?" I said to myself. So, I bought a copy of the Gospels and read it from the first page to the last.

This is how I converted. I wanted to follow Jesus, love Him, serve Him, and know Him even more. First, I decided to change my lifestyle, and then I met with a priest. I rediscovered true happiness and a great love for the Church. This was the start of a long journey.[44]

— Sylvie

[44] *Il est vivant,* 19.

Thérèse, a Beacon in the Night

I'm fifty years old. I'm married and the father of three children. I've had problems for many years that have driven me to darkness and despair. I became addicted to alcohol and led a disordered life in order to numb my anxiety. I was tempted to kill myself. I joined a cult and almost lost my marriage because of it.

Then, one day in 1982, while I was desperately trying to find meaning in life, a name mysteriously entered my mind: Thérèse. This was a name that often came up in my thoughts. When I was younger, I had read some lives of the saints, including Thérèse, but I had forgotten about her. After her name came to mind, I started to look for a book about her. I came across a book written by Msgr. Guy Gaucher: *The Story of a Life: St. Thérèse of Lisieux*. I devoured the book in no time at all. Then I read *Story of a Soul* — the writings of Thérèse. This illuminated my life. Since opening that book, I have become a different man!

Nothing at all has been the same for me. I wrote a book to talk about this experience,[45] and if my testimony, through God's grace, touches hearts, all I can say, despite everything, is that it's the pale reflection of

[45] André Pighiera, *Un phare dans la nuit* [A beacon in the night] (Paris: Editions du Cerf, 2000).

what I felt when I was reading Thérèse. It seemed to me that Thérèse broke into the most intimate part of my soul to open the doors and windows and let God's sun shine on it. A peace that was unknown to me until then overwhelmed me in a wonderful moment. It swept away all my worries. This peace made the loneliness that had shadowed me since I was a very young child disappear. Thérèse went down into this thickest night, where I had been struggling for so long, to show me the way out. She freed me like a doctor of the soul from the ills that were causing me to feel continually hopeless. She told me that God loved me in a unique way, that He was a Father, and that I was His child. This was a sure thing. I knew that what she was saying was true and that from then on, it was impossible to doubt it.

I had complicated my life in the past. It's safe to say that I looked for God in this life's disorders. But I was frantically agitated and running in all directions, whereas I needed to stop. Thérèse showed me her "little way," and her childlike spirit touched me. I had to become a child again! Thérèse's teaching, which was drawn from the very heart of the gospel, seemed to me to be obviously simple: "For simple souls there must be no complicated ways."[46] She placed before my eyes the blazing triptych of childhood, confidence, and abandonment, crowned by honor. I finally had the remedy for my ailment! Yes, I could follow this "little way"!

What carries me to Thérèse and fills me with enthusiasm today is that she taught me to pull out all the stops every day of my life. In fact, she taught me that "everything is grace" when we know that God is always looking at us. So how can we be worried? This has nothing to do with a philosophical fatalism that would make us toys of a blind God. Thérèse's abandonment isn't a subjugation. I'm not submitting to a capricious God. I'm being placed under the protection of a loving

[46] St. Thérèse of Lisieux, Manuscript C, 33v, in *Story of a* Soul, 254.

God who has only one plan for me: my happiness. Thérèse's God is a Father who loves us with a mother's heart. Thérèse's genius, which came to her from the Holy Spirit, was meant to disperse the mists of Jansenism, which had moved God away from people. The originality of Thérèse's "little way" is to have made the path toward holiness visible and accessible to everyone. Since then, I seem to have been "flying from victory to victory" with her.

The old man in me isn't dead, but I know that in Thérèse's school of thought, "a Christian isn't someone who never falls, but someone who always gets back up." If I sometimes regret the past or fear the future, she always tells me that "the past no longer belongs to us, that the future doesn't belong to us, and we must live in God's eternal presence." I'm a willing student but not a brilliant one. If I happen to drag my feet after her, she never gets tired of me. She's as patient as an angel with me.

We've been walking together for twenty-one years. She hasn't left me for one day. This accompaniment is completely aimed toward a single goal: Christ, her Unique Love. Thérèse, through her presence, doesn't hide what's essential. She's at my side to guide me toward Heaven.

Hadn't she promised to win innumerable souls for the Lord? This child from another century had promised that she would "spend her heaven doing good on earth." She got everything she desired. "Ah! In spite of my littleness, I would like to enlighten souls as did the Prophets and the Doctors. I have the vocation of the Apostle."[47] She was elevated to the rank of Doctor of the Church on October 19, 1997! I was very glad to be in Rome that day. In her wisdom, the Church gave herself this child as a spiritual teacher for our time. It was a great day for me — the triumph of childhood that's turned toward the Father — the triumph of love! With all my heart, I was able to repeat with Thérèse in St. Peter's

[47] St. Thérèse of Lisieux, Manuscript B, 3r, in *Story of a Soul*, 192.

Square that day: "I thank Thee Father, Lord of heaven and earth, that Thou hast hidden these things from the wise and understanding and revealed them to babes" (Matt. 11:25).

— André Pighiera, 2002

We'll stop the list of testimonies here. We could continue it at length. In their variety, they give us an idea of the "shower of roses" that the Father favors His children with through the prayer of St. Thérèse of the Child Jesus and the Holy Face. You'll find testimonies of other healings from different countries in the third part of this book — about the world trips of St. Thérèse's relics.

We give thanks for this by recalling the boldness of Thérèse, who said at the end of her life: "God will have to carry out my will in heaven because I have never done my own will here on earth."[48]

[48] *Yellow Notebook,* July 13, 2, 91.

Part 2

Thérèse the Doctor

Women doctors are not to my liking.

—Molière, *The Learned Ladies,* act 1, scene 3

Saint Thérèse of Lisieux . . . I proclaimed a Doctor of the Church precisely because she is an expert in the scientia amoris.

—John Paul II, *Novo Millenio Ineunte,* no. 42

Among all the astonishing events of John Paul II's long pontificate, which started in 1978, there's one that has hardly been stressed. Everyone has noted that he's the pope who has beatified and canonized the greatest number of people in the past two thousand years.

Pope John Paul II has said, "I thank the Lord that in these years he has enabled me to beatify and canonize a large number of Christians, and among them many lay people who attained holiness in the most ordinary circumstances of life."[49]

[49] Apostolic letter *Novo Millenio Ineunte* (January 6, 2001), no. 31.

Another striking event occurred on October 19, 1997. John Paul II proclaimed a new Doctor of the Church: "a young woman — a contemplative" — St. Thérèse of the Child Jesus and the Holy Face. She was the youngest of all the Doctors.

There are still few people who have assessed this event on the theological and spiritual levels. Some of them have sensed its importance. But nobody can predict the meaning of such a proclamation in the future. Time must do its work.

It's useful to specify briefly what a Doctor of the Church is:

1. The person must be a canonized saint, which is already a mark of orthodoxy and basic wisdom.
2. Then — and this is hard — the candidate must bring a standard to the universal Church: an "eminent doctrine"[50] that's useful for everyone. This implies a critical examination of the future Doctor's writings.
3. The Church, of course, has to decide on this "eminent doctrine." The pope, ultimately, does so after four successive examinations that go before the theologians and cardinals of the Congregation for the Causes of Saints and the Congregation for the Doctrine of the Faith.

We must not confuse the Fathers of the Church with the Doctors of the Church. Not all of the Fathers are Doctors, and vice versa. The Fathers of the Church are writers, most of them saints, from the first six centuries who are noteworthy for their theological role in the development of Church doctrine. There were only thirty Doctors of the Church — who were all men — for nearly two thousand years of Christianity. Then, in 1970, Pope Paul VI proclaimed two women Doctors of the Church: St. Teresa of Jesus (of Ávila), a sixteenth-century Spanish woman, and St. Catherine of Siena, a fourteenth-century

[50] The official text says "*Eminens doctrina.*"

Italian woman. This was a very important event that, alas, almost went unnoticed![51]

Theology, in fact, remained almost exclusively "masculine" for several centuries. Women, in the vast majority of cases, didn't contribute to philosophical and theological knowledge. There were, of course, some exceptions, such as Hildegard of Bingen and the Fontevraud abbesses.

We can, of course, include innumerable saints throughout the centuries and great mystics who had very profound divine experiences. But quite often, they didn't express any academic or scientific knowledge. The fact remains that Catherine of Siena and Teresa of Ávila had something to say about God that surpassed theologians' thoughts to a large extent.

Let's not forget that Catherine of Siena was illiterate and that everything we have from her (letters, revelations) was written down by her enthusiastic disciples. So Paul VI did something earthshaking in 1970 when he declared this person to be a Doctor of the Church. Thus, it's possible to be illiterate and be a Doctor of the Church!

The image of the master theologian who is covered with degrees, is the author of ponderous summas, and teaches from the pulpit was suddenly seriously challenged. All the criteria of an "eminent doctrine" were to be revised. They had been laid out by Benedict XIV in the eighteenth century.

St. Teresa of Jesus, the Spanish foundress of the Carmelite reform in the sixteenth century, wrote her masterpieces only out of obedience. Her *Life, The Way of Perfection,* the *Foundations,* the *Exclamations, The Interior Castle,* and so many other marvels sprang up out of necessity.

The Carmelite moaned about her lack of education throughout her writings, which were often composed in inconceivable conditions

[51] See "Catherine de Sienne et Thérèse d'Avila," *Vie spirituelle* , no. 718 (March 1996).

(of health, place, schedule, and so on).[52] The fact remains that Teresa knew more about God through experience than many of her directors.

Women have found their way to universities and have accessed teaching chairs since the twentieth century. So to do without the specifically feminine contribution to the knowledge of God would seriously impair theology.

During the conferences that were given at Notre-Dame in Paris in 1973, on the occasion of the centenary of the birth of St. Thérèse of Lisieux, Fr. Hans Urs von Balthasar declared:

> It's significant that a whole procession of holy women have silently protested against this masculine theology from the Middle Ages to the modern era (this is about eternal salvation) and that they have been extremely hopeful, thanks to the boldness of their hearts and a direct access to the mystery of salvation. To limit ourselves to the greatest names, let's mention Hildegard, Gertrude, Mechthild of Hackeborn, Mechthild of Magdeburg, Lady Julian of Norwich, Catherine of Siena. We could probably add Catherine of Genoa, Marie of the Incarnation, and even Mme. Guyon. But the theology of women has never been taken seriously by the brotherhood. Yet we should finally think about it in the current redevelopment of dogma after [Thérèse of] Lisieux's message.[53]

[52] E.g., "It's hard to explain oneself in spiritual things for people like me who didn't study" (*Life* 11:6). "The rest of us, who are women, aren't educated" (*Life* 26:3). "I'm uneducated. My ignorance is incapable of expressing anything" (6 D, 4:9). "The rest of us, who are women, aren't scholars" (C 28:10).

[53] "Actualité de Lisieux" [News from Lisieux], in *Thérèse de Lisieux, Conférence du Centenaire (1873–1973)*, special edition (May 1973), News from the Institut catholique, 121.

This is what is being done thirty years later. The road is long.

"If men and women experience their being differently in the world, they also go to God in their masculine and feminine ways. We need to understand this spiritual dimension better in order for the Church to breath according to all its aspects."[54]

This is a very serious issue concerning female Doctors in the Church. More than thirty years after Pope Paul VI's prophetic act, the awareness of the indispensable feminine contribution to the mystical knowledge of God is still unfolding too slowly.

But there are no longer only two female Doctors. The last, littlest, and youngest one has arrived in order to reinforce women's official teaching in the Church.

She was far from being illiterate. She had left the Benedictine school when she was thirteen and a half[55] to take private lessons until she went into the Carmel on April 9, 1888, when she was fifteen years and three months old.

Nine years later, she died of tuberculosis as an unknown person. About thirty people accompanied her body to the cemetery in Lisieux on October 4, 1897. Her sister Léonie led the mourning.

Sr. Thérèse of the Child Jesus and the Holy Face had been unknown for her whole (brief) life: by her family — who loved her a lot — her schoolmates, her Carmelite sisters, her chaplains, her spiritual director (who was living in Canada), and her bishop.

What had she "produced"? She had, like her Spanish mother, the Madre, out of obedience, written her childhood memoirs in two notebooks that contained 86 and 36 pages; 54 poems — most of which she

[54] "Homme et femme devant Dieu" [Man and woman before God], *Christus,* no. 190 (April 2001).

[55] At that time, education for girls usually ended when they were sixteen. They were taught, above all, to become a good wives and mothers and experts in household tasks.

was ordered to write — 8 plays to entertain and edify her Carmelite sisters; and 21 prayers. This left her with 266 letters, two of which were added to her manuscripts when, on October 21, 1898, the Carmel published a book titled *Story of a Soul*. Two thousand copies were printed and sent to all the Carmels in France and to some friends.

All that had been written with a basic fountain pen in notebooks that cost ten centimes and in conditions that were as difficult as those of her Spanish mother — often at night in the light of a little gas lamp. She was in very poor health when she wrote the last manuscript. The small pencil that replaced the fountain pen fell from her hands in early July 1897. She was at the end of her rope.

This is the work that earned the young Carmelite the title of Doctor in 1997, after meticulous theologians had examined it with a magnifying glass exactly one hundred years after her death.[56]

But we must not forget that the 1932 request for Thérèse to become a Doctor had been turned down. The Jesuit Paul Droulers, a professor at Gregorian University who died in 1992, told the in-depth story of how St. Thérèse of Lisieux was not permitted to be named a Doctor at that time.[57] I'll summarize that story.

As soon as Sr. Thérèse of the Child Jesus and the Holy Face was canonized, voices were raised around the world to suggest that the young Carmelite could be declared a Doctor of the Church. Hadn't the pope said she was "a Word of God for the world"?[58]

Thus, during a conference that was held in Lisieux from June 26 to July 3, 1932, for the official opening of the basilica's crypt, Fr. Gustave Desbuquois, a Jesuit and one of the founders of *L'Action Populaire*,

[56] Out of the thirty-three Doctors, only St. Alphonsus Liguori had been declared a Doctor more quickly: only eighty-four years after his death.

[57] *Ephemides Carmeliticae* 24 (1973): 86–129; taken up again in *Vie thérésienne*, no. 132 (1993): 243–279.

[58] February 11 and April 30, 1923.

suggested that Thérèse become a Doctor. Not only did he have to highlight the importance of Thérèse's doctrine (which had already been emphasized by Popes Benedict XV and Pius XI), but he also had to provide arguments for a woman to be able to be a Doctor of the Church. The Jesuit thought that, at the time, when women were demanding more rights (including the right to vote), the Church would show her openness with this decision.

The assembly, which was made up of eminent cardinals, bishops, and theologians, rallied behind this proposition. The newspaper *La Croix* passed this request on to France, and different countries reacted favorably to it. A collection of signatures was organized, which started in Canada; 342 bishops had signed it by the spring of 1933.

Fr. Desbuquois was encouraged. He created a file and sent it to Pius XI, who had made Thérèse the "star of his pontificate." He had beatified her on April 29, 1923, and canonized her on May 17, 1925 (an unusually short time frame). On December 14, 1927, on his own authority — for his entourage hardly favored it — he had declared Thérèse to be the Patroness of the Missions, like St. Francis Xavier. That is to say, Pius XI was the twentieth century's most "Theresian" pope.

But when Desbuquois's report landed on his desk, the pope clearly refused to proclaim his star a Doctor. He had already refused the Carmelites' request of February 1, 1923, to have Teresa of Jesus proclaimed a Doctor. Yet St. Teresa's statue stands in St. Peter's Basilica with the inscription "Mother of spiritual leaders."

The pope said, "*Obstat sexus*" — "her gender is opposed to it." It was also inconceivable that she would be a Doctor before her Spanish mother. Pius admitted that the issue would be taken up again by his successors. So everything came to a halt. Cardinal Pacelli, the secretary of state (the future Pope Pius XII), wrote to Mother Agnès of Jesus (Pauline Martin), prioress of the Carmel of Lisieux, that they need not bother to talk or think about Thérèse's becoming a Doctor.

It was necessary to wait almost forty years for Pope Paul VI to take the plunge in favor of two women, as we've said. From then on, the obstacle about the feminine problem fell. The only thing left to do was to "demonstrate" little Thérèse's "eminent doctrine."

The most diverse theologians had been working on this since 1925. A lot of spiritual leaders paid heartfelt tributes to Thérèse's doctrine.

Three very different men — a Carmelite, a Dominican, and a member of the Congregation of the Holy Spirit — very impressively prophesized Thérèse's future between 1923 and 1932.

I will note that the cause of beatification of one of them, Fr. Marie-Eugène of the Child Jesus, has been opened, and that the third one, Daniel Brottier, was beatified in 1984. Their writings, which aren't well known, deserve to be cited because they powerfully anticipated the future — not only the one we're experiencing (about seventy years after their writing) but the future of the twenty-first century and beyond.

Fr. Marie-Eugène of the Child Jesus (1894–1967), a Carmelite and the founder of the Secular Institute of Notre-Dame de Vie, wrote in October 1923, after Pius XI had beatified Sr. Thérèse:

> Thérèse goes all over and settles everywhere with the amiable ease of a little queen. The majestic Roman court didn't know how to resist her childlike charms. Thérèse was led inside this very formidable and enormous tribunal for important people. She had said: "The little ones won't be judged." While her smile won the hearts of her judges, her power made light of their severity. She was enthusiastically beatified, and it was said that they were looking forward to canonizing her. In fact, Thérèse is ambitious, and she has expressed her expectations by increasing miracles since April 29. She wants supreme honors. She wishes to climb the highest pulpit available in

> order to preach her doctrine with more authority and direct the spiritual struggle for love against hate.
>
> To preach a doctrine — what big words! Isn't it true? Yet these big words aren't at all pretentious. Thérèse has a doctrine. We said that the Chaplain called her his "little doctor."[59]

Thérèse of the Child Jesus would be the Doctor of the little way near Teresa of Jesus, the great Doctor of mystical paths.

As we have said, the Dominican Fr. Hyacinthe Petitot (1880–1934) wrote the first theology book on St. Thérèse in 1925 — *Sainte Thérèse de Lisieux, une renaissance spirituelle* (St. Thérèse of Lisieux: a spiritual rebirth) (Desclée et Cie). He wrote these prophetic lines seven years later:

> The life of St. Thérèse of the Child Jesus, though it was internal and hidden, was one of the most faithfully and universally apostolic lives that the Catholic Church can boast of. St. Thérèse of the Child Jesus' apostolate — the range of its breadth and depth — is immeasurable.
>
> St. Thomas Aquinas, using traditional philosophy, taught that every causality belonging to a superior order includes — possibly very simply — the multiple energies that are contained in lower causes. St. Thérèse of the Child Jesus' very brief life was completely angelic and even divine. She'll need a lot of time to develop her latent potential that's still partly unsuspected. This life's efficiency will be practiced in all the orders — mystical, ascetic, moral, social, spiritual, temporal, esthetic, artistic, etc.

[59] A text that was cited in *Thérèse au milieu des Docteurs* [Thérèse in the midst of the Doctors], symposium at Notre-Dame de Vie, September 19–22, 1997 (Éditions du Carmel), 13.

> This is why we will be able to appreciate the extent of our saint's prodigious and multiple influences only in a few centuries. We'll then recognize that St. Thérèse of the Child Jesus was the providential promoter of a new era. We'll then talk about the spiritual renewal that was launched and carried out under her auspices, just as the historians talk about the century of Augustus, Leo X, and the Renaissance, which occurred in the literary, artistic, and scientific fields in the fifteenth century.
>
> Those of us who are watching in wonder at the dawn of this spiritual renewal, like spectators or poor, humble workers, will be able to glimpse its fulfillment — like the sun when it's beaming at noon.[60]

Finally, Blessed Daniel Brottier (1876–1936), whom Thérèse had protected during the First World War (1914–1918) and who had been appointed to oversee the Orphans Apprentices of Auteuil in 1923, was one of the first to dedicate a chapel in Paris to her (rue La Fontaine). He wrote these astonishing lines:

> She's one of the greatest saints who has ever appeared in the Church's firmament. We'll never praise her glory enough because her merits, which appear under a smiling and kindly virtue, surpass those of the greatest contemplatives, missionaries, and saints. To summarize everything in a few words, I don't think I'm exaggerating by saying that Thérèse participates in the glory of the prophets, in addition to her other titles. Yes, the word may be inexact, but it seems to me she received a sublime and divine vocation — that she was the Lord's "spokesperson" — and that God invested her with a doctrinal mission

[60] *Etudes et Documents* (Lisieux, 1932), 19.

that was completely adapted to our time. Moreover, she said straight out: "I feel that my mission has begun — that of giving my little way to souls."

She offers a sure and straight path to our contemporaries, who are full of pride and independence, are motivated by money, and are so often on the verge of being discouraged or in despair. It's the simplicity and humanity of childhood, total trust in God, and God's filial love.... God gave this child, who died when she was twenty-four years old in the Carmel's depths and was unknown by everyone, an incredibly powerful apostolate. More than ten million copies of *Story of a Soul* were printed, and [the book was] translated into every language. What writer or academician can boast of such success in bookstores? Doesn't that prove that God's finger was there?...

This isn't all. We find — on the lips and under the pen of this extraordinary child — statements that would have been considered reckless, arrogant, or crazy if they hadn't been accomplished in full view or confirmed by God via the most dazzling miracles.

What saint, I ask you, has dared to write this? "Everyone will love me!... The good Lord will have to accomplish my will in Heaven since I've never done my own will on earth.... After my death, you will see, there will be what seems like a shower of roses.... I will spend my heaven doing good on earth. No, I will not be able to rest until the end of the world, as long as there will be people to save."

This little saint's last statement deserves a special kind of attention. The other saints were popular for a while, which means that we've prayed to them for a certain period of time or in some countries. Then we forget about them. I think it will

> be different for little Thérèse. I'm convinced that the Catholic Church's faithful will still be praying to her in a thousand years and that she will continue to shower her roses all over the world. She wouldn't have so solemnly asserted the power of her respect in Heaven — she who was so humble — if she hadn't received an absolute assurance from the very mouth of God.
>
> This is why I dared to say that we must place St. Thérèse of the Child Jesus in the first ranks of Christian heroes after the Virgin Mary and the giants of holiness named St. Joseph, St. John the Baptist, and Sts. Peter and Paul.[61]

Many theologians from different countries have studied and emphasized Thérèse's doctrinal contribution since the 1920s and 1930s. We can only list them here.

Cardinals: Désiré Mercier (1851–1926), Jean Daniélou (1905–1974), Gabriel-Marie Garrone (1901–1994), Charles Journet (1891–1975), Narcís Jubany (1913–1996), Yves Congar (1904–1995), François Marty (1904–1994), Albert Decourtray (1923–1994), Emmanuel Suhard (1874–1949), Godfried Danneels (1933–2019), Jean-Marie Lustiger (1926–2007), Carlo Maria Martini (1927–2012), Lucas Moreira Neves (1925–2002), Paul Poupard, Joseph Ratzinger (Pope Benedict XVI; 1927–2022), Christoph Schönborn . . .

Theologians: Fr. Maurice Zundel (1897–1975), Hans Urs von Balthasar (1905–1988), Ambroise-Marie Carré (1908–2004), François de Sainte-Marie (1910–1961), Réginald Garrigou-Lagrange (1877–1964), Erich Przywara (1889–1972), Emile Mersch (1890–1940), Marie-Michel Philipon (1898–1972), Emile Rideau (1899–1981), André Combes (1899–1969), Stéphane Piat (1899–1968), Philippe

[61] Quoted without a reference in *Thérèse au milieu des Docteurs*, 14–15.

de la Trinité (1908–1977), François-Xavier Durrwell (1912–2005), Louis Bouyer (1913–2004), Marie-Dominique Molinié (1918–2002), Marie-Joseph Le Guillou (1920–1990), Jean-François Six, René Laurentin (1917–2017), Bernard Bro (1925–2018), Pierre Descouvemont, Conrad De Meester, François-Marie Léthel …

Let's notice the variety of religious in this list: Dominicans, Carmelites, Franciscans, Jesuits, Oratorians, Redemptorists, the French Mission, diocesan priests … This list is obviously not exhaustive. But it clearly shows the theological impact of Thérèse's works. Let's emphasize that the majority of these teachers weren't able to benefit from all of Thérèse's works, which have been available in the critical edition of her complete works only since 1992.[62]

On the Way to Becoming a Doctor

In 1973, the centenary of Thérèse's birth, during a conference in Venasque, Cardinal Garrone asked a question and gave a clear answer to it: "Could St. Thérèse become a Doctor of the Church someday? I unhesitatingly say yes. I'm encouraged by what happened to the great St. Teresa and St. Catherine of Siena."[63]

Fr. Simeon of the Holy Family, who was a postulator general of the Discalced Carmelites, posed the question to Cardinal Raimondi, the prefect of the Congregation for the Causes of Saints, on December 15, 1974. The Carmelites' prior general worked for the investigation of the cause six years later (December 23, 1980).

At Fr. Simeon's request, Cardinal Roger Etchegaray, president of the Bishops' Conference of France, sent a postulatory letter to Pope John Paul II with this in mind on June 25, 1981.

[62] *Nouvelle Edition du Centenaire*, Cerf-DDB, 8 vol. It was honored by the Prix Cardinal Grente de l'Académie française on June 1, 1989.

[63] *Vie thérésienne*, no. 136 (1994): 239–252.

Eight years went by. Msgr. Pierre Pican, the bishop of Bayeux and Lisieux, asked his assistant to follow up on the Doctor issue on February 8, 1989.

I'm somewhat embarrassed to admit it, but at first, I asked my Carmelite brothers what they thought. They had gathered in a general chapter and sent a request to John Paul II on April 19, 1991, in favor of having Thérèse become a Doctor. We were encouraged, and along with Bishop Pican, we asked the French bishops to discuss this issue during their assembly in Lourdes. The assembly voted for this secretly after a brief debate on October 29, 1991. We must say that the letter of Fr. Yves Congar (who was confined to his sickbed at the Invalides Hospital), which I read in the assembly, had played a decisive role. This theologian of immense prestige responded very clearly to the statement I made on June 9, 1989: "I don't think there's any doubt that St. Thérèse of Lisieux can be named a Doctor of the Church." The Dominican, who emphasized the three requirements that were needed to become a Doctor, concluded with an "absolutely positive response."[64]

Other world bishops' conferences very rapidly joined the French Church's request. It's impossible to list them all. This was an obvious sign that it wasn't a French idea. The 260 bishops in Brazil, for example, unanimously signed the request!

During a private audience on February 18, 1993, we, along with Bishop Pican and Fr. Zambelli, offered to the Holy Father the eight volumes of *Nouvelle Edition du Centenaire*. At the same time, we brought them to Cardinal Felici, the prefect of the Congregation for the Causes of Saints, and to Cardinal Ratzinger, the prefect of the Congregation for the Doctrine of the Faith.

Cardinal Ratzinger emphasized that the complete works in a critical edition were needed for those candidates who were to become Doctors.

[64] Letter to Guy Gaucher, June 17, 1989.

This simple remark seriously encouraged us. This is an opportunity to stress that this long collaborative work, which had started in 1969 and ended in 1992, and totaled 6,200 pages, was an essential basis for St. Thérèse's becoming a Doctor.

At first, while we were working with Sr. Cécile de l'Immaculée of the Carmel of Lisieux, and Sr. Geneviève, a Dominican, under the direction of Fr. Bernard Delalande, the Carmelite provincial, we weren't thinking of Thérèse's becoming a Doctor. But when we were pressured by Fr. Bernard Bro, O.P., director of Editions du Cerf, we envisioned a critical edition of all of Thérèse's works, along with Jacques Lonchampt's decisive contribution. We discerned that this work would be a useful basis for Thérèse's becoming a Doctor in the future.

Some fifty bishops' conferences around the world asked the pope to have Thérèse declared a Doctor. More than 250,000 signatures from members of the People of God from 107 countries must be added to this.

Let's examine one very characteristic testimony among thousands of them.

When Cardinal Lucas Moreira Neves, the bishop of Salvador and the president of the Episcopal Conference of Brazil, came to preside over the Theresian feasts in Lisieux in September 1996, he wanted to write a letter to John Paul II to ask him to proclaim Thérèse a Doctor. Here's a section from the homily he gave on September 26 before the crowd that was gathered in the basilica:

> I see Thérèse as a Doctor, but a Doctor of Life and of Love — love for God, neighbor, and the Church.
>
> I see Thérèse as this daughter of the Church, who becomes a Doctor in the heart of the Church through love. It's in this sense that I asked my brother bishops in Brazil . . . to sign a petition to the Holy Father to proclaim Thérèse of Lisieux a Doctor

of the Church. I'm writing a personal letter to him now from Lisieux to beg him to move forward and to proclaim Thérèse as a Doctor of the Church as soon as possible. I'm telling him this in complete confidence: "Most Holy Father, we know that the Church already has a lot of great Doctors from throughout the centuries. But if you declare Thérèse of the Child Jesus a Doctor of the Church, you'll give the entire Church the joy of being sure of the doctrine of confidence, love, and spiritual childhood. You'll make Catholic women very happy by proclaiming a third woman to be a Doctor of the Church, and you'll give much joy to the young people you love by proclaiming a very young lady — and not an elderly pastor — as a Doctor of the Church. She'll be the youngest Doctor of the Church — even younger than Catherine of Siena, who was [only] thirty-three years old. The world, which includes so many young people and is sometimes concerned about the paths they follow, will gain a young female Doctor of the Church at the dawn of the third millennium. I'm sure the Holy Father will listen to so many bishops and the humble voice of a humble Brazilian pastor who loves Thérèse just as the Holy Father himself proclaimed his love for this young saint here."

Here, dear brothers and sisters, is the humble testimony that I wanted to give Thérèse of Lisieux. I want to encourage you to give your testimony of love, devotion, and confidence to St. Thérèse of Lisieux in front of Thérèse's sacred relics.[65]

I want to give a different point of view, on a theological level, about the request to have Thérèse proclaimed a Doctor. It's a very amazing analysis that's attributed to Fr. Bro.

[65] *Thérèse de Lisieux* (January 1997): 15–17.

In his remarkable book *Thérèse de Lisieux, sa famille, son Dieu, son message* (Thérèse of Lisieux, her family, her God, her message), he affirmed: "We all hope that Thérèse will be declared a Doctor of the Church."[66] He gave theological reasons for this in an abridged version that must be quoted in full:

> A lot of theologians since 1932, in the wake of Fr. Desbuquois, indicated why it would be good to have Thérèse declared a Doctor. This blessing wouldn't call her doctrine into question. She doesn't need it. The proof of her eminent quality has been evident for seventy years. But this declaration will really help rebalance theology — first of all, in its scientific role as a light for the Church and a "switchboard operator," as it were, for the transmission of the Faith. Thérèse of Lisieux's life and works move us off-center and require us to rediscover magnetic north — at least on some decisive points.
>
> - Trinitarian life — the source and end of all human life.
> - The radical newness of Jesus' coming in the Incarnation and therefore the importance of everyday life in the very name of God's transcendence. For Thérèse, this rediscovery results in her clear love of the Church in her institution.
> - The imitation of Christ — not only because He became a man whom people could gaze at but because He is the Word of God who reveals Himself and invites every human being to imitate His Father's "behavior" and receive the fruits of the Spirit. Thérèse restores the dynamism of the virtues of His divine status — and

[66] Bernard Bro, O.P., *Thérèse de Lisieux, sa famille, son Dieu, son message* (Paris: Fayard, 1996), 260.

not just the human one — to everyone through her understanding of love.

- The unity of a contemplative and missionary life through its Trinitarian and filial source. Thérèse leads us beyond an anonymous Christianity that suggests that the Beatitudes are one more social or humanitarian movement that have no theological rootedness in the contemplation of the living God.
- The role of "works" — the meaning of the offering of all suffering and sacrifices. This gives a sense of purpose to merits because, thanks to the "little way," they are real only in the life of abandonment and confidence. In taking up God's audacity and "begging in Jesus Christ," Thérèse has abolished all stoicism, Puritanism, Jansenism, and Pelagianism. She transfigures all fear as an opportunity for self-discovery. The myth of the "adult" Christian has come to an end. Long live the children of God!
- The news of hope in the heart of a lost world.
- Finally, the only possible and really universal ecumenism that's beyond the religions of the Book and the different types of monotheism — the communion and ecumenism that's drawn from mercy. It's understood not only as compassion but as the center of one's very life and the source of the originality of all Christian mysteries.

Thérèse works at an introduction to the "practice" of theology in that she requires the three essential tasks of every catechism and all accounts of the Christian mystery:

- the purification of our ideas so that they don't diminish God

> - the manifestation of the coherence and connections of the mysteries among themselves
> - finally, the proof of the nourishing worth and possibility of a universal and "Catholic" language of faith
>
> Wouldn't Thérèse, along with the Curé d'Ars, be the best reading guide for the Second Vatican Council and its continuation?[67]

The Discalced Carmelites' prior general, Fr. Camilo Maccise, hastily summoned a working committee in Rome right after the French bishops' *ad limina* visit in February 1997. This occurred after the Congregation for the Causes of Saints gave the green light to write quickly a *Positio* to have the saint from Lisieux become a Doctor. This was a huge report that was historical, theological, and spiritual. It justified the request.

Twelve Theresian specialists immediately started working and handed in their copy in record time. Nothing would have been possible without computers, fax machines, and the Internet. It was still necessary to drop off, on May 15 (in May, when there are many long weekends in France), 500 copies of 978 pages that were bound in red — that is to say, 489,000 printed pages — to the Congregation for the Causes of Saints. The printing company Roger Rimbaud de Cavaillon would push its presses to the limit to manage it. The challenge would be met.

Now Thérèse would need to take the four examinations mentioned earlier, and she brilliantly passed them. The Holy Father decided on June 18 to proclaim St. Thérèse of Lisieux a Doctor. She would become

[67] Ibid., 260–262. See also his book *Le Murmure et l'Ouragon. Une femme de genie* [The whisper and the hurricane: a female genius] (Paris: Fayard, 1999).

the youngest Doctor of the Church — only one hundred years after her death.[68] That was a record.

At World Youth Day in Paris, on August 24, 1997, at 12:20 p.m., at the end of the closing Mass on the Longchamp racetrack, John Paul II announced his intention to proclaim Thérèse a Doctor of the Church in Rome on Mission Sunday on the following October 19. Immense applause arose from the crowd of 1.2 million young people. It lasted a long time. "This was an unforgettable ovation! When John Paul II confirmed that Thérèse of Lisieux would become a Doctor of the Church in Longchamp a century after her death, the young modern crowd cheered: 'little Thérèse' from the other century."[69] The pope declared:

> Therese's teaching, a true science of love, is the luminous expression of her knowledge of the mystery of Christ and of her personal experience of grace; she helps the men and women of today, and she will help those of tomorrow, to be more aware of the gifts of God and spread the Good News of his infinite love.
>
> Carmelite and apostle, mistress of spiritual wisdom for many consecrated persons and laypeople, patroness of the missions, St. Thérèse has a privileged place in the Church. Her eminent teaching deserves to be considered among the most fruitful.[70]

[68] Usually, there must be time to appreciate a Doctor's influence. Thus, it took 310 years for Robert Bellarmine to be declared a Doctor, 328 years for Peter Canisius, and 335 years for John of the Cross.

[69] Bruno Frappat, "Oui, la modernité," *La Croix*, September 27, 1997, supplement, 1.

[70] Introductory remarks of the Holy Father, World Youth Day, Longchamp, August 24, 1997, Society of the Little Flower, https://ca.littleflower.org/therese/doctor-of-the-church/pope-john-paul-iis-statement/.

St. Peter's Square

The pope proclaimed St. Thérèse of the Child Jesus and the Holy Face a Doctor of the Church during a Mass with about sixty thousand people in attendance on Sunday, October 19. She was the third woman to receive this title, the thirty-third in the history of the Church, and the youngest one. It took only sixty-five years for this title to be granted her after Fr. Desbuquois's request.

Once again, the young Carmelite shook up the Roman dicasteries. This started very quickly. Her beatification process was opened in 1909, barely thirteen years after her death, despite the First World War, which hampered connections between Bayeux, Lisieux, and Rome. Cardinal Vico, who was prefect of the Sacred Congregation of Rites (which takes care of saints' causes), confided this to the Carmelites in Lisieux: "We must hurry to glorify the little saint if we don't want the people's voice to get ahead of us. If we were in the early times of the Church, when the beatifications of God's servants were done by acclamation, the little sister would have been raised to the altars a long time ago."[71]

Later, when bishops from several countries asked that Thérèse be declared the Patroness of the Missions (they noted the effective help she brought to missionaries), the pope's cabinet hardly encouraged it. Pope Pius XI passed over it.

We might think it would take centuries for St. Thérèse to become a Doctor. In any case, 1997 seemed to be an impossible date. In the apostolic letter *Divini Amoris Scientia* (The science of divine love), the pope justified his decision. It's a major text that emphasizes the importance of Thérèse's "eminent doctrine":

> Shining brightly among the little ones to whom the secrets of the kingdom were revealed in a most special way is Thérèse of

[71] Documentation from the Carmel of Lisieux.

> the Child Jesus and the Holy Face, a professed nun of the Order of Discalced Carmelites, the 100th anniversary of whose entry into the heavenly homeland occurs this year.
>
> During her life Thérèse discovered "new lights, hidden and mysterious meanings" (Ms A, 83v) and received from the divine Teacher that "science of love" which she then expressed with particular originality in her writings (cf. Ms B, 1r). This science is the luminous expression of her knowledge of the mystery of the kingdom and of her personal experience of grace. It can be considered a special charism of Gospel wisdom which Thérèse, like other saints and teachers of faith, attained in prayer (cf. Ms C, 36r)....
>
> From careful study of the writings of St. Thérèse of the Child Jesus and from the resonance they have had in the Church, salient aspects can be noted of her "eminent doctrine", which is the fundamental element for conferring the title of Doctor of the Church.
>
> First of all, we find a special charism of wisdom. This young Carmelite, without any particular theological training, but illumined by the light of the Gospel, feels she is being taught by the divine Teacher who, as she says, is "the Doctor of Doctors" (Ms A, 83v), and from him she receives "divine teachings" (Ms B, 1r).[72]

The pope listed the areas of spiritual theology in which Thérèse contributed in her specific style — the love of the Trinity (with her Act of Oblation, for instance, on June 9, 1895 — a major stage of her spiritual life), the absolutely central Christology, which implied a realistic approach (very feminine) to the mystery of the redeeming Incarnation (summarized in the religious name of Thérèse of the Child Jesus

[72] St. John Paul II, apostolic letter *Divini Amoris Scientia* (October 19, 1997), nos. 1, 7.

[and] the Holy Face), an ecclesiology of communion that places Love in the center of everything, a Mariology that was very much ahead of her time, "achieving results very close to the doctrine of the Second Vatican Council, in chapter 8 of the Constitution *Lumen Gentium*, and to what [John Paul II himself] taught in the Encyclical Letter *Redemptoris Mater* of 25 March, 1987."[73]

We must also emphasize her astonishing sense of the Word of God for her time and religious condition. "Under the influence of the Holy Spirit she attained a profound knowledge of Revelation for herself and for others."[74] What other Carmelite from her convent — and even of her time — wished to learn Hebrew and Greek to deepen her understanding of the letter and spirit of the Scriptures?[75]

Pope John Paul II recognized her "inadequate training," but this was largely exceeded and compensated for by the depth of her experience:

> Thérèse's teaching expresses with coherence and harmonious unity the dogmas of the Christian faith as a doctrine of truth and an experience of life. In this regard it should not be forgotten that the understanding of the deposit of faith transmitted by the Apostles, as the Second Vatican Council teaches, makes progress in the Church with the help of the Holy Spirit: "There is growth in insight into the realities and words that are passed on . . . through the contemplation and study of believers who ponder these things in their hearts (cf. Luke 2:19 and 51). It comes from the intimate sense of spiritual realities which they experience. And it comes from the preaching of those who have

73 Ibid., no. 8.

74 Ibid., no. 9.

75 Process of the Ordinary, 275. See *Conseils et souvenirs* [Advice and memories], 80, and St. Thérèse of Lisieux, *Yellow Notebook*, August 4, 5, 132.

received, along with their right of succession in the episcopate, the sure charism of truth" (*Dei Verbum*, no. 8).

In the writings of Thérèse of Lisieux we do not find perhaps, as in other Doctors, a scholarly presentation of the things of God, but we can discern an enlightened witness of faith which, while accepting with trusting love God's merciful condescension and salvation in Christ, reveals the mystery and holiness of the Church.

Thus we can rightly recognize in the saint of Lisieux the charism of a Doctor of the Church, because of the gift of the Holy Spirit she received for living and expressing her experience of faith, and because of her particular understanding of the mystery of Christ.[76]

The Science of Love

One week after Thérèse was proclaimed a Doctor, in St. Peter's Square, John Paul II received the sixty participants of the Plenary Assembly of the Congregation for the Doctrine of the Faith. Cardinal Joseph Ratzinger, the congregation's president, addressed the Holy Father. The latter responded to this prestigious body of international theologians with this recommendation:

> I am especially glad to conclude this meeting with you today by recalling Thérèse of the Child Jesus and the Holy Face, whom I had the joy of solemnly proclaiming a Doctor of the Church last Sunday. The witness and example of this young saint, the Patroness of the Missions and a Doctor of the Church, helps us to understand that there is an intimate unity between the task of understanding the Faith and the one that is truly missionary, of announcing the Gospel of salvation. Faith wants in itself to be understood and accessible to everyone. So the Christian

[76] Ibid., no. 7.

> mission always aims to make the truth known. Real love toward the neighbor manifests itself in its most accomplished and elevated form when it wants to give the neighbor what man most essentially needs — the knowledge of the truth and communion with it. Supreme truth is the mystery of the one and triune God, which is definitely and unequally revealed in Christ.
>
> When the missionary desire runs the risk of becoming impoverished, this is particularly due to the loss of interest in and love for the truth with which the Christian faith connects us.
>
> On the other hand, knowledge of Christian truth intimately recalls and internally asks for the love of the One to which it has given its assent. St. Thérèse of the Child Jesus' sapiential theology points to the master path of all theological reflection and every doctrinal approach. The love that the law and the prophets depend on is a love that tends toward the truth, and in this way, it is kept as an authentic *agape* toward God and man. Today, it is theologically important to rediscover the sapiential dimension that completes the intellectual and scientific aspects through holiness of life and the contemplative experience of the Christian mystery. Thus, St. Thérèse of Lisieux, a Doctor of the Church, indicates the path that today's theology must follow to reach the heart of the Christian faith, through her wise reflection, which was fed by Sacred Scripture and divine Tradition. This is in full compliance with the Magisterium's teachings.[77]

In sum, we can say that John Paul II indicates a path for theologians to follow — that they study theology in the spirit that was St. Thérèse of Lisieux's. She, of course, hadn't gone through any specialized studies. But she spontaneously went to the heart of the divine mystery under the Holy Spirit's influence.

[77] *L'Osservatore Romano*, French ed., no. 44, November 4, 1997, 3.

Theology and spirituality have been separated for too long. But we know that there's a "theology of saints" and that their writings — if those saints weren't theologians by trade — have opened up infinite horizons concerning the mystery of God and His connections with the world.

If theology is a word (logos) about God, how can we neglect what those who have a personal experience of Trinitarian intimacy can say?

That's why we need to pay attention again to "the theology of the saints," which John Paul II mentioned in his apostolic letter *Novo Millennio Ineunte*: "Faced with this mystery, we are greatly helped not only by theological investigation but also by that great heritage which is the 'lived theology' of the saints. The saints offer us precious insights which enable us to understand more easily the intuition of faith, thanks to the special enlightenment which some of them have received from the Holy Spirit."[78] John Paul II cited two Doctors of the Church, both women — St. Catherine of Siena and St. Thérèse of Lisieux — to confirm his intention.

Fr. Hans Urs von Balthasar once lamented this gap between dogma and the spirituality of the saints: "Theology was, as long as it was a praying theology, kneeling in adoration. This is why its contribution to prayer, its fruitfulness for prayer, and its ability to arouse it, have been immeasurable."[79]

The theologian also remarked: "If little Thérèse had had to write more than a pious autobiography that was, moreover, adapted to her sisters' liking, we could have heard some even more astonishing things than the ones she put down on paper."[80]

Decades went by and, if some theologians were still reticent about allowing women who weren't academics to become Doctors, the

[78] *Novo Millennio Ineunte,* no. 27.

[79] *Théologie et sainteté,* 122.

[80] Ibid., 106. Balthasar couldn't have known about the complete works of Thérèse in 1948. At that time, he had only the 1898 version of *Story of a Soul.*

horizon was cleared and led to a broad understanding of this indispensable feminine contribution to theology for our times.

Now that three women have become Doctors, a new era of theology can open up. We don't perceive it yet because a feminine theology isn't a feminist theology. It consists not in feminizing a masculine theology but in the emerging of woman's specific originality in her complementarity. This reality is being recognized more and more from various sides:

> Thérèse of Lisieux has been a Doctor of the Church since 1997. In this respect, she's more than ever for the twentieth and twenty-first centuries. Thus, we'll need to return to her to understand the contribution she brings to the very contemporary debate about the place and vocation of women in the Church.[81]

> It's the responsibility of today's Church to work for a new union between the masculine and the feminine so that the gospel can still excite believers in our world tomorrow.[82]

> To this day, we're probably far from exploring everything that femininity can reveal about God's richness, as we think we've done with masculinity.[83]

> Society's evolution has made us discover that we can't offer a word of life if we exclude women, who play such an important role in our lives' creation. Our theology for the

[81] Anne-Marie Pelletier, *Le Christianisme et les Femmes* [Christianity and women] (Paris: Éditions du Cerf, 2001), 158.

[82] Robert Scholtus, "Une foi transmise par les femmes," *Christus*, no. 190 (2001), 141.

[83] André Gouzes, O.P., *Une Eglise condamnée à renaître* [A theology that is doomed to be reborn] (Saint-Maurice, Switzerland: Editions Saint-Augustin, 2001), 73.

> third millennium is inadequate if it's not steeped in women's wisdom.[84]

> This mystic (Thérèse), who was engaged in a unique experience, also possessed an elderly spiritual father's wisdom.... She was a beacon who enlightened this darkened twentieth century.[85]

This brief anthology on women's specific contributions to spiritual theology can be easily amplified.

Let's end by returning to John Paul II, who, in 1978 — in order to honor the Doctor of the Church that Catherine of Siena became in 1970 — declared:

> I see in Saint Catherine a visible sign of the woman's mission in the Church. I want to say many things about this, but the short space of this day doesn't allow me to. The Church of Jesus Christ and the Church of the Apostles is simultaneously the Mother Church and the Church as a Bride. Such biblical expressions clearly reveal how profoundly the woman's mission is inscribed in the Church's mystery. May we together discover the multifaceted significance of the woman's mission. May we also rely on the richness that the Creator put in women's hearts from the start and on the admirable wisdom of this heart that God wanted to manifest in St. Catherine of Siena.[86]

We can already perceive in the pope's thinking what would orient him to proclaim another woman a Doctor of the Church nineteen years later.

[84] T. Radcliffe, O.P., *Je vous appelle amis* [I call you friends] (Paris: Éditions du Cerf, 2000), 66.

[85] Claude Langlois, "Spiritualité au féminin," *Christus*, no. 190 (2001): 206.

[86] *L'Osservatore Romano*, French ed., no. 45, November 5, 1978.

It's rather revealing to note that in his letter *Divini Amoris Scientia*, which proclaimed St. Thérèse of Lisieux a Doctor, John Paul II referred to St. Catherine of Siena:

> We can apply to Thérèse of Lisieux what my Predecessor Paul VI said of another young Saint and Doctor of the Church, Catherine of Siena: "What strikes us most about the Saint is her infused wisdom, that is to say, her lucid, profound and inebriating absorption of the divine truths and mysteries of faith.... That assimilation was certainly favoured by the most singular natural gifts, but it was also evidently something prodigious, due to a charism of wisdom from the Holy Spirit" (AAS 62 [1970], p. 675). (no. 7).

Five years later, John Paul II cited these two female Doctors side by side. He called on the saints' "experienced theology" in his apostolic letter *Novo millennio ineunte*:

> The saints offer us precious insights which enable us to understand more easily the intuition of faith, thanks to the special enlightenment which some of them have received from the Holy Spirit, or even through their personal experience of those terrible states of trial which the mystical tradition describes as the "dark night." Not infrequently the saints have undergone *something akin to Jesus' experience on the Cross* in the paradoxical blending of bliss and pain. In the *Dialogue of Divine Providence*, God the Father shows *Catherine of Siena* how joy and suffering can be present together in holy souls: "Thus the soul is blissful and afflicted: afflicted on account of the sins of its neighbour, blissful on account of the union and the affection of charity which it has inwardly received. These souls imitate the spotless Lamb, my Only-begotten Son, who on the Cross was both

> blissful and afflicted." In the same way, *Thérèse of Lisieux* lived her agony in communion with the agony of Jesus, "experiencing" in herself the very paradox of Jesus' own bliss and anguish: "In the Garden of Olives our Lord was blessed with all the joys of the Trinity, yet his dying was no less harsh. It is a mystery, but I assure you that, on the basis of what I myself am feeling, I can understand something of it." What an illuminating testimony![87]

John Paul II's decision to proclaim this humble Carmelite a Doctor opens out on the vast horizon of theological works which will continue to increase. There are already many of them.[88] They are increasing. "The feminine genius" that John Paul II spoke about is attracting researchers. The list of master works is accumulating in every language. We'll specifically note a doctoral thesis at the Pontifical Gregorian University by Fr. Recardo José Salvador Centelles: *En el corazon de la Iglesia, mi Madre, yo seré el amor: Jesus y la Iglesia como misterio de Amor en Teresa de Lisieux*.[89] It's remarkable that this thesis received the Bellarmine Prize for the best thesis of the year in Rome.

A Universal Influence

She hasn't stopped leaving a profound mark on *saints*, and those on the way to canonization, outside the strictly theological field: St. Raphael of St. Joseph Kalinowski, O.C.D. (1835–1907), St. Maximilian Mary

[87] *Novo millennio ineunte*, no. 27. The pope quotes no. 78 of St. Catherine's *Dialogue* and St. Thérèse of Lisieux, *Yellow Notebook*, July 6, 4, 75.

[88] Books on Thérèse already number five thousand titles. Of course, the academic works are in the minority to this day. We can, in French, refer to the work created by Loys de Saint-Chamas: *Sainte Thérèse de l'Enfant-Jésus, Dieu à l'oeuvre* [St. Thérèse of the Child Jesus: God at work] (Éditions du Carmel, 1998), 501–616.

[89] In the heart of the Church, my Mother, I will be love: Jesus and the Church as a mystery of Love in Thérèse of Lisieux.

Kolbe, O.F.M. (1894–1941), St. Teresa of Jesus (of the Andes), O.C.D. (1900–1920), St. Teresa Benedicta of the Cross, O.C.D (1891–1942), St. María Maravillas of Jesus, O.C.D. (1891–1974), Daniel Brottier (1876–1936), Elizabeth of the Trinity, O.C.D. (1880–1906), Titus Brandsma, O.C. (1881–1942), Dina Bélanger (1897–1929) Faustina Kowalska (1905–1938), Mother Teresa (1910–1997), John Vicent of Jesus and Mary, O.C.D. (1862–1943), Édouard-Jean Poppe (1890–1924), Fr. Marie-Joseph Lagrange, O.P. (1855–1938), Dom Columba Marmion, O.C.S.O (1858–1923), Fr. Romuald of St. Catherine, O.C.D. (1866–1936), Cardinal Raffaele Rossi (1876–1948), Fr. Marie-Eugène of the Child Jesus, O.C.D. (1894–1967), Fr. Jacques de Jésus, O.C.D. (1900–1945), Marthe Robin (1902–1981), Madeleine Delbrêl (1904–1964), Fr. Marcel Van, C.Ss.R (1928–1959), Jacques Fesch (1930–1957), and so on.

We could cite long lists of spiritual leaders who adhered to Thérèse's spirituality, from Maurice Zundel (1897–1975) to Jacques Loew (1908–1999), Mother Yvonne-Aimée of Jesus (1901–1951), and Fr. Christian de Chergé, O.C.S.O. (1937–1996), and so on.

In addition, we must recall that this young woman didn't stop fascinating *writers* outside the strictly theological field: Paul Claudel, Lucie Delarue-Mardrus, Giovanni Papini, Marie Noël, François Mauriac, Georges Bernanos, Marcel Moré, Stanislas Fumet, John C. H. Wu, Julien Green, Henri Daniel-Rops, Raymond Queneau, Giorgio Papasogli, Maxence Van der Meersch, Thomas Merton, Fernand Ouellette, Catherine Rihoit, Sven Stolpe, Ingemar Leekiux, Majken Johansson, and so on.

Philosophers: Henri Bergson, Maurice Blondel, Emmanuel Mounier, Jacques Maritain, Jean Guitton, Jean Daujat ...

Politicians: Charles Maurras, Marc Sangnier, Jean Le Cour Grandmaison, Augustin Ibazizen, Giorgio La Pira, François Mitterrand ...

Artists: Édith Piaf, Robert Hossein, Candice Patou, Michael Lonsdale, Brigitte Fossey, Daniel Facerias ...

Playwrights: Henri Ghéon, Gilbert Cesbron, Marcelle Maurette, Geneviève Baïlac, Jean Favre …

Movie directors: Julien Duvivier, Philippe Agostini, Alain Cavalier, Fabrice Maze, Jean-Daniel Jolly Monge …

Painters: Georges Desvallières, Maurice Denis, Henri de Waroquier, Rodolphe Duguay, M. A. Couturier, Isabelle Rouault, Alfred Manessier, Nicolas Greschny …

Sculptors: Fr. Marie-Bernard, E. Manfrini, Jean Lambert-Rucki, Jean Touret …

Journalists: Bernard Gouley, Rémi Mauger, François de Muizon …

Doctors, psychoanalysts: Louis-François Gayral, Alain Assailly, Robert Masson, Pierre-Jean Thomas-Lamotte, Jacques Maître, Denis Vasse, Maurice Bellet, Bernard Dubois …

Recently, the academy itself, in the person of Claude Langlois, the director of studies and president of the Religious Science Department of the École pratique des hautes études, has become interested in the Carmelite from Lisieux. He has so far published three books and has become especially attached to Thérèse the writer. He sees her not as a young girl with a mushy style but an author whose Manuscript B (September 1896), which he called "the poem of September," can compete with the prose poems of Rimbaud and Claudel.[90]

Let's end with a reflection about the Carmel's history. Have we sufficiently noticed and emphasized that the twentieth century was punctuated by the proclamation of three Carmelite Doctors by three popes?

- Pius XI declared John of the Cross (1542–1591) a Doctor of the Church in 1926.

[90] Éditions du Cerf, 2002. It would be easy to give the references for all the other cited names. But this would significantly weigh down these pages.

- Paul VI proclaimed St. Teresa of Jesus (1515–1582) a Doctor in 1970.
- Finally, John Paul II proclaimed St. Thérèse of Lisieux (1873–1897) a Doctor in 1997.

Thus, a religious order whose specific feature is to be entirely devoted to contemplation in a hidden life gave the Church and the world three Doctors, including two women.

Human history can't be limited to factual history. Our history is also a holy history, which is written in lives that are often totally ignored by the media. Thus, it would surely be productive to wonder about the meaning of these three papal decisions. They punctuated a terrible century, during which the heights of horror were reached in the extermination of millions of human beings.

The beginning of an answer may be coming from the life of another Carmelite whom the Polish pope canonized on October 11, 1998. She was Sr. Teresa Benedicta of the Cross (Edith Stein), a German Jew who converted to Catholicism, became a Carmelite, and ended her life in a gas chamber in Auschwitz on August 9, 1942.

The tragedy of this century is manifested in her. Edith Stein was a woman with exceptional human qualities, a very high-level philosopher, and one of Edmund Husserl's students. Husserl saw in her the one who would continue his work on phenomenology. She was a strong feminist who changed dramatically after reading the *Life* of St. Teresa of Ávila one night and declared the following morning: "This is the truth."

She, with the rigor of her logic and constancy in her search for the truth, asked to be baptized and entered the Carmel in Cologne (October 14, 1933). She sacrificed everything to discover Jesus Christ.

She and her sister had to go even further, to the point of giving their lives when they were arrested by the Gestapo on August 2, 1942. They left the Carmel of Echt (Netherlands), where they had taken refuge, with these words of Sr. Teresa Benedicta of the Cross: "Come, we're leaving for our people!"

She was the one who had replied to a friend who had admitted to her that she didn't like the style of *Story of a Soul:*

> What you're writing me about little Thérèse surprises me. Up until now, I'd never even thought we could approach her in this way. The only impression I had was that I found myself facing a human life that was uniquely and completely full of love of God to the end. I don't know anything greater than this, and I want, as much as possible, to transport a little of it into my life and into the lives of those who are surrounding me."[91]

In her martyrdom, Sr. Teresa Benedicta of the Cross, a hidden contemplative Carmelite, sealed her vocation of prayer for the world in the wake of the three Carmelite Doctors who were recognized in the twentieth century as universal spiritual teachers.

Cardinal Joseph Ratzinger rightly emphasized the place of these two Carmelites in John Paul II's theological and spiritual reflection:

> I think I can assert that two women, who were both Carmelites, can help us understand the sapiential dimension that underlies this pontiff's theological reflection. They are a saint whom he declared a doctor and a doctor whom he declared a saint.... The first one, St. Thérèse of the Child Jesus, was a young girl who manifested her holiness in the simplicity of her young heart. She revealed herself to be so wise that she was proclaimed a Doctor of the Church, thanks to John Paul II. The second one, Teresa Benedicta of the Cross, was a young philosophy student. She learned, through her knowledge of the

[91] Letter of July 17, 1933.

> Cross and her freely accepted martyrdom, this mysterious wisdom that emerges from a holiness that is lived out. One is the Patroness of the Missions, which is a sign of the universal openness of salvation. The other one is a Jew who was converted to Catholicism, which is a sign of the reunion between the Father and the Son. We find, in the lives of both of these, the holiness that becomes wisdom and the wisdom that becomes holiness. This is in a unique plan of love and salvation for people. Both are sages; that is to say, they know this wisdom that is revealed only to those who have found the cornerstone of the meaning of their existence in the Cross.[92]

This is a great opportunity to highlight the fact that no pope has given women such a place in the Church since Christianity began. Let's recall his remarkable apostolic letter *On the Dignity and the Vocation of Women* (August 15, 1988), his *Letter to Women* (June 29, 1995), and his *Letter to Priests* (Holy Thursday 1995) on "The Importance of Women in a Priest's Life."

There are three men who are patron saints of Europe: Sts. Benedict, Cyril, and Methodius. John Paul II named three women patron saints of Europe via a *motu proprio* on October 1, 1999: Sts. Catherine of Siena, Bridget of Sweden, and Teresa Benedicta of the Cross (Edith Stein).

The pope consistently emphasized the importance of the "feminine genius."

> The Church gives thanks *for all the manifestations of feminine "genius"* which have appeared in the course of history, in the

92 *Théologie sapientielle: sollicitude de Jean Paul II pour le troisième millénaire* [Sapiential theology: John Paul II's solicitude for the third millennium], Angelicum University, November 5, 1998, for the fiftieth anniversary of Karol Wojtyla's obtaining a doctorate.

> midst of all peoples and nations; she gives thanks for all the charisms which the Holy Spirit distributes to women in the history of the People of God, for all the victories which she owes to their faith, hope and charity; she gives thanks for all *the fruits of feminine holiness.*[93]

John Paul II recognized this feminine "genius" in the only Doctor he proclaimed in the twenty-five years of his pontificate — a woman:

> Thérèse is a *woman,* who in approaching the Gospel knew how to grasp its hidden wealth with that practicality and deep resonance of life and wisdom which belong to the feminine genius. Because of her universality she stands out among the multitude of holy women who are resplendent for their Gospel wisdom.[94]

93 John Paul II, Apostolic Letter on the Dignity and Vocation of Women *Mulieris Dignitatem* (August 15, 1988), no. 31.

94 *Divini Amoris Scientia,* no. 11.

Part 3

Thérèse the Missionary

Ah! In spite of my littleness, I would like to enlighten souls as did the Prophets and the Doctors. I have the vocation of the Apostle. I would like to travel over the whole earth to preach Your Name and to plant Your glorious Cross on infidel soil. But O my Beloved, one mission alone would not be sufficient for me, I would want to preach the Gospel on all the five continents simultaneously and even to the most remote isles.

—Thérèse of Lisieux, Manuscript B, 3r

This third section, which is a succinct account of the passage of St. Thérèse of Lisieux's relics in twenty-seven countries, differs from the first two sections. This is due, first of all, to the fact that this unique spiritual epic is far from over. Also, I was able to refer only to the incomplete reports that we received concerning the Lisieux pilgrimage. Some countries were lavish with them, and we thank them very much. Others sent briefer information. This explains the variety in the chapters that follow.

I took the risk in publishing them now because we couldn't wait for several years to report on such a religious phenomenon. The time will come when we'll be able to push the informative, historical, pastoral, and spiritual work much further.

Yet this allows us to attempt the first provisional outline and to ask some questions at a time when popular religion encounters the new evangelization on a global scale.

One day in 1994, I was in the office of Fr. Raymond Zambelli, the rector of Paris's pilgrimage, and he mentioned for the first time the idea of the travels of St. Thérèse's relics. I couldn't imagine for an instant the international scope that this unexpected initiative would take on.

We received a letter from an Indian bishop who asked us what we were preparing for the centenary of Thérèse's death. He suggested that each continent honor the saint of Lisieux for a year in its own way. But he didn't talk about relics.

I mentioned that the relics had toured France from 1945 to 1947 in the euphoria after the Liberation. The tour was astonishingly successful. On May 3, 1944, Pope Pius XII had declared St. Thérèse of Lisieux the Secondary Patroness of France, on a par with Joan of Arc. This was done at the request of the French bishops.

The relics had then come to Paris from February 27 to March 8, 1945, under the leadership of Cardinals Emmanuel Suhard, the archbishop of Paris, and Achille Liénart, the archbishop of Lille, among others.[95] In November 1946, they toured the country's eastern dioceses. They went to those of the west and south from February to April 1947. They then went to those of the north in October 1947. Finally, they went to Brittany in November.

[95] Thérèse of France, *Les Réliques de sainte Thérèse de l'Enfant-Jésus à Paris* [The relics of St. Thérèse of the Child Jesus in Paris] (February 27–March 8, 1945), *Compte rendu, Documents et Discours,* Ed. des Annales de Lisieux, 1945.

Bishop Germain, the rector of the pilgrimage, which had followed the journey, summarized it in this way: "The passage of St. Thérèse's relics stirred up immense, enthusiastic, praying crowds everywhere."[96]

But that was fifty years earlier. The context was very different in 1994. Society and the Church had considerably changed since then. Who would still care about relics?

Yet Fr. Zambelli reflected out loud: "Why not offer to have the three great cities of France that Thérèse visited during her trip in 1887 — Marseilles, Lyons, and Paris — receive the relics as a token? And why not offer to have a capital on each continent receive them as well?"

This last point seemed to me to be ideal. But why not try it first in France? So I decided to meet with the bishops of those three cities: Lyons, Marseilles, and Paris.

[96] Details of this trip are in the *Annales de sainte Thérèse de Lisieux*, 1947–1948. See the diocesan *Semaines religieuses*.

Lyons (October 14–15, 1994)

Bishop Albert Decourtray welcomed me very warmly. Yes, he wanted the relics to come to the basilica in Fourvière, which Thérèse visited on December 1, 1887, when she returned from Italy. (A slab of marble bears witness to it.) He even suggested that different speakers give Lenten homilies in the crypt. Thus, Fr. Pierre d'Ornellas, Fr. Conrad de Meester, Fr. Raymond Zambelli, and I gave talks. Fr. François-Marie Léthel held a conference on Theresian Christology in the School of Theology in Lyons.

The Carmel of Fourvière swung into action and alerted all of Thérèse's friends to organize and participate in the basilica's prayer vigil on October 14. This consisted of stage plays for children and young people; talks — two ex-convicts spoke about the mission in Africa and Prado; and a choir, which sang Thérèse's poems. Various groups had gathered to help and to participate.

To everyone's surprise, the basilica was crowded with about twelve hundred people, and four thousand passed by during the day. Alas, Cardinal Decourtray had passed away on September 16. Msgr. Abel Cornillon, the vicar-general, declared: "The cardinal, an enthusiastic supporter of Thérèse's becoming a Doctor, is now a powerful intercessor for this cause that he'll help to bring to fruition in 1997."

This first test was very encouraging. There was one regret — that the visit was so brief. Carmel was receiving calls from Annecy and Chambéry: "Can we come and see Thérèse's relics?" The reply was: "Alas, no, they have left!"

After meeting Cardinal Robert Coffy, who received the relics at Notre-Dame de la Garde, I told myself that the stay in Marseilles had to be prolonged.

Marseilles (November 18–29, 1994)

There is a plaque that recalls Thérèse's visit to the basilica of Notre-Dame de la Garde on November 29, 1887.

For this visit, too, the Mission of the Sea, the Christian Movement of Retired People, the Little Sisters of the Poor, families, prayer groups, the Missionary Workers of Living Water, the Our Lady of Life Institute, the Community of the Beatitudes, and others swung into action. There was a magnificent exhibition of thirty-four panels that retraced Thérèse's life and message. A procession toward the sanctuary brought together four hundred young people.

About four thousand people blocked the parking lot. Fr. Bertochi, the rector, had rarely seen so many people. Alas, Cardinal Coffy, who was sick, couldn't preside over the feasts. He was replaced by Msgr. Bernard Panafieu, his assistant.

Of course the relics visited the Carmelites of Marseilles and the Institute of Our Lady of Life, which was founded in 1932 by a Carmelite, Fr. Marie-Eugène of the Child Jesus, whose cause for beatification has been opened. The relics attracted some of the faithful from Carpentras, Avignon, Montélimar, Apt, and Venasque.

The astonishing success in Marseilles opened up some new perspectives. We went from one surprise to another. This was only the beginning.

Paris (March 29–June 12 and September 16–25, 1995)

There was a third city to visit — the capital. Cardinal Jean-Marie Lustiger, like his colleagues, accepted Thérèse's arrival and named a work commission to organize a stay in Paris that was spread out — with interruptions — in about a dozen parishes from March 29 to June 12.

The first one was the Church of St. Ferdinand des Ternes and St. Thérèse of the Child Jesus, from March 29 to April 2. On the following two days, there was a trip to the Trinity International Church of Paris (Emmanuel Community), with a brief passage to the Carmelite convent of the Institut Catholique (April 4). Since we knew the love of the Martin family for Our Lady of Victories, we had to go to that sanctuary, where Thérèse received some great Marian graces on November 4 or 5, 1887.[97] The multiple initiatives of Fr. Duloisy and his pastoral team attracted crowds from April 30 to May 20, 1995.

[97] See Thérèse of Lisieux, Manuscript A, 56 v-57r in *Story of a Soul*, 122–123. For Thérèse, "the wonder" of the capital was Our Lady of Victories.

And of course we had to go to the Orphelins Apprentis d'Auteuil, given the connection between the saint of Lisieux and Blessed Fr. Brottier, their founder.[98]

A procession of the relics was organized on May 29.

This procession, which was followed by about a thousand people, crossed Paris and even the Place de la Concorde, which is usually closed to demonstrations. Some prayer breaks punctuated this very long processions. Photos showed people going to Confession while leaning on parked cars.

The relics remained in Auteuil until May 28 and then went to different Parisian parishes that had requested them. There was another stop in St. Ferdinand des Ternes and St. Thérèse of the Child Jesus Church (May 28–31). Its pastor, Fr. Jean-Yves Riocreux, testified:

> Having participated in the preparation of the feasts in honor of St. Thérèse in Paris and having received the grace of welcoming the relics on two occasions, I can bear witness here to the fruits of Thérèse's presence among us.
>
> It is good, first of all, to emphasize how the delicate and complicated situation had unraveled a few days before the relics' arrival, as if by a miracle. It allowed many parishes to join these feasts.
>
> This is how we were able to benefit, thanks to St. Thérèse, from continual prayer, real conversions, and a spiritual renewal.

98 During the First World War, Fr. Brottier, who was the chaplain of the French soldiers, was unknowingly protected by Sr. Thérèse, as his bishop later showed him. He was named the head of the Orphelins Apprentis d'Auteuil (an adoption organization) in 1923, and he immediately placed the work under the protection of Thérèse — "the little mother of orphans." He built a chapel for her in 1923, and it opened in 1925.

A long book very movingly compiles these conversions and graces that were received in this powerful movement of prayer.

Priests, deacons, and laypeople who participated in these feasts can also testify about them. Priests remained available to hear Confessions and to welcome parishioners and pilgrims coming from St. Thérèse's crypt during the six days of Thérèse's presence.

Moreover, a real pastoral fruit for our parish was that of a greater ecclesiastical communion between the twenty people who were a part of the parish's St. Thérèse committee and the parishioners. The latter also discovered the story of the crypt that was dedicated to St. Thérèse on this occasion. It was built before and during the war, when the pastor often went to the Carmel of Lisieux to meet St. Thérèse's two Carmelite Sisters.

Thérèse had prophesized, "The whole world will love me."[99] How true this was in our country on the occasion of these Theresian celebrations (January 19, 1996).

A banker had lent a nine-hundred-meter site in order to host a Theresian exhibition on Our Lady of Victories square. He also added thirty-two parking spots and had a telephone line installed at his expense.

The Church of Saint-Louis d'Antin received the relics from May 31 to June 3, with the participation of Msgr. Jean Badré, the retired bishop of Bayeux and Lisieux. Then the relics returned to the Trinity International Church of Paris from June 3 to 11. This included a program that was loaded with conferences, shows, and the commemoration of the centenary of Thérèse's Offering to Merciful Love, many

[99] We see these words only in *The Last Conversations and Confidences of Saint Thérèse of the Child Jesus: May–September 1897*, August 1, 1897 (Long Prairie, MN: Neumann Press, 1952), 75.

Eucharistic celebrations, and vigils. The sacrament of Reconciliation was received by numerous people during the closing Mass; seventeen priests heard confessions.

Fr. Patrice Vivarès testified the following in the June 29, 1995, issue of the newspaper *La Croix*:

> Whenever I take one of my godsons for a walk in Paris, I like to suggest that we go into a church for a little visit. This is how — passing by chance in front of the Trinity International Church — I suggested to Mark, a thirteen-year-old, that we look in at this newly renovated building. We were surprised when we entered it. St. Thérèse's relics were being exhibited in a shrine, and many faithful people were forming a procession before kneeling, two by two, for a time of prayer. In the process, the pilgrims could take rose petals to deposit on the case and little pieces of paper to write prayers on and place near the relics.
>
> At first, I instinctively distanced myself from this spectacle, but my godson changed my mind. He spontaneously headed toward the procession, patiently joined the line, and took a rose petal and a small sheet of paper to write his prayer. This otherwise boisterous teenager enthusiastically took part in this spiritual devotion that others would have thought sanctimonious. I myself got into the line with those people who acknowledged that St. Thérèse of Lisieux was a simple and very holy model.
>
> In our modern world, many Catholics aren't satisfied with living their faith in a purely spiritual way. They want to rediscover tangible devotions. Visits of saints' relics are all the rage because they are a visible expression of faith.
>
> These practices and traditional rites don't dispense us from developing an understanding of the Faith that can face the

contemporary world's challenges. It's not enough to venerate relics. We have to approach the profound meaning of our existence as believers in an indifferent world. But a simple faith continues to be an essential component of the Christian undertaking — even for intellectuals. The Gospel presents these simple gestures as pure gems. The widow who puts a coin in the temple treasury, the sick woman who touches Jesus' clothing, and many other figures express a step of faith expressed through a bodily gesture.

In our world, in which people value things that are short-lived, we need to follow the saints who preceded us on the path to the Kingdom. St. Thérèse of Lisieux represents a clear figure of strong, humble faith. Her relics are a sign and an indicator that orient our hearts toward this figure of faith in order that we, in turn, may place our confidence in God as the foundation of our lives.

While the car was returning the reliquary to Lisieux on June 12, 1995, we stopped in front of 9 de la rue Frédérick-Le-Play and told François Mitterand, the former president of France, about the relics' stopover in Paris when he was going on his daily morning walk. He came over right away, and we showed him the reliquary. We told him about its past and current history and offered him some rose petals after a few moments of silence. The street was almost deserted that morning except for a few police officers. Very few of us witnessed this encounter.[100]

[100] Various media echoed this event, but with some mistakes. For example, in his book *Les Derniers Jours de François Mitterand* [The last days of François Mitterand], Christophe Barbier said the meeting occurred on December 3, 1995, when François Mitterand was very ill. He died on January 8, 1996.

The Carmel of Montmartre welcomed its sister from September 16 to 21 after a vacation break. Then St. Peter's Parish and, finally, the Basilica of the Sacred Heart did so. "After having devoted ourselves to the Sacred Heart in the Basilica of Montmartre, we left for Paris on the morning of Monday, the 7th," St. Thérèse said.[101] A plaque commemorates her November 1887 visit in the basilica's crypt. Later, Thérèse offered her gold bracelet to be melted down to form part of the monstrance that would be used in the church.

Finally, the reliquary completed its Parisian journey in St. Francis Xavier parish on December 3. Here are a few comments:

> Thérèse's fame is surprising. Despite the clichés and negative images that are attached to her, which stem from a poor understanding of her message, Thérèse is incredibly popular. Generations and cultural and social backgrounds don't have much to do with it.[102]

Fr. Michel Gitton, pastor of Saint-Germain-l'Auxerroir, reported this:

> We welcomed St. Thérèse's relics from April 28 to 30. It was a short stay during the vacation period, yet people didn't fail to respond and, at certain times, they filled the church's choir. (That is where the shrine had been placed.) The priest was obviously surprised to see unknown crowds who were attracted by little Thérèse's fragrance rush into the church. The simple piety of those who came to light candles and touch and kiss the relics coexisted with the more discreet attitude of other visitors who meditated nearby. We noted that some people in

[101] Manuscript A 56r, in *Story of a Soul*, 121.
[102] Laurence Dario, *Paris Notre-Dame*, no. 793 (September 7, 1995).

the crowd (especially young people from the dechristianized West) were merely curious: "So, who is this Thérèse whom you talk about so much?" The area where candles and books were sold was often used to answer such questions.

When the procession started, it was followed by a huge crowd, which once again confirmed that big public gatherings have a role in our Church and bring joy and pride to Christians.

Fr. Francis Kohn, pastor of the Trinity International Church of Paris, testified: "We've witnessed some true conversions."

Many testimonies were gathered in these parishes. We'll cite some of them:

> I'm unemployed and have no money. Yesterday, I stayed in bed almost all day. But a mysterious strength pushed me to get up and go to the Church of St. Ferdinand at around 5:00 p.m. I bought a book about St. Thérèse and prayed in front of her relics. Today, I no longer feel like killing myself and have regained my equilibrium. I'm thinking of my future. I never would have thought that my life would be changed in one evening in front of these relics. Thank you, St. Thérèse! —*André (excerpt from the notebook of intentions)*

> A succession of Thérèse's "winks" makes me say that I now know what saint I'll dedicate myself to. When I was in Lisieux last summer, Thérèse gave me the grace to meet Claire, whom I'm about to marry. I was there because Guy Gilbert was to speak there. This priest had been an inspiration in my spiritual life since the day I discovered him on Radio Notre-Dame.
>
> I met Claire on the anniversary of Thérèse's exhumation, August 9, at the St. Amour feast (a love feast, which you can't

make up). But this isn't all. I experienced a lot of professional turmoil in the early part of the year that led me to look for a new assignment in my company. I knew the relics were going to come to Paris, and I decided to entrust these shifting sands to Thérèse. The list of the company's vacant positions was to be published in mid-June. But there was a lead, and it came out on June 9, the day of Thérèse's Offering to Merciful Love! I had a month to explore. Going back and forth in front of the relics calmed and encouraged me. I had a positive response on July 13, the anniversary of the wedding of Thérèse's parents, whom Claire and I had often prayed to! —*Jean-Yves*

I only knew Thérèse via Alain Cavalier's film. I thought she was a rather crazy young woman. While listening to her poems, I realized, on the contrary, that she was one who understood everything! —*Bruno, one of Our Lady of Victory's volunteers*

The parish mission that took place at the Trinity International Church of Paris from March 25 to April 3 last year was under the patronage of St. Thérèse of Lisieux, the Patroness of the Missions.

The parish's priests and laypeople, who were devoted to Thérèse, had prepared its last mission for a long time. Her relics' arrival in the church had been announced in the special issue of the newspaper *Du côté de la Trinité* [On the side of the Trinity]; thirty-five thousand copies were distributed for the parish mission. The mail carriers deposited them in the buildings' mailboxes in our parish's area. In addition, thirteen thousand holy cards of St. Thérèse were printed for the mission.

Thirty young people from École international de formation et d'évangélisation's and some parishioners visited in pairs the buildings on the 105 neighborhoods streets, as well as the merchants and many offices in that area. In addition to going from door to door, some street evangelization groups met at noon and in the evening, near the Opéra and the Saint-Lazare station, the Place de Clichy and the Place Pigalle. Everyone we met during the week received a St. Thérèse holy card.

We noticed how often Thérèse opens doors — and hearts. First, she's indisputably famous. It's estimated that 95 percent of the people we met in buildings or on the street, including those from Jewish and Muslim families, knew and loved her.

It was often thanks to her that we were able to contact people and engage in conversations. Here are some choice examples:

> One woman was virulently against the Church. The young people prayed silently. They talked to her about St. Thérèse of Lisieux and gave her a holy card and the newspaper *Du côté de la Trinité*. The woman calmed down. Her husband arrived with the newspaper *L'Humanité* under his arm. He had clearly decided to dismiss the young missionaries, but his wife told him, "Let them come in. It's St. Thérèse of the Child Jesus!" And the conversation started.
>
> A young person we meet in a café who was apparently uninterested and didn't take part in the conversation, finally asked for a picture of St. Thérèse.
>
> A man on the street who saw a picture of St. Thérèse on a badge that a young missionary was wearing on his jacket shouted: "Ah, no, I've sinned too much!"
>
> One man whom we met in an office elevator introduced himself as being HIV-positive and said that he had converted to Buddhism. But he accepted the holy card of St. Thérèse, made the Sign of the Cross, recited the Hail Mary, and left with a smile!

> Damien, a young man from the School of Evangelization, said: "This saint's influence takes my breath away! So many people know this little Carmelite from Normandy — French people, foreigners, and even some from other religions! As soon as we talked about her, faces lit up and people remembered Lisieux. Jews and Muslims — everyone willingly took St. Thérèse's holy card!"

Interiority, peace, enthusiasm, and simplicity abounded. There was an admirable crowd of pilgrims of all races and from every walk of life who confidently bowed before Thérèse:

> A young woman who wasn't baptized came to pray to St. Thérèse with her children, including a seven-year-old girl who asked her mother to write her prayer intentions as she dictated it to her:
>
> 1. St. Thérèse, find me a good husband.
> 2. May everyone in my family believe.
>
> The young women, who was astonished and moved by her daughter's boldness, commented on the event to her mother-in-law: "I've never thought that prayer could be so powerful!"

> "A young women came to pray to St. Thérèse. She was sad and discouraged because her daughter had turned away from the Faith and the Church. In the basket of intentions she put her request to the Lord for her daughter to join her. What a surprise it was for her to notice her coming to attend the prayer vigil that very night! This was a prayer that was immediately answered" (Fr. Francis Kohn, April 18, 1995).

There is a long, well-informed article titled "Thérèse's Relics Fill the Nave" by Philippe Rochette in the May 15 issue of *Libération*. This was what the Parisian priests who welcomed Thérèse thought. It's true that all expectations had been largely exceeded. We discovered that a whole group of people was very interested in her. They came together from all walks of life and all social classes for the humble Carmelite from Lisieux.

The Spirituality of the Relics

How can we still transport and venerate relics at the dawn of the third millennium? Isn't this going back to superstition, obscurantism, and magic? Isn't this maintaining the wrong kind of popular devotion?[103]

Downward spirals and excesses are certainly possible. The spontaneous movements of devotion and enthusiasm must be evangelized and refer to the Christian mystery.

Without going into a scholarly history of the devotion to relics, let's emphasize the Church's consistency throughout the centuries in venerating the bodies of martyrs and saints. This was confirmed starting with Polycarp's martyrdom in the middle of the second century. His bones were collected and thought to be "more valuable than precious stones and more to be esteemed than gold."[104]

[103] See Frédéric Munier, "Reliques" in *Dictionnaire des miracles et de l'extraordinaire chrétiens* [Dictionary of Christian miracles] (Paris: Fayard, 2002).

[104] Eusebius, *Church History*, bk. 4, chap. 15, no. 43, in *Nicene and Post-Nicene Fathers*, Second Series, vol. 1, trans. Arthur Cushman McGiffert, ed. Philip Schaff and Henry Wace. (Buffalo, NY: Christian Literature, 1890), revised and edited for New Advent by Kevin Knight, http://www.newadvent.org/fathers/250104.htm.

St. Augustine (who died in 430) and St. Gregory the Great (who died in 604) thought along the same lines. The latter declared that saints' remains could accomplish miracles. The cult of saints experienced its apex specifically between the eighth and twelfth centuries. There were, of course, some abuses, thefts of relics, and shameful trafficking, but these misdeeds only showed the strong interest in saints' relics.

From the Carolingian era onward, each altar that was consecrated in a church had to contain relics of saints. The altar was the symbol of Christ, and the relics signified the belief in the final resurrection. This has continued to this day.[105]

Thus, people began making pilgrimages to honor saints where their remains were located. The most famous one is Compostela, in honor of James the Apostle.

The *Catechism of the Catholic Church,* in speaking about popular religion, mentions the veneration of relics, which it says is legitimate but follows through with important recommendations:

> Besides sacramental liturgy and sacramentals, catechesis must take into account the forms of piety and popular devotions among the faithful. The religious sense of the Christian people has always found expression in various forms of piety surrounding the Church's sacramental life, such as the veneration of relics, visits to sanctuaries, pilgrimages, processions, the stations of the cross, religious dances, the rosary, medals (cf. Council of Nicaea II: DS 601; 603; Council of Trent: DS 1822), etc.
>
> These expressions of piety extend the liturgical life of the Church, but do not replace it. They "should be so drawn up

[105] "The practice of placing relics of Saints, even those not Martyrs, under the altar to be dedicated is fittingly retained." *General Instruction of the Roman Missal,* no. 302.

> that they harmonize with the liturgical seasons, accord with the sacred liturgy, are in some way derived from it and lead the people to it, since in fact the liturgy by its very nature is far superior to any of them" (*SC* 13 § 3).
>
> Pastoral discernment is needed to sustain and support popular piety and, if necessary, to purify and correct the religious sense which underlies these devotions so that the faithful may advance in knowledge of the mystery of Christ (cf. John Paul II, *CT* 54). Their exercise is subject to the care and judgment of the bishops and to the general norms of the Church. (1674–1676)

Fr. Zambelli, in an enlightening article, recalled that relics give us a profound sense — of which we are aware — that "we're not pure spirits, and we need signs."

The saints' relics are only very poor, fragile signs of what their bodies were like. In the presence of these relics, therefore, we can more easily bring their human condition to mind. The saints acted, thought, prayed, worked, and suffered with their bodies.

So God wants to use these tenuous and, at times, almost ridiculous signs to manifest His presence and make His power and glory shine. For He's the one who acts through these signs. God's logic is different from the world's logic. This is what Paul reminded the Corinthians of: "God chose what is foolish in the world to shame the wise, God chose what is weak in the world to shame the strong" (1 Cor. 1:27). But hadn't the same apostle just declared: "For the foolishness of God is wiser than men, and the weakness of God is stronger than men" (1 Cor. 1:25)?

Let's come back to Thérèse's specific case. It's a fact that God, who had received so many signs of love from her through her humanity, is pleased, in return, to manifest His love in the presence of and through contact with her poor mortal remains (which are like the remains of a plucked rose).

Her saving power is revealed and manifested through these poor signs. To be convinced of this, it's enough to read the volumes of testimonies about favors and healings obtained through Thérèse's relics as well as the large quantity of mail that arrives in Lisieux every day. Who can say how many people preciously preserve a picture bearing the note "touched to the saint's relics"? We are dealing very much with another kind of logic, as it appears in the words of Jesus: "I thank thee, Father, Lord of heaven and earth, that thou hast hidden these things from the wise and understanding and revealed them to babes" (Luke 10:21).

Fr. Zambelli cited a convincing example — that of Blaise Pascal. This mystic and thinker, who was brilliant in so many fields, revealed his thoughts about relics that he himself venerated with profound respect. It's true that he had been deeply moved by witnessing the miraculous healing of his niece, who had a lacrimal fistula and was instantaneously healed when she came in contact with the Holy Thorn. The miracle was authenticated by the Church in Paris. This is why Pascal wrote: "As God has made no family more happy, let it also be the case that He find none more thankful."[106]

In his correspondence with his friends the Roannezes, Pascal wrote this after he had received a relic as a gift:

> It's true that the Holy Spirit rests invisibly in the relics of those who died in God's grace until He visibly appears in the Resurrection. This is what makes the saints' relics really worthy of being venerated. For God never abandons His own — not even in the tomb, where their bodies, although dead in men's eyes,

[106] Blaise Pascal, *Pensées* (New York: E. P. Dutton, 1958), no. 855.

> are more alive before God because sin is no longer there. Sin's fruits aren't still there. This unfortunate root, which is inseparable from it during life, makes it so that they can't be honored then, for they are rather worthy to be hated. This is why death is necessary, so that this unfortunate root is entirely mortified, and that's what makes it desirable.

In light of these lines, it seems to me that the attitude we must have toward relics is admirably described by the same Pascal in this other fragment of his *Pensées*: "The external must be joined to the internal to obtain anything from God, that is to say, we must kneel, pray with the lips, etc., in order that proud man, who would not submit himself to God, may be now subject to the creature. To expect help from these externals is superstition; to refuse to join them to the internal is pride."[107]

Fr. Jean-Robert Armogathe gave a conference titled "A Christianity of Flesh and Blood: The Cult of the Relics." He gave the conference on the occasion of the loan of the relics of Christ's Passion to the Cathedral of Notre-Dame in Paris on June 1, 2001. Those relics are usually housed in the magnificent reliquary that is the Sainte-Chapelle, which was built by St. Louis IX (who died in 1270).

Fr. Armogathe recalled that the Catholic Church, despite the attacks on relics in the sixteenth century, never abandoned her devotion to relics. He then reminded us that in December 1563, the Council of Trent required all bishops to teach the faithful the right way to engage

[107] *Pensées*, no. 250. *Thérèse de Lisieux*, no. 742 (February 1995): 18–19, 33. See Fr. Zambelli's communication in the Symposium in Lisieux 2001. "Thérèse de Lisieux, apôtre de la nouvelle évangélisation, l'accueil des reliques de Thérèse dans le monde: histoire et signification [Thérèse of Lisieux, apostle of the new evangelization. the reception of Thérèse's relics in the world: its history and significance], which appeared in *Vie Thérésienne*, no. 165 (2002): 33–53.

in "the intercession of the saints and their invocation, the honors due to the relics, and the legitimate use of images."

Two basic truths come together in devotion to relics: the communion of saints (the spiritual solidarity that unites us with one another as members of Christ) and the resurrection. "The veneration of the relics of a body that's promised [to be restored] in the heavenly Jerusalem is, first of all, an act of faith in the resurrection of the flesh — that of the Firstborn leading saved humanity, whose saints are the tangible fulfillment [of the passage] from this world into glory."[108]

Prudence and discernment are recommended, but the Council "serenely reaffirmed the importance of relics associated with images and statues."

Fr. Armogather, who is an alumnus of the École normale supérieur, posed a good question: "Why does the Church, despite so many misfortunes, maintain the cult of relics?"

> The answer is simple, and history itself provides it for us. It's because Christianity has a history. It's a history of flesh and blood — because Christianity arose from God's election of a people and the birth of God Himself in His people's flesh. Christianity isn't made up of abstract ideas and isn't a philosophical system. It's a religion of flesh and blood. There's no Resurrection without death and no salvation without an Incarnation.

Thus, he can draw this conclusion:

> The Church's presentation of holy relics is a deliberate choice to affirm the integration of faith in the history of the world

[108] Alain Grau, "Faut-il brûler les reliques?" [Must we burn relics?], *France catholique*, no. 2403 (May 14, 1993): 16.

> and the integration of its God in human history. It's not about conceding to popular practices or being condescending toward an uninformed piety. To suggest praying in front of the Passion's holy relics is to assert that our faith isn't disembodied and that the invitation to believe — this invitation that the Church presents to the world — is nourished with the Flesh and Blood of God made man. The relics are gifts that God has given us to assist us in the groping of faith through the reality of the objects that accompanied the exhausting task of salvation that God undertook on the earth.

What is said here about objects also applies to saints' remains, which have been honored since Christianity began.

The body of Thérèse of the Child Jesus and the Holy Face was first exhumed on September 6, 1910, according to the rules of a beatification process. On August 10, 1917, it was unearthed another time for the second process, which is known as the apostolic process. Only bones remained of the Carmelite's body. Finally, her remains were exhumed a third time to bring her back triumphally into her Carmel on March 26, 1923. The hearse drove between a crowd of fifty thousand people, and the remains were placed in a shrine that was especially prepared for them.[109] They have been there ever since.

The *Directory on Popular Piety and the Liturgy*, which was published in December 2001 by the Congregation for Divine Worship and the

[109] We were lucky to find an eight-minute newsreel in 1997 that showed the exhumation in the Lisieux Cemetery and the trip to Lisieux. See "La translation des reliques de cimetière de Lisieux au monastère du Carmel, le 26 mars 1923 [The transfer of the relics of the Lisieux Cemetery to the Carmel Convent on March 26, 1923] in *La Bienheureuse Thérèse de l'Enfant-Jésus, sa beatification* [Blessed Thérèse of the Child Jesus: her beatification] (Imprimerie des Orphelins Apprentis d'Auteuil, 1923), 61–92.

Discipline of the Sacraments, recognizes the legitimacy of the cult of saints' relics. It emphasizes that "the faithful deeply revere the relics of the Saints." Thus, an "adequate pastoral instruction of the faithful about the use of relics" is necessary. The text concludes:

> The various forms of popular veneration of the relics of the Saints, such as kissing, decorations with lights and flowers, bearing them in processions, in no way exclude the possibility of taking the relics of the Saints to the sick and dying, to comfort them or use the intercession of the Saint to ask for healing. Such should be conducted with great dignity and be motivated by faith.[110]

[110] Congregation for Divine Worship and the Discipline of the Sacraments, *Directory on Popular Piety and the Liturgy* (December 2001), no. 237.

Belgium (November 17–27, 1995)

Then another unexpected letter arrived in Lisieux. Msgr. André-Mutien Léonard, the bishop of Namur, Belgium, requested the relics for his diocese. This caused a predicament for the Carmelites in Lisieux. When was the reliquary finally going to return home? Now it was a question of the relics' leaving France, which was a first. But how were we to say no in light of Bishop Léonard's enthusiasm and his reasons for the request?

Thus, from November 17 to 27, 1995, Thérèse visited St. Aubin's Cathedral in Namur, the Sanctuary of Our Lady of Beauraing, St. Martin's Church in Arlon, and six Carmels. The visit exceeded all expectations. Twenty thousand people crowded St. Aubin's Cathedral, and more than ten thousand flocked to Beauraing and Arlon.

The Belgian press was unanimous and ran the headline "Namur Pays Tribute to the Little Thérèse." How were we to explain the great attraction to St. Thérèse?

The Wallonia conference center's monthly *Confluent*[111] remarked:

> Little Thérèse attracted large crowds during the visit of her shrine to Namur. This success was repeated in Beauraing and

[111] No. 232, December 1995.

> Arlon. It was astonishing! In fact, we have noticed a decrease in religious practice (to the point of taking up the issue of reallocating "empty churches"). Also, criticisms are being expressed everywhere against the Church — particularly in the Diocese of Namur — and against "traditional" positions adopted by its bishop. So how do we explain that the cathedral hasn't been emptied for five days and five nights — with an unexpected resurgence of enthusiasm? This seems to refute the narrative about the Faith's setback. Do we explain it by the attraction of a saint whose words speak more to people's hearts than sermons about the world's miseries do? If so, this change might indicate a certain demotivation of Christians in the realm of social action. Do we explain it by the strong impression that we feel when participating in high-quality liturgical ceremonies?

A lay organizer placed the statement in its ecclesiastical context:

> The reception of the relics of St. Thérèse of the Child Jesus in the Diocese of Namur is part of the pastoral activity for Christian communities preparing for the 2000 Jubilee.
>
> In accordance with the episcopal council, the bishop of Namur, who had learned about the tour of the shrine containing the saint's mortal remains, jumped at the opportunity to offer this beneficial visit to his flock. Thus, the Diocese of Namur could, in the presence of the relics, celebrate Mass, adore the Blessed Sacrament, pray the Rosary, bring targeted audiences together, sing Thérèse's poems, experience the sacrament of Reconciliation, hear lectures by specialists on saints, and so forth.
>
> A young philosopher also wondered:
>
> People want to connect with the profound meaning of their existence while they speak to Thérèse. The inner life is like a

> battery that must not be allowed to run out. Otherwise, we won't live anymore. A nun explained that "Thérèse allows everyone to recharge their batteries." This is what the saint undoubtedly represents in the eyes of her faithful ones: a path toward meaning, a return to the source of our position in the world and our position before the divine, and an oasis in the growing desert of social problems.

The bishop who organized the visit and practically accompanied the reliquary for ten days expressed his enthusiasm in an article with an unequivocal title: "Thérèse is a hit!"

> I expected that Thérèse of the Child Jesus' visit to the Diocese of Namur would be a great spiritual success, but not to this extent!
>
> The crowds' interest exceeded all expectations. Few events have mobilized so many people in our two provinces — and not only for a one-time gathering but for ten days in a row. I was especially impressed by the participants' simple joy. Many of them spontaneously approached the organizers to express their happiness and their thanks — emotionally at times.

On January 3, 1996, Bishop Léonard would draw, in hindsight, some very perceptive pastoral conclusions regarding this first visit of St. Thérèse's relics outside France:

> The ten-day sojourn of Thérèse's relics in the Diocese of Namur continues to be a significant pastoral event.
>
> Thérèse's presence enabled what very rarely happens. People from very different classes and backgrounds enthusiastically participated in the same spiritual event. All ages were included — children, teenagers, young couples, middle-aged people, and senior citizens. All social classes

were there — from the bourgeoisie to the poorest of the poor and the middle and working classes. There were intellectuals as well as manual Laborers. All vocations were represented — laypeople in crowds, priests, deacons, consecrated people, and old and new communities that gathered together in a great fraternal communion.

Thérèse achieved a splendid evangelization mission among us during this remarkable popular gathering. She completely fulfilled her mission as a "Doctor." She did this not by teaching an academic theology (which is indispensable elsewhere) but by living the "theology of the saints" (according to von Balthasar's beautiful expression) among us. For who, in truth, can speak better to us about God than the saints?

This young Carmelite took thousands of people by the hand for ten days. She taught them about God's merciful love and the paths of prayer and the experience of simple truths whose richness they hadn't seen until then. This is a very uncommon and unusually deep training for a diocese, and it's far from being over! All the diocese's schools had received a study guide on Thérèse. Thanks to her visit's immense success, students in many classes are starting to study Thérèse and discover the living God through her.

There has also been a great theological impact on the sacramental and liturgical levels. Mass was enthusiastically celebrated in meticulous and lively ways — beautiful and fraternal. We experienced very fervent celebrations of Reconciliation. We adored the Blessed Sacrament. We sang Lauds and Vespers in packed churches. Never in the memory of St. Aubin's Cathedral had Vespers been sung with more than six hundred people in the cathedral! What a splendid introduction of an entire people to the beauty of liturgical prayer!

> Thérèse's visit also had a definite impact on the preparation of the 1996 Eucharistic Jubilee (the 750 years of the institution of Corpus Christi in Liège) and of the Great Jubilee in 2000.
>
> Thérèse's arrival taught us again about the joy of experiencing a beautiful Church event together, coming from very different backgrounds.
>
> The main part, however, defied every evaluation beyond this measurable pastoral impact. Who could appreciate the secret conversions, the renewed impulses of generosity, the thousand hidden devotions, and the tears of repentance, healing, and joy? Only the Father knows all that. He sees in secret. But isn't God's secret the first and last ingredient of pastoral theology?
>
> Frankly, I wish that every bishop would know the joy of being able to have his diocese live through such a deep pastoral experience. Thanks to the Carmel and the pilgrimage of Lisieux for making this possible throughout France and even outside France, praise God!

The reliquary had just returned from Belgium when some Parisian parishes requested it from November 29 to December 10.

Pamiers (December 10–23, 1995)

But Thérèse couldn't linger in Paris because the French bishop in Pamiers in Ariège asked for the relics "to evangelize his diocese." This was Msgr. Albert-Marie de Monléon, a Dominican who was installed as bishop in Pamiers on October 1, 1988, and who entrusted his people to Thérèse as soon as he arrived. He had the idea and "audacity" — according to his own expression — of asking to have Thérèse's relics visit Ariège during the seventh centenary of his diocese's foundation.

On December 10, 1995, the reliquary would fly, for the first time, in a single-engine Cessna Centurion plane from Toussus-Le-Noble to the airport in Pujols. The bishop was on board. There was another very striking premiere — a visit to twenty prisoners in the Foix detention center. One of them, who had been sick in his cell, couldn't approach the shrine. At his request, his friends carried it to him through the maze of corridors.

There was a youth meeting as well as a street procession. A Mass filled the cathedral on Sunday, the seventeenth. During the celebration, Bishop de Monléon proclaimed Thérèse the patroness of a group of young people known as Ariège Terre Promise (Promised Land).

Fr. Marc Prigent, pastor of Saint-Girons, testified:

The first thought that inspires me about this Theresian mission — with the hindsight of six months — comes directly from the Gospel: "The poor have good news preached to them" and "Blessed are the poor in spirit, for theirs is the kingdom of heaven" [Matt. 11:5; 5:3].

Thérèse speaks directly to those who resemble her in one way or another. This includes the poor and prisoners, who were very much affected by this highly intense and moving visit, but also, of course, the Carmelites, her sisters, older people, children, and young people. They, in particular, were deeply touched by Thérèse's presence and message and, more so, by her personality. The young people's evangelization received a renewed and decisive boost from Thérèse's being proclaimed patroness of the group Ariège Terre Promise. A direct fruit of this was the pilgrimage of the young people to Lisieux last May.

I can attest to Thérèse's impact in my mission with young people every day — through her eyes and her face, which speak to hearts, and her message about mercy, the love of the Father, trust, abandonment, and the spirit of childhood. She quietly gains entry everywhere — without any manifestation or loud or brilliant demonstration — through young people and children, and in families, homes, and hearts.

In this spirit, I'd like to emphasize another observation. Thérèse's active presence in evangelization (and in all environments) gives her a great yet very gentle strength, which leads to a deep-rooted faith, and a more staunch, powerful, and interior Christian life. In fact, I notice this astonishing depth and faithfulness among all the young people whom she

> directly touched — daily prayer, Mary's stronger presence, a regular sacramental life, and the desire for commitment and service in the Church. Yes, Thérèse makes people love the Church. She teaches her "novices" the spirit of offering and the gift of oneself. I've also observed that she strengthens budding vocations, to say nothing of the ones she has already kindled.
>
> As she had prophesied, Thérèse is loved by everyone — with strength, tenderness, and conviction. Even those who do not know her very well are touched by her presence and the simple mention of her life or the sight of her face. For example, the reference to her message or the singing of her poems in the liturgy (even the liturgy of the deceased) gives rise to a distinctive meditation or, to speak another language, a very strong "anointing."
>
> The passage of Thérèse's relics hasn't, therefore, been a "flash in the pan." On the contrary, it has been the source of a deep, lasting renewal of our faith and, in concrete terms, of the mission in Ariège — not in a spectacular way but in a very interior one. Consequently, we haven't finished seeing the fruits of it — far from it.

After hearing about these astonishing events, the abbot of a Benedictine monastery asked for the relics and emphasized how much the monks really loved St. Thérèse. Fr. Zambelli asked him to find out whether any other monasteries were interested. A few weeks later, the abbot responded that he had found thirty-four interested monasteries.

This meant that if Lisieux agreed to it, the reliquary would go to at least thirty-four French dioceses. But how was it to go only to Cistercian and Benedictine monasteries when there were Carmelites in every diocese? As soon as the Carmelites heard the news, they responded vigorously: "We want to welcome our sister!"

Bordeaux welcomed Thérèse on the initiative of Bernard Peyrous, of the Emmanuel Community, from December 17 to 23, 1995. Fr. Peyrous was the pastor of Sacred Heart Parish, and he greeted Thérèse in the presence of Archbishop Pierre Eyt. The relics would go to St. Eulalie Church, where Louis, the son of Captain Martin, who was garrisoned in Bordeaux, was baptized on August 23, 1823.

It was suggested that two police officers in civilian clothes drive Thérèse back to Lisieux.

Sixty-Seven French Monasteries (January 8–May 1, 1996)

In 1996, Thérèse's visits to French monasteries would increase. She left Lisieux on January 8 and would not return there until the end of May. She stopped in forty-five monasteries and twenty-two Carmels. Let us mention, among others, the great Soligny-la-Trappe, Saint-Benôit-sur-Loire, Port-du-Salut, Kergonan, Solesmes, Sept-Fons, Rimont, Chambarand, Our Lady of the Snows, Bonneval, Belloc, St. Wandrille, Bellefontaine, and Timadeuc.

We then received a call from bishops in Belgium and in Luxembourg. The other Belgian dioceses had undoubtedly heard about the considerable success of the relics' visit to the Diocese of Namur. They wanted to benefit from this evangelical mission to prepare for the centenary of the French saint's death. Thérèse was going to cross the border for the second time.

Belgium (May 11–18, 1996) and Luxembourg (May 18–20, 1996)

Conrad De Meester, a Flemish Carmelite and an eminent Theresian, organized this Belgian journey. It would reach Brussels, Louvain, Banneux, Gand, Ypres, Anvers, Bruges, Tournai, and Mons, along with a three-day stay in Luxembourg.

Let's turn the spotlight on some characteristic and memorable moments. These include the great procession in Hanswijk on May 12 and the celebration of the Ascension in the Basilica of Koekelberg, which Cardinal Godfried Danneels presided over, in the presence of many Belgian Carmelites (Thérèse visited all of these monasteries).

We also won't forget this astonishing fact. On June 9, Thérèse's reliquary was placed near the tomb of Jansénius (Cornelius Jansen; 1585–1638). He was the instigator of a very complex spiritual trend known as Jansenism, which devastated the Church — particularly in France. Thérèse's life and doctrine were the perfect antidote.

Cardinal Danneels was very much present at these celebrations. He retraced Thérèse's life in his pastoral letter of Easter 1996 and declared her "little way" a "Copernican" revolution in the search for holiness. He announced the relics' arrival in Belgium in the final round and concluded as follows:

Thérèse's relics will come to various places around the country for a few weeks in May. The more or less mocking thoughts won't fail to spring up: "Let's leave Thérèse in peace." "Is this kind of marathon of a deceased person's body really necessary?" There will be many other similar thoughts.

Rest? Thérèse can't rest. One of the main theological and spiritual perspectives she brought to our era — among others — was that she shook up preconceived ideas about life after death from top to bottom. Eternity isn't peaceful and somnolent. Thérèse died when she was twenty-four. But her mission hadn't ended: "I can't rest as long as there are souls to be saved." "I do not intend to remain inactive in Heaven. I want to continue to work for the Church and for souls." She has done so for one hundred years. Thérèse rest? Come on!

But her relics? The Church has preserved the relics of martyrs in her altars from the very beginning. By the way, isn't it remarkable that the humble faithful never ask these critical questions? Might it be the characteristic of children and those who are like them to hold on to everything that reminds them of those they have loved? To their bodies, first of all. It's enough to see the joy of all the humble people wherever the relics go. It's a sign that does not deceive. For they — the poor and the little ones — often can't afford to travel to Lisieux.

It's true that the real place where Thérèse rests isn't, first of all, her shrine, but the Church and the childlike hearts of people who pray to her and connect with her compassion and the offering of herself for the world's salvation. But it's not astonishing that we find this Church and this kind of person wherever her reliquary goes. "As a deer longs for flowing streams . . ." [see Ps. 42:1].

His appeal for the faithful to come during the visit of the relics was heard, and the response exceeded his pastoral expectations.

At the request of Msgr. Fernand Franck, the reliquary crossed the Grand Duchy of Luxembourg's border for a stay from May 18 to 21. The cathedral was packed on May 18 and 19.

They would also be venerated in the Carmel in the presence of Maria Teresa, the Grand Duchess, and of Princess Sibilla. Jean Favre's play *Thérèse of Lisieux*, with Corinne Lechat and Anne Vassallo, was performed in the chapel on the evening of the twentieth.

France (June 17–August 19, 1996)

After this long, moving interlude outside France, Thérèse's relics could resume their journey in French monasteries from June 17 to September 23. This was the day before the celebrations of the centenary of the death of the saint of Lisieux.

Thirteen monasteries and thirty-nine Carmels were visited during these months. But some parishes (especially those dedicated to Thérèse) also asked for a visit. Sometimes these were new communities, such as the Béatitudes in Nouan-le-Fuzelier (July 17–20) and the Emmanuel Community, which requested the relics for the sessions in Paray-le-Monial — visited by thousands of people (July 28–29, August 1).

Germany (August 8–11, 1996)

We must also note a detour outside of France. This was during a gathering of young people from the Emmanuel Community in Germany at the Shrine of Our Lady of Alltötting, from August 8 to 11. The theme of this gathering was "Therefore, Choose Life!" — a preliminary to the 1997 World Youth Day in Paris, which gathered eight thousand young people together. The speakers — Sr. Emmanuelle, Fr. Guy Gilbert, and Msgr. Christoph Schönborn — venerated the relics in the presence of Cardinal Friedrich Wetter, the archbishop of Munich, who presided over the Mass in honor of Thérèse on August 8.

Fr. Francis Kohn wrote:

> The most famous guest of this first International Youth Forum in Altötting was a little French woman who came from Lisieux! The presence of St. Thérèse's relics was an immense blessing. It was actually the first time that the one whom the Church has declared the Patroness of Missions and who dreamed so much during her life in the Carmel of going to evangelize the world came to Germany. In a country marked by rationalism, her simple language touched hearts where they needed it most. As soon as she arrived, the doubts and fears of some people

were erased, through the simplicity of her presence. The young people gathered near her in the evening and during the night while her relics were exposed in the basilica.[112]

On August 15, while the International Forum was taking place in Paray-le-Monial with five thousand young people, Pope John Paul II published his invitation letter to World Youth Day 1997 in Paris. He concluded it in this way:

> On 30 September 1997 will occur the centenary of the death of St. Thérèse of Lisieux. Hers is a figure that, in her own country, cannot fail to draw the attention of a great many young pilgrims; Thérèse, precisely, is a young Saint, and her message today is simple and suggestive, brimming over with amazement and gratitude: God is Love; every person is loved by God, who expects to be welcomed and loved by each one. This is a message, young people of today, that you are called to receive and to shout aloud to those of your own age : "Man is loved by God! This very simple yet profound proclamation is owed to humanity by the Church" (cf. *Christifideles Laici,* 34).
>
> From the youth of [Thérèse] of the Child Jesus spring forth her enthusiasm for the Lord, the intensity of her love, the realistic daring of her great projects. The charm of her holiness is confirmation that God grants in abundance, even to the young, the treasures of his wisdom.
>
> Walk with her the humble and simple way of Christian maturity, at the school of the Gospel. Stay with her in the "heart" of the Church, living radically the option for Christ.[113]

[112] *Il est vivant,* no. 127, 30.

[113] Message of the Holy Father to the Youth of the World on the Occasion of the XII World Youth Day (August 15, 1996), no. 9.

We'd see that this message would be heard.

But Thérèse wasn't going to leave Germany without visiting her sisters in the Carmel in Dachau, near Munich. These were very intense moments that were experienced on Sunday, August 11. The Carmel of the "Precious Blood" was built inside the concentration camp where two hundred thousand people from forty nations perished between 1933 and 1945.

The next day, August 12, we celebrated the feast of Karl Leisner, whom John Paul II had beatified in Berlin on the preceding June 23. He was arrested by the Nazis and confined in Dachau. He supported, aided, and comforted the dying. He was nicknamed "The Angel of Dachau," and he was clandestinely ordained a priest in the camp by the bishop of Clermont-Ferrand, Msgr. Gabriel Piguet, who was deported on December 17, 1944. Karl Leisner died on August 12, 1945.

Fifty years later, Thérèse's relics were venerated in this death camp, in communion with this young German martyr.

Italy: Rimini (August 20–25 1996)

The relics' travels would not have been so successful without some very motivated people who loved Thérèse passionately. Fr. Giuseppe Scarpellini was one of those. He was the pastor of a small parish on Italy's Adriatic Coast, near Rimini. He dreamed about receiving the relics in his church, dedicated to St. Giustina, and so fervently did he request it that St. Thérèse went there three times in one year.

He had prepared everything magnificently with his parishioners' enthusiastic support. There were banners, posters, streamers, and a plane that dragged the announcement on a banner above the coast, where thousands of vacationers were crowded. Fr. Scarpellini had the support of the religious authorities, civilians, and members of the military. There was a huge tent behind the church, along with various booths, a bookstore, exhibitions, and fireworks. The days were very full. They consisted of celebrations, conferences by reputable Theresians, performances by parishioners of Thérèse's plays, dancing, and so on. More than ten thousand people eagerly attended.

This period coincided with the huge conference that the Communione e Liberazione in Rimini offered on the theme of friendship.

We had planned for a large exhibition on St. Thérèse of Lisieux to prepare for the centenary of her death. The Carmel of Lisieux had lent us some of Thérèse's belongings that had great symbolic value. The exhibition was very successful. Usually, around 500,000 people visited this gathering. The number rose to 750,000 that year. Was it because of the Theresian exhibition? It was entitled "Closing the most distant borders." Some youth groups gathered to listen to Thérèse's writings, under the leadership of Fr. Antonio Sangalli, a Carmelite. Guided tours went through the exhibition until midnight.

Various activities were added among the many conferences, as well as a roundtable on Thérèse of Lisieux in which the following people participated: Msgr. Schönborn, the archbishop of Vienna; Fr. Camilo Maccise, prior general of the Discalced Carmelites; and Fr. François-Marie Léthel, a Carmelite, theologian, and professor in the Teresianum. Fr. Scarpellini invited me as well, and I participated in this roundtable in front of a packed hall of about three thousand people. Many couldn't get in.

Evidently, this crowd, knowing that the relics were being venerated in St. Guistina Church, hastened to come. The municipality had made free shuttles available to it. Many bishops came to celebrate in the church.

France (August 26–September 23, 1996)

After this very stirring Italian episode, Thérèse would resume her journey in France through the south (Avignon, Carpentras, Cavaillon, Orange, Montpellier, and Toulouse), the center (Le Puy), and the east (Metz, Nancy, Troyes, and Sens). She ended it in her diocese (Bayeux and Caen). She finally reached Lisieux on September 23 — when the centenary's feasts were about to start. St. Thérèse had just visited sixteen Carmels, seven monasteries, and several St. Thérèse parishes. She saw 142 French monasteries in all — without taking the parishes into account.

The Carmelites in Lisieux were happy to see the reliquary return to its usual place and participate in the feasts, which were exceptional that year. The route from the Carmel to the basilica seemed very modest after the relics had traveled thousands of miles, but it didn't fail to attract thousands of pilgrims.

Cardinal Frédéric Etsou, the archbishop of Kinshasa (Zaire), an enthusiastic Theresian, presided over the opening Mass on Sunday, September 29. Msgr. Mario Tagliaferri, the apostolic nuncio, rounded out the celebration on the following Sunday.

During the week, there was an international symposium titled "A Saint for the Third Millennium." The speakers included four cardinals from three countries: Moreira Neves from Brazil, Etsou from Zaire, and Lustiger and Poupard from France; three women: Virginia Azcuy from Argentina, Yvette Périco, and Sr. Noëlle Hausman; some laymen: Henri Hude and Jean Vanier; an English bishop, Msgr. Boyce; the Romanian Msgr. György Jakubinyi; Camilo Maccise, the Mexican prior general of the Order of Discalced Carmelites; and a priest named Pierre d'Ornellas. These speakers revealed the universal nature of Thérèse's thought and influence.[114]

It seemed that everything was going to return to normal after such a high point — that is to say, that Thérèse would "rest" in her Carmel. This didn't take her missionary enthusiasm into account.

It's true that there was a break for a few months. But the 1997 World Youth Day in Paris was already looming. John Paul II was calling young people from the entire world by highlighting the young Thérèse. We had to get organized in order for her to be present in Paris in August 1997, the year of the centenary of her "entrance into life."[115]

[114] This symposium was published by the Éditions du Carmel in 1997.

[115] St. Thérèse of Lisieux, Letter 244, to her spiritual brother Fr. Bellière in *Letters of St. Thérèse of Lisieux*, vol. 2, 128.

World Youth Day in Paris (August 20–24, 1997)

I remember the huge procession — between the Trocadéro and the Champ-de-Mars — of a portrait of Thérèse from when she was fifteen years old. It was flapping in the midst of five hundred thousand young people from all countries who were waiting for Pope John Paul II to arrive.

During these days, Thérèse's relics were in the sanctuary of Our Lady of Victories, where they were venerated by thousands of young people, accompanied by their bishops.

But the summit of the Theresian story of World Youth Day in Paris was the Angelus message on August 24 in Longchamp, where John Paul II announced the future proclamation of Thérèse as a Doctor of the Church in the presence of 1.2 million young people, who applauded the news.[116] Thus, the young Thérèse was a prominent figure at the Paris World Youth Day.

At the same time, some sixty thousand young people swamped Lisieux. They prayed and celebrated in different languages, wherever they found a suitable place, which was often outside. In its long history,

[116] For texts that John Paul II gave on October 19, see part 2, on the Doctor issue.

Lisieux had undoubtedly never welcomed so many people within its walls.

But before the relics went to the Eternal City, Cardinal Martin, the archbishop of Milan, had submitted an urgent request to welcome the relics in his huge diocese. With 155 priests from Milan, he had come to Lisieux in February 1997 on a traveling retreat whose theme was "Thérèse and the Tragedy of Unbelief."[117]

The cardinal wanted the relics to visit the big San Vittore Prison in Milan, which they did on October 7, 1997. The next day, they were venerated by a huge crowd in the cathedral that Thérèse had visited on November 9, 1887, "in its smallest details." She was always the first one, along with her sister Céline, "to see everything regarding the saints' relics" and "to hear the descriptions," especially in regard to "the tomb of St. Charles" [Borromeo].[118]

[117] Original text that was published by the Éditions Ancora (Milan, 1997) and then in French by the Éditions Saint-Augustin (1997) with a preface by Msgr. Pierre Mamie.

[118] Manuscript A, 58 v, in *Story of a Soul*, 126.

Proclamation as Doctor, Rome (October 19, 1997)

On November 20, 1887, a young lady, accompanied by her father and her sister, disturbed a beautifully organized tribute to Pope Leo XIII. Despite efforts to keep her from speaking to the very tired elderly man,[119] she asked him for permission to enter the Carmel of Lisieux when she was fifteen years old. It was a "fiasco," according to her sister Céline. Two guards lifted the kneeling Thérèse and carried her away in tears into the next hall.

One hundred ten years later, this saint's relics occupied the center of St. Peter's Square. They faced Pope John Paul II, who was celebrating Mass and proclaiming Thérèse a Doctor in the presence of the crowd of pilgrims who were Thérèse's friends.

The Holy Father had chosen this date, World Mission Sunday, as the new Doctor had been Patroness of the Missions since 1927. It was also the beginning of the school year for Rome's colleges and universities.

[119] That very evening, Thérèse, in tears, recounted the audience to her sister Pauline, a Carmelite: "The good Father was so old that it seemed as if he was dead. I would never have pictured him like that. He can hardly say anything else." Letter 36 to Sr. Agnes of Jesus (Pauline), in *Letters of St. Thérèse*, vol. 1, 356.

St. Peter's Basilica was completely empty and was used as a sacristy for the concelebrants. After the celebration, the reliquary was carried into the basilica by the seminarians of Caen's interdiocesan seminary. The pope stopped to pray before the reliquary for a few moments before it was placed amid the glory of Bernini in the back of the nave. The crowd of pilgrims and Italians venerated it there for a few days.

Her brothers and sisters from the Carmel couldn't let her leave Rome without decorating her with her new title, according to the academic custom. After the customary speeches, the reliquary was covered with the doctoral ribbon in the Teresianum (Rome's Carmelite University) on October 22 in the midst of the professors, some students, and friends of the Carmel.

Switzerland (November 3–15, 1997)

Switzerland received Thérèse's reliquary the following month. The young traveler had enthusiastically admired the country's mountains while crossing them by rail on November 8, 1887.[120]

Everything started in the Hauterive Abbey on November 8, 1997. The monks expected thirty to sixty people. Three hundred came. It was impossible to explain what was occurring in Geneva, Lausanne, Zurich, and Cazis. A large prayer weekend was organized by Pray and Witness at the University of Freiburg, and three thousand people participated in it.

[120] Manuscript A, 57v -58r, in *Story of a Soul*, 124–125.

Austria and Slovenia (November 15–24, 1997)

From November 15 to 24, Thérèse visited Austria — Innsbruck, Salzburg, Linz, Mayerling, Vienna, Eisens, Graz, Bärnbach, Himmelau, and Klagenfurt. She traveled more than three thousand miles.

Her relics were in St. Stephen's Cathedral in Vienna on November 20, under the jurisdiction of Cardinal Christoph Schönborn, an enthusiastic Theresian.

The passage into Slovenia was quick but important for this country (November 25–27), especially in Ljubljana, where there was limited space for the Mass that Msgr. Franc Rodé, the local archbishop, presided over.

Then something very important happened: the Episcopal Conference of Brazil asked for the reliquary. It was going to leave Europe for the first time. The car trips were over. The tour of the relics was taken to an entirely new level.

This time, the Carmelites of Lisieux were seriously worried. Could they risk letting the shrine cross the ocean? But how could we refuse?

Brazil (December 14, 1997–December 17, 1998)

Thérèse's relics crossed the Atlantic Ocean for the first time. In Brazil, the means of transportation would be diversified — civilian and military airplanes, helicopters, boats, and trains — depending on the places that were visited (megacity, sertão, or Amazon forests).

Thérèse would visit ninety cities during one year, including Salvador, Brasilia, Belo Horizonte, Rio de Janeiro, São Paulo, Rio Grande do Sul, and Porto Alegre. She traveled more than twelve thousand miles.

A close connection has existed between Brazil and Thérèse since after the First World War.[121] An abridged translation of *Story of a Soul* was published in 1914. There is a small city in Brazil called Santa Teresinha on the edge of the huge Araguaia River. And Brazil is the country that gave the Carmel of Lisieux the famous shrine that contains the relics. In 1924, Msgr. Lemonnier, the bishop of Bayeux and Lisieux, wrote to the ambassador of Brazil in France: "What a triumph to see

[121] See the conference that Cardinal Moreira Neves held in Lisieux on September 30, 1996, "Au Brésil: un peuple et une Eglise a l'école de Thérèse de Lisieux [In Brazil: A people and a Church in Thérèse of Lisieux's school of thought], which was published in *Une sainte pour le troisième millénaire* [A saint for the third millennium] (Éditions du Carmel, 1997), 17–30.

that our blessed woman is seen, loved, and honored in your nation, which has taken the lead in South America." The bishop called this "a true Theresian explosion."

Henri Rubillon, a Jesuit who was born in the Diocese of Bayeux in 1866, was sent to Brazil as a teacher. He became an ardent friend of Thérèse in connection with the Carmelites of Lisieux in 1910. He founded groups of "Legionnaires of St. Thérèse."

Having taken up a collection, he sent the Carmelites a Brazilian flag in a big chest that was made out of jacaranda (a very precious wood) on which was carved Thérèse's coat of arms. This masterpiece is called "the wonder of Brazil" in the Carmel. Hence, the idea of asking Fr. Rubillon for a reliquary shrine made out of gilded silver. Dom Sebastião Leme da Silveira Cintra (who was later the archbishop and cardinal of Rio) and about thirty bishops raised about 81,000 contos de remis, which is a considerable amount, for its construction. H. Brunet, the goldsmith, would make a shrine — in fact, two of them. The first one, which was made out of gilded silver, would be the more famous one. It would be used for Theresian feasts and the tour of France from 1945 to 1947, along with the trips that were undertaken from 1994 to November 1997. But it would be too risky for this reliquary to cross the ocean. So?

A happy solution would emerge. The second shrine, which was made of wood and gilded silver and was a copy of the first one, would receive a unique relic and travel across the world. The first relic would no longer leave Lisieux. This solution was ideal.[122] People got into the habit of calling the silver shrine "Brazil's shrine" and the wooden one the "centenary's shrine."[123]

[122] In regard to the story of these reliquaries, see Fr. Fernando Guimaraes's works and his article in *Vie thérésienne* 150 and 151 (April–July, 1998).

[123] The dimensions are approximately 4.9 by 3 by 2.8 feet with the protective casing and the weight approximately 291 pounds. The wooden shipping crate is approximately 5.2 by 3.4 by 3.9 feet and the weight

The second shrine would now cross this huge country and so many others later. This was a significant coincidence. The synod that was dedicated to the America's new evangelization was ending when the reliquary took off from the Roissy [Charles de Gaulle] Airport for Brazil on December 12, 1997.

After returning from the synod, Cardinal Neves took the same plane as Thérèse from the Varig airline to land with her in Salvador de Bahia. He was the archbishop of this huge city. Forty thousand of the faithful were waiting for them in the Fonte Nova Stadium. The cardinal presided over the Mass, which was concelebrated by 130 priests, during which 1,000 young people and adults were baptized. A helicopter spilled a shower of roses onto the stadium at the end. On December 21, the cardinal built a new parish called St. Thérèse, Doctor of the Church.

Knowing how Brazilians like to celebrate, we can imagine their enthusiasm for Thérèse's presence. Local radio and television stations covered the itinerary. The conferences had been prepared several weeks in advance. The mayor of Madeiro had decreed a public holiday for the relics' arrival. Motorcyclists, brass bands, songs, firecrackers, and dances escorted the relics everywhere. But the teachings and conferences about the life and message of Thérèse and the republication of *Story of a Soul* in Portuguese were more important.

There was a flood of confessions all over Brazil.

It was impossible to follow every detail of this itinerary for twelve months!

The same reverberations recurred in all the diocesan reports. There were crowds that went beyond all expectations. The relics went to hospitals, retirement homes, seminaries, and prisons. The churches were open all night. There were long, peaceful lines of people who waited

---

approximately 254 pounds. The total weight of the reliquary and the shrine is approximately 545 pounds.

to approach the relics, and there were healings all along the way. It was hard to verify them at times, but those who benefited from them were not very worried about medical certificates.

Others were concerned about expressing thanks for the gifts that they received. A priest from Holy Spirit parish in the Diocese of Nazaré da Mata was to have a kidney stone operation. It had been planned for the day the relics arrived in the cathedral. The priest was sorry and apologized to his bishop for his absence. But he and the doctor got a surprise in the hospital. There was no more kidney stone and no need to intervene! The priest rushed to the cathedral to give thanks and bear witness.

A woman who had been suffering from a cancerous tumor in Caxias felt intense heat in her body when she touched the reliquary. An X-ray revealed that the tumor had disappeared. Msgr. José Mendes, the local bishop, testified in writing: "I herewith send you the two medical certifications of a miraculous healing on the occasion of the presence of St. Thérèse's relics in our city. The first certificate proves the existence of the malignant tumor. The second one confirms the nonexistence of this tumor, one week after the relics' visit. Let's give thanks to God."

The Brazilian Air Force in the Diocese of Belém offered the transportation. Belém's municipal chamber and the state's legislative assembly gave Thérèse the status of "citizen of Belém and citizen of the state of Pará." Twenty-five thousand people participated in the closing Mass.

The city that carries the saint's name — Santa Teresinha — is in the Diocese of Uruaçu. Two hundred cars escorted the reliquary across the city. We learned that some politicians who had not been speaking to each other reopened their dialogue on this occasion.

The Archdiocese of Uberaba in the state of Minas Gerais had prepared for the relics' arrival for several months. Thirty-five thousand of the faithful went into the thirteen parishes that the relics went through in four days.

The legislative assembly in Divinópolis that welcomed Thérèse proclaimed her as the city's "godmother." Msgr. José Belvino do Nascimento, the diocesan bishop, wrote the following: "The relics were welcomed as if they were a living person in the midst of the people who applauded her, prayed, cried, and sang. But Thérèse also entered into the secret places in people's hearts.... We've received testimonies of graces, conversions, healings, solutions to material problems, and so on, and we give thanks to God."[124]

The mayor handed over the city's keys to Bishop José de Lima in front of the cathedral in the Diocese of Sete Lagoas as a sign of the people's devotion to Thérèse. Twenty thousand people participated in the festivities.

Eighty-eight Brazilian bishops had asked to receive the relics in their diocese. Some of them started too late. One of them, who didn't wish to welcome them, saw the faithful in his diocese leave in droves to see the relics in the neighboring diocese.

Cardinal Eugênio de Araújo Sales, the archbishop of Rio de Janeiro, distributed an important announcement about Thérèse's relics in Brazil in July 1998, and it was taken up by the city's newspapers. He reminded people about the traditional meaning of the veneration of relics and emphasized that this important event that touched Brazil was an excellent opportunity to review the devotion to the saints and correct possible mistakes. He concluded that this was also God's blessing.

After receiving Thérèse's relics in their dioceses for an entire year (from December 14, 1997, to December 17, 1998), the bishops published the following assessment during their annual assembly in Itaici:

> We've had the joy of receiving the relics of St. Thérèse of the Child Jesus in our dioceses for one year, and we're better able

[124] *Thérèse de Lisieux*, no. 783 (November 1998): 19.

to evaluate this visit's significance, its importance, and its consequences.

St. Thérèse of the Child Jesus came among us as a missionary. She attracted crowds and touched the hearts of enthusiastic Catholics, awakened the faith of a lot of indifferent people, brought countless people who had no religious practice to their Lord and Master, and reached many men and women of other religions. The testimonies of miracles and favors of all kinds increased during her visit. The greatest one was indisputably the endless lines of people waiting to venerate her relics day and night. How many times did we ask ourselves: What's the secret of this attraction? How is it possible to reach such a variety of people — young people and infants, adults and elderly people, simple people and cultured ones who found that her message spoke to them?

It's true that she had promised to make a shower of roses fall after her death, but we think more deeply that her power of attraction actually resides in the intensity of her union with Christ. Jesus said: "He who abides in me, and I in him, he it is that bears much fruit" (John 15:5). We want to testify and proclaim that we have seen the confirmation of these words of our Savior in St. Thérèse of the Child Jesus.

Her relics' travels have been a blessing for our dioceses. This is why we're thankful to the Carmel of Lisieux for having given us the possibility of welcoming them, and we joyfully commit ourselves to keep the flame of her presence among us lit. We'll do it for the good of our specific Churches. We'll especially do it for the glory of God.

Itaici, Brazil, April 15, 1999 (101 signatures follow).

Netherlands (January 20–February 22, 1999)

This was a change of scenery. Thérèse returned to the European continent, and, to our great surprise, a small country requested her. We didn't think the Netherlands would be interested in the Norman Carmelite after all the turmoil that Catholicism had experienced there.

Cardinal Adrianus Simonis, president of the Bishops' Conference of the Netherlands, Fr. Marc Timmermans of the Emmanuel Community, Fr. Conrad De Meester, and Miss Danielle Prins held a press conference and presented the program of the reliquary's trip. It was favorably received and widely distributed in the media, including the KRO (Catholic) and NOS — a national station — and the radio stations. Millions of people were in the know. A witness noted this: "On the whole, the media were very kind, but what was most surprising was their interest in the month-long trip. It was very surprising to see so much attention in a press that's generally quite critical toward the Catholic Church."

The pastor of St. Joseph's Church's in Tilburg, who was in his sixties, declared having experienced "the most beautiful event of his priestly life."

There were powerful moments. The relics entered the Carmel of Echt on February 2, the World Day of Prayer for Consecrated Life. This is where Edith Stein (St. Teresa Benedicta of the Cross) had lived as of January 1, 1938. She and her sister, accompanied by the Gestapo, left there on August 2, 1942, to go to Auschwitz to die. The Carmelites of Echt spent the night praying silently.

On February 3, a lady confided her pain to the nuns in the monastery of the Benedictine Sisters of Jesus Crucified in Brunssum. She hadn't heard from her daughter in ten years. A sister told her: "We're going to entrust this to Thérèse." The mother got a phone call from her daughter the next day.

On Sunday, February 7, a thousand people defied the cold to go to the cathedral of Bois-le-Duc, the country's biggest diocese, and about a dozen priests heard confessions. This kind of turnout hadn't been seen in a long time. Unbelievers and Muslims came to ask what was going on.

Eindhoven's newspaper reported on the testimony of a thirty-nine-year-old man who converted three years earlier after seeing a picture of Thérèse and reading her manuscripts: "My life completely changed!"

The Church of "Papegaai" (the parrot) in Amsterdam is on a very busy street in the heart of the city. People from all countries visit it. Many of them are touched by the liveliness of the songs, plays, and testimonies of the young people from the Emmanuel Community there.

Here again, confessions kept many priests busy. The pastor would later learn about several conversions. "We've never seen anything like this in the Netherlands."

Cardinal Johannes Willebrands, the former archbishop of Utrecht, celebrated Mass.

The program was modified so that the relics could visit the Sisters of Mother Teresa in Amsterdam. The reliquary couldn't fit through the narrow chapel door, so it remained in the common room, where the sisters served meals to those in need and let them spend the night with them, near Thérèse.

In many places, churches were opened all day — and even at night — for Thérèse, whereas they were usually closed. The parish of the Nativity of the Virgin Mary in Nijmegen brought together 450 people for an evening of mercy and confessions. Such a celebration had never taken place in that church.

An evening that was organized for young people gathered seventy (whereas four to ten would ordinarily attend).

Sunday, February 21 was the relics' last day in the Netherlands. The church received 550 of the faithful, at the most, at Christmas and Easter and about 180 on Sunday. But there were 900 people on that day.

Fr. Timmermans concluded: "Thérèse gave hope to the Church in the Netherlands, which is so affected by secularism. There are already many visible fruits, and it seems that the harvest will be abundant."[125]

[125] *Thérèse de Lisieux*, no. 789 (May 1999): 14.

Russia (February 24–May 5, 1999)

The most famous picture of the relics' travels around the world is undoubtedly the one that shows the reliquary being carried by six Kremlin guards in front of a former KGB building. It was viewed around the world, and it especially impressed American newspapers.

This was really new — Thérèse in Russia!

In the face of the terrible ravages of Stalinism after 1925, Pope Pius XI had entrusted this country to the one he had just declared Patroness of Missions (December 14, 1927).

The Russicum, the seminary that would train Catholic priests who would be sent to Russia, had been built in Rome in 1929, at the Carmel of Lisieux's expense. Many of those priests were arrested and executed.

The sudden demise of communism in Russia in 1991 was an extraordinary event. Seeing people regain their freedom, including the freedom of conscience and religious freedom, after seventy years of a horrible dictatorship, seemed to be a dream. But this dream was a reality, even if the conditions for its fulfillment were strained by habits that had been created during decades of lies, concealment, and denunciation.

Also, when three Catholic bishops — Msgr. Tadeusz Kondrusiewicz, Russia's apostolic administrator; Msgr. Joseph Werth, bishop of

Siberia; and Msgr. Jan Paweł Lenga, bishop of Kazakhstan — requested the relics for those huge territories, we had a hard time believing it! We were really facing the unknown. How would all this be done?

An important meeting had been scheduled in Lisieux, and it would unite a Russian delegation with those in charge of the pilgrimage. Msgr. Kondrusiewicz was accompanied by Msgr. Clemens Pickel; Fr. Michaël Shields, pastor in Magadan; Fr. Bernard Le Léannec, rector of the Church of St. Louis of the French in Moscow; Fr. Pierre Dumoulin, vice rector of the St. Petersburg Seminary; two Russian nuns; and two Assumptionist priests.

Msgr. Kondrusiewicz presided over the feast of the Assumption on August 15, 1998, and delivered the homily. He reminded people that before 1917, the Catholic Church in Russia had 150 parishes, 2 dioceses, 250 priests, an ecclesiastical academy, and 2 major seminaries that graduated 700 priests, including 62 bishops and 2 cardinals. But darkness submerged all of that. How many were shot dead or were in the gulags, like their Orthodox brothers?

After arriving in Moscow in 1991, the new bishop found only 6 parishes, 3 priests, 2 churches, and 2 chapels. In 1998, he counted 93 parishes, 115 priests (including eight Russian ones), 127 nuns who came from seventeen countries (including ten Russian ones), a middle school with 300 students, and a major seminary with 60 students. He ended his homily by commenting that he expected a lot from the arrival of Thérèse, who protects Russia.

We had to wait for months of preparations and talks. The relationships between the Orthodox Church and the Catholic Church continued to be difficult. The Orthodox Church, which was weakened by persecution, didn't favor the arrival of foreign clergy and different sects after the fall of communism. The fear of "proselytism" was strong. The Catholic authorities thought it might be better to cancel Thérèse's visit to Russia at some point.

Yet the Orthodox people like two Catholic saints — St. Francis of Assisi and St. Thérèse of Lisieux. In fact, icons of Thérèse circulated underground during the reign of communism. And so the green light was given. Sr. Tamara, from the Community of the Beatitudes, had spoken to Pope John Paul II about the project on March 26, 1998. He'd said to her: "May God bless your initiative."

Finally, a plane from Aeroflot-Russian Airlines took off from the Charles de Gaulle Airport in Paris for Moscow on February 24, 1999. Everything started with a few bureaucratic difficulties. Even though they had been informed by the nuncio, the customs officers dragged out the formalities. They weren't used to letting a 550-pound package containing human bones go by. They wanted to ask for confirmation — from a veterinarian!

Some women resolved the situation. An employee in the embassy of France, the wife of the Guatemalan ambassador, and one of her friends arrived and convinced the customs officers to let Thérèse enter Russia. It was snowing, and it was really late, so the relics' first night in Russia was spent in the Guatemalan embassy!

In the morning, Msgr. Kondrusiewicz celebrated Mass in front of the reliquary. Then we took the reliquary to St. Petersburg — almost five hundred miles away. It was escorted by the Guatemalan ambassador, who drove his own car. The relics made their long journeys in a new Espace car, which was offered by a European member of Parliament during a Theresian session in Luxembourg.

Sr. Tamara and Sr. Christelle of the Community of the Beatitudes stayed with the relics during the entire trip. The bishop of Moscow had officially charged them with the organization. They would be the most important witnesses of this incredible adventure that would lead into Siberia, on a journey of more than eighteen thousand miles.

Fifty seminarians emotionally welcomed Thérèse in the St. Petersburg Seminary. They had learned to sing Thérèse's poems in Russian.

Sylvie Buisset, of the Community of the Beatitudes, sang them in French. A crowd overwhelmed the seminary and venerated the relics. More than five hundred people participated in this event. Many of them cried.

The Church of the Sacred Heart, like so many other churches, had been divided into floors and offices by Stalin's regime. A section of the main floor and the third floor had been returned to faithful Catholics. The reliquary was to be honored in Lenin Hall, but it couldn't fit through the narrow door. So the relics were kept in the hallway, and hundreds of people went by for hours on end while singing hymns. Sick persons were brought there.

Thérèse visited the Catholic parishes of St. Petersburg, St. Stanislas, and Our Lady of Lourdes for a week. Confessions overwhelmed the priests because many penitents were returning to the Faith after being brought up in radical atheism. People even asked to be baptized.

The relics went to St. Peter and St. Paul Church in Novgorod on March 7.

Fr. Xénon, an Orthodox iconographer, made an icon of Thérèse for this trip in Pskov. It did not leave with the reliquary but would return much later to the Carmel of Lisieux, where it would be displayed near the shrine.

Smolensk was 280 miles farther on. It was impossible to go into the big church, which had not yet returned to being a place of worship. It sheltered the Komsomol Archive. Fr. Yatsk, a Franciscan, received the reliquary in a garage that had been converted into a chapel. Some people who had come from far away prayed all night long.

There was a passage through Katyn, where thousands of people had been massacred by the Russians in 1940.

After traveling for nearly 220 miles on icy roads, we stopped at the home of five Franciscan brothers in Kaluga. An Orthodox priest and seminarian came to pray there, as well as a Protestant pastor and his wife, who would stay the whole night.

Finally, 93 miles farther on, we returned to Moscow to the Church of St. Louis, the only church, besides Our Lady of Lourdes, to stay open during the religious persecution. It wasn't far from the Lubyanka Building — the notorious prison — which was surrounded by KGB buildings. A camera from a balcony was filming those who went into the church.

On March 13, 1999, Fr. Bernard Le Léannec, the pastor and his parishioners thought they were dreaming. Six Kremlin guard cadets were carrying the reliquary. Snow was falling. A blue banner decorated the pediment: "Welcome, St. Thérèse." The church wouldn't be empty for three days. It was filled with rich and poor, diplomats and students, Catholics and Orthodox.

Msgr. Kondrusiewicz celebrated Mass in the Church of the Immaculate Conception, which had been a church for Polish Catholics and then was transformed into a factory in 1935. Major construction would make it a place of worship again, and it became Moscow's Catholic cathedral. For the moment, the reliquary was carried past the huge building site's pipework.

The bishop prayed:

> St. Thérèse, teach us about the greatness of the love of God and neighbor. Help all Christians to be one family. Request for us the grace of conversion and a return to the Father, so that we can experience the virtues of faith, hope, and love. Request for us the grace that, following your example and your little way, we will know how to receive God's mercy and return to spiritual childhood. May the veneration of your relics be the opportunity for a true spiritual renewal for us through the huge Russian Catholic communities, at the dawn of the third millennium and the great Jubilee!

Then it was time to go to the Volga and Siberia.

It's impossible to retrace at length a journey of this magnitude from April 5 to 20. It went from Orenburg to Tomsk, passing through Omsk and Novosibirsk (about twenty-three hundred miles) to Western Siberia and then to Eastern Siberia from April 22 to May 5, going through Irkutsk (nine thousand miles).

Let us ponder this astonishing image: Thérèse's presence in these places of unspeakable suffering for millions of deportees. This vast area has been a place of suffering and death for the many undesirables who were sent there. The czars had started this. The communist regime continued it on a larger scale. It organized those famous and terrible gulags that Thérèse would visit — as far as Magadan and Sakhalin Island.

I can provide my testimony here. I had been invited by Msgr. Jerzy Mazur, a young bishop from Eastern Siberia — one of the vastest dioceses of the world. He organized a pastoral meeting from April 25 to 30, 1999, with all of his clergymen and sisters — that is to say, twenty-four priests and fourteen sisters. He invited me to participate in it when the relics were in Irkutsk (a city of seven hundred thousand).

He welcomed me in his residence, on the fourth floor of a housing project in squalid surroundings. The pastoral meeting was held in a church that had been confiscated by Stalin and transformed into a concert hall. Thus, it had to be rented for a few days and reorganized for our use. For five days, we experienced prayer, brotherhood, and a deep, modest joy.

Almost all of the people who came to venerate Thérèse's relics were children of deportees or of people who had been shot or had disappeared.

Msgr. Mazur understood that he'd never be able to retrieve his church, so he decided to build one. He had bought some property and buried a medal of Thérèse in the ground there.[126]

[126] The miracle occurred. One year later, on December 8, 2000, a cathedral was built there with a bishop's residence and some meeting rooms.

Another one of Msgr. Mazur's projects was to build in Kamchatka a church dedicated to St. Thérèse under the title Doctor of the Church.

There was an exterior stone path that was scattered with black boxes containing dirt from the gulags. Some former members of those camps were present at the church's consecration. Alas! We know that Msgr. Mazur's visa was refused without an explanation on April 19, 2002, despite the Vatican's protests. Msgr. Mazur was stopped in Poland and continued to contact his distant diocese before being named bishop of Ełk in Poland in April 2003.

Kazakhstan (May 5–June 28, 1999)

The journey in Kazakhstan was undoubtedly the most difficult one, but it included many blessings for these populations that still suffered after some terrible years.

Kazakhstan, a former member of the USSR, has been independent since 1990. It is five times the size of France and has seventeen million residents. The first people living there were Kazakhs, who are now only 50 percent of the population. The rest is made up of Russians (30 percent), Ukrainians, Germans, Poles, Tartars, Belarusians, Turks, Koreans, and others. Altogether, there are more than a hundred nationalities. They are descendants of deportees or are deportees themselves. Forty percent of the country is steppe land. The main religion is Islam. There are two million Catholics.

Though rich in various minerals, Kazakhstan is economically ruined. There are some big mining and steel centers, which were built by deportees at the cost of millions of lives.

Msgr. Lenga, the Catholic bishop (he spent ten years in the camps), has fifty priests for this huge country. Finding Catholics is like looking for a needle in a haystack.

These poor little communities were amazed when they saw Thérèse arriving in their homes!

Srs. Tamara and Christelle shared testimonies they had collected. They left Pavlodar on May 5, 1999, and arrived in Astana, the new capital (280,000 residents) on June 26, having stopped in twenty-three cities and districts. They traveled all the way in a minibus in very difficult conditions. (The reliquary would fly to Astana to get to Moscow.)

Four hundred fifty open-air atomic experiments occurred in this country. The Aral Sea shrunk by 35 percent because of pollution. There are labor camps (Akmola and ALZHIR) near the city of Malinovka, where thousands of women died while working in a huge chicken coop.

Sr. Christelle wrote:

> Their bodies are resting under our feet. They were dumped into a small lake near or buried in this prairie where we need only to scratch the ground in order to find human bones.
>
> These obviously very small Catholic communities received Thérèse after traveling long distances on impossible roads in a landscape of plains and black earth, fields, forest, and steppes. There's nothing else on the horizon but these hedges of trees that were planted to slow the wind down and stop the dust. The wind blows there all the time.
>
> You have to resist feelings of sadness and hopelessness in this region, which can clutch your heart. How is so much suffering possible? There are many unemployed people there today.

There continue to be poignant testimonies of this exceptional journey. You have to perceive the tragedies that all these residents experience. These aren't insignificant events. Everyone's life here is a dark novel — often a horror novel.

Let's give a few examples:

Irena is an elderly grandmother who was deported from Ukraine. Her parents and brothers and sisters died when they arrived here. She stayed by herself with her little six-month-old brother and was sent to an orphanage when she was six years old.

We asked her: "Have you forgiven all those who harmed you so much and who are at the root of all the suffering in your life?

She simply replied: "If I hadn't forgiven them, I couldn't have lived."

Macha belongs to the intermediary generation that arose from deported families. As young people, they were indoctrinated in communism. They then experienced a life without God, in which having faith is considered to be a crime and the Christian religion is seen as despicable. Marriage was but a formality for them. Faithfulness didn't exist, and abortions weren't a problem. Macha, who became a leader of her region in Kazakhstan, always carried a revolver and was skilled in handling it.

By chance, she went into a church two years ago. She experienced a conversion and opened her heart to Fr. Christopher. She progressed in the Faith with giant strides. Today, she works in the priest's home and was the one who very warmly welcomed us. Thérèse deeply moved her heart and gave her the key to bear her life of misery and her alcoholic husband and to care for her children: "I put so much love into small ordinary things that they became extraordinary."

Gregor is a young man from the region. He lived out Thérèse's school of thought in the Institute of Our Lady of Life in Venasque for three years. Then he returned to his country and was ordained a priest. He was the one who came to welcome Thérèse in the cathedral.

Fr. Laurenz came to meet us in Tonkochourovka. He was the dean of Berlin's largest parish. On the day of his retreat, he declared: "This is a new beginning for me!"

He decided to give ten years of his life to Kazakhstan. This is how he landed in the northern part of the country's most distant and desolate region in 1990. He had to look for some parishioners, build the church, and persevere in some very precarious conditions despite his age and sickness. He was almost finished doing his work for the Lord.

Thérèse's visit was an opportunity to unite the parishioners from all the neighboring villages. The brand-new church was packed. This was a beautiful opportunity for Fr. Laurenz to catechize because many of them had never seen a church in their lives!

Rosa is one of the babushkas (grandmothers) whom Stalin exiled in 1936. She was secretly baptized, and she catechized children and welcomed the priests who passed through. One day, a mysterious person, clothed in black, visited her and said: "Go to Moscow to meet such and such a person and ask for permission to build a church." Brezhnev had all the churches demolished in the 1970s. But nothing would stop Rosa. She was illiterate and didn't know anything about the big city, but she left for Moscow. After four days on a train, she presented her request to the central government's Ministry of Worship, and, against all odds, she got permission. Christians could build a house as long as there was no exterior sign, steeple, or visible cross, and as long as there was a fence around the building to keep bystanders from seeing it. The village started to work even amid persecutions, and Kazakhstan's first church saw the light of day. It was dedicated to St. Francis, who thus became the country's patron saint. A red glass cross was put in the church, which defied the ban.

To decorate the church, Rosa brought from Vilnius two huge ceramic angels that weighed 220 pounds each and a set of porcelain Stations of the Cross that weighed 33 pounds each. She traveled alone with her cumbersome load, but this didn't bother her. She called the militiamen on the station platform to help her.

Only elderly women and children were in the church when Thérèse's relics arrived. Middle-aged people, whom the atheist regime had silenced, didn't practice the Faith. But Rosa was going to fill that church. Unfortunately, after all her preparations, this woman who was so happy about this exceptional event, became deathly ill when Thérèse arrived. Fr. Pchémislav had the whole parish pray for Rosa during the Mass to welcome Thérèse's relics, but Rosa died. She was buried on the day of the feast of the Immaculate Heart of Mary, which coincided with Thérèse's departure. All of St. Francis's parishioners were there. The beautiful ceramic angels were shining, and Thérèse touched people's hearts. People returned to the church to say farewell to Thérèse after Rosa's burial.

During these months, 1.3 million images and posters of St. Thérèse were freely distributed in Russia and Kazakhstan, along with texts in Russian, the autobiographical manuscripts translated in Russian, twenty thousand copies of my book *The Story of a Life*, and fifty thousand booklets about Thérèse. The latter included songs, prayers, and poems. We noted that many people who had been raised according to the principles of communism requested these books and pictures.

Msgr. Kondrusiewicz had Moscow's Catholic cathedral consecrated on Sunday, December 12, 1999, after this astonishing journey. As I mentioned earlier, this was Moscow's Polish church, which Stalin had transformed into a factory in 1935.

The work of transformation and restoration was smoothy conducted. The apostolic administrator wrote to Fr. Raymond Zambelli, rector of the Basilica of Lisieux:

> I want to thank you again for your hospitality and especially for all that you did for the pilgrimage of St. Thérèse's relics in Russia.
>
> In turn, I want to invite you to my cathedral's consecration. I've planned to reserve a place of honor for St. Thérèse for the relic that you offered us.... The presence of the Catholics' protector in Russia — in Moscow — isn't only about Catholics but also about our Orthodox brothers. Many of them venerate her greatly.

Cardinal Angelo Sodano, the pope's legate, presided over the consecration in Moscow on Sunday, December 12. He was surrounded by thirty bishops and eighty priests. We experienced a historical and moving three and a half hours. This was especially due to the fact that among those present in the crowded cathedral were former gulag prisoners and people who recalled when the church had been a factory. The Eucharist came back to the tabernacle on that day after a break of sixty-four years.

An altar in the right transept was topped by a relic of St. Thérèse, Russia's protector, which was offered by our diocese. We've come full circle when we recall the arrival of the Russian delegation in Lisieux on August 15, 1998.

"Little" Thérèse still has a lot to do for the millions of residents of this huge country, which made the world tremble, so that the country's people can rediscover the "Russian soul's" deep spirituality.

At the end of her mission in Kazakhstan, two French priests who had participated in it — the Jaccard brothers — testified:

> Little Thérèse's witness and example were very striking for the people who had experienced years of atrocious suffering in famine, cold, and misery. But when they came to venerate the relics, all of them thanked her while crying and telling her: "Thank you for being our Hope!"
>
> We will keep in our hearts the image of the crossroads in the steppes where some Christians, whose children, with arms loaded with flowers from the fields, were waiting for the minibus that Thérèse, Srs. Tamar and Christelle, and both of us were in. The kneeling Christians prayed for a few moments during the minibus's stop and greeted us by kissing us (often while crying). Then, we left again, knowing that Thérèse had deeply marked the souls of all these poor people.
>
> The arrival in the village was such a celebration! Some of the people asked us: "How is it that you come to see us, and

how can St. Thérèse be here in our midst?" Thérèse herself answered them: "Love's characteristic is to humble oneself." Such a response changes your heart.

Cardinal Danneels used this expression from Fr. De Meester's preface in *Story of a Soul*: "Thérèse is a phosphorescent light. She's like a beacon along the way of people who are looking for God." We spoke about her sometimes three or four times a day. At that moment, we felt that the Carmelite from Lisieux was, according to Pius X's expression, "a word of God" for these Christians from the catacombs or from the secrecy and horror of deportations and gulags.[127]

[127] Raymond-Marie and Pierre-Marie Jaccard, report of the mission in Kazakhstan, June 29, 1999.

Argentina (July 9–October 3, 1999)

Argentina was quite a contrast with Russia! The reliquary had confronted temperatures of negative twenty-two degrees Fahrenheit in Siberia! It landed in Argentina in July in very hot weather.

Once again, the program was impressive. Over three months, the reliquary would visit sixty-four dioceses and forty monasteries, including twenty-eight Carmelite ones.

Msgr. Antonio Baseotto, bishop of Añatuya and president of the Episcopal Commission on Mission, and Dr. Juan Laprovitta, secretary of worship for the Presidency of the Republic, were in Lisieux on July 7. They would bring the relics to Argentina from the Charles de Gaulle Airport on July 8.

The relics' itinerary honed in on Argentina's cultural heritage. Here's the decision of the secretariat general of the nation's presidency:

> Buenos Aires, June 3, 1999
>
> In view of file no. 4184/99 from the register of the General Secretariat of the Nation's Presidency, we ask that the travels that will take place with the relics of St. Thérèse and of St. Roque Gonzales of the Holy Cross be declared in the national interest.

That the aforementioned travels will be carried out in different places in our country with the goal of preparing the Argentinian people for the sixth Missionary Latin American Congress — COMLA 6th — and the first American Missionary Conference — CAM 1st. This is an event that is internationally important.

That the impact of this event — via its social, cultural, historical, and religious effects — will help enliven an authentic spiritual celebration and an exchange that is conducive to the awareness of the defense of fundamental values that make up the essence of man and his condition, in the framework of a communal integration.

That the reasons that inspire those who are requesting the event deserve that it be declared in the national interest.

That THE SECRETARIAT GENERAL FOR CULTURE OF THE PRESIDENCY and the MINISTRY OF FOREIGN AFFAIRS, INTERNATIONAL TRADE AND WORSHIP favor this.

That this measure is in accordance with the faculties that are conferred by Article 1, Paragraph II of the 101/85 decree with its modification.

For all that

THE SECRETARY-GENERAL

OF THE PRESIDENCY OF THE NATION

IS DECIDING THAT:

ARTICLE 1 — The trips that will take place in different places in the country with the relics of St. Thérèse of the Child Jesus and St. Roque Gonzalez of the Holy Cross, from July 9 to September 26, 1999, are declared to be in the national interest.

ARTICLE 2 — The declaration that is conferred by Article 1 of this same administrative act does not result in any budgetary distribution of the 2001 jurisdiction — GENERAL SECRETARIAT — PRESIDENCY OF THE NATION.

ARTICLE 3 — That this be registered, published, communicated, and handed back to the official and archived register's national board.

RESOLUTION S.G. No. 721.

Dr. Alberto Antonion Kohan, Secretary-General

Thus, what was going to occur in Santa Cruz, Buenos Aires, Córdoba, or Santa Fe would become an official national event. Thérèse was going to be welcomed as a very important person. All of the state's services, including the army, would be mobilized to support her arrival in twenty-two cities and regions, in the framework of preparing for the Jubilee Year 2000.

Her passage would be part of an important event: the sixth Latin American Missionary Congress, which would occur in Paraná from September 28 to October 3, 1999. (This time frame include the dates of Thérèse's death, September 30, and of her universal feast, October 1.) It would be open to both Americas for the first time.

The Patroness of the Missions is associated with a martyr of evangelization: St. Roque González, who was born in Asunción, Paraguay. This Jesuit was a missionary to the Guaraní people. He died on November 15, 1658, at age fifty-two, when he and some fellow Jesuits were killed by a shaman's followers. They were Río de la Plata's first martyrs and were canonized by John Paul II in Asunción in 1988.

When the relics arrived in the Buenos Aires Metropolitan Cathedral, Msgr. Estanislao Karlic, president of the Bishops' Conference of Argentina, emphasized that Thérèse's arrival coincided with the celebration of Argentina's Independence Day.

The historical summit of Thérèse's visit in this country was obviously the gathering of the missionary congress in the Club Patronato in

Paraná, where three thousand missionaries and two hundred bishops assembled.

On August 7, Msgr. Bernardo Witte declared in Concepción, Tucumán, that he was experiencing "his episcopate's most marvelous day." The pastor of the Santa Teresita del Niño Jesus parish in Jujuy was given the city's keys on August 10.

Then the reliquary flew from Buenos Aires to New York.

United States (October 9, 1999–January 28, 2000)

Fr. Donald Kinney, an American Carmelite from San Jose, was in charge of the tour of the relics in the United States.

The program was finally ready after months and months of very detailed preparation. It included twelve pages that listed the 89 cities (128 stops), regions, and monasteries in 23 states that had requested Thérèse's relics. This journey would last more than three months. It affected all of the country's big cities. The reliquary would cross the huge American continent from east to west (from the Atlantic to the Pacific), and from north to south (from Wisconsin to Louisiana).

In this large country, nothing would be too big in order to welcome "little" Thérèse with dignity. The organizers themselves were astonished by everything that was being prepared. They gave the dioceses and the media a press kit that contained a multitude of information on the life of Thérèse Martin, her writings and message, the meaning of her becoming a Doctor, her relics' world travels, the object of such travels, and so forth.

Everything started with the Archdiocese of New York. The *New York Times* described the reception at JFK Airport as "Simply awesome!"

Here are some striking episodes.

A crowd in which all races mingled invaded Fifth Avenue and produced a traffic jam on Sunday, October 17. Six young bearded

Franciscans from the Bronx entered the cathedral with the reliquary. We saw through the door behind the procession the statue of the giant Atlas lifting the earth, at Rockefeller Center. How were we not to think of this phrase from St. Thérèse, quoting Archimedes: "Give me a lever and a fulcrum and I will lift the world"?[128]

Thérèse went in front of Atlas. The police presence was overwhelming. Alas, Cardinal O'Connor was already very ill and couldn't see the people of God surging toward Thérèse night and day. Msgr. Patrick Ahern, New York's retired auxiliary bishop[129] gave the homily. An exhibition and a "St. Thérèse group" made up of volunteers greeted the people.

Here is what some journalists reported:

> A superstar of the Catholic Church arrived in New York today. This was one of the numerous stops of a tour that was worthy of a rock star, and Fr. Michael Faulkner is more than ready.
>
> "We've spent three years preparing for her arrival," said the priest of the Church of Our Lady of the Scapular–St. Stephen on the Lower East Side. The faithful in his church would be able to venerate the remains of St. Thérèse of Lisieux for two days. They were contained in a wooden reliquary decorated with gold-plated silver....
>
> There are five churches dedicated to St. Thérèse in New York's five boroughs....
>
> "I thought of her a million times during my life," Fr. Faulkner said. "But I'd never seen her before last week, when she arrived at Kennedy Airport. I had goosebumps!"[130]

[128] Manuscript C, 36r in *Story of a Soul*, 258.

[129] Author of *Maurice and Thérèse: The Story of a Love* (New York: Image Books, 2001).

[130] Charles W. Bell, *Daily News*, October 16, 1999.

The Saint Who Stopped Traffic on Fifth Avenue!

Another star and another traffic jam. They are used to it in New York. Is the president in town? Don't approach the Waldorf! Is Ricky Martin stopping in Times Square? Avoid the neighborhood! But how many New Yorkers would have imagined having to avoid Fifth Avenue because of a box containing bones?

A certain number would — especially if they were Catholics. They would not have been surprised by the excitement of the reliquary' arrival at nightfall in front of St. Patrick's Cathedral. Some women cried while trying to touch it. The faithful followed it with their candles. They ended up having to close Fifth Avenue for half an hour. This had never happened to the Beatles!...

She undoubtedly has a tremendous ability to attract people. Crowds of the faithful came to venerate her at every stop. The luckiest ones managed to touch the plexiglass dome that covered the reliquary or to press their lips to it.

Her popularity isn't hard to explain. Her life was simple. She did no great works or miracles while she was alive. So she's accessible to everyone today.

"It's not often that we can see a saint or at least a saint's relics," said Gerry Olsen while leaving St. Patrick's Cathedral yesterday. She had come with her husband, Bill, simply to see the reliquary in front of the altar. "We feel close to her." ...

"I can really feel her presence," said Roz Romero, a Wall Street broker. "She's telling us that everyone can become a saint."[131]

[131] David Usborne, *Independent* of London, October 19, 1999.

St. Thérèse, Superstar

St. Thérèse of Lisieux has posthumously started a four-month tour of North America that promises to be triumphant. The saint's relics arrived at New York's JFK Airport and were welcomed with all the honors due to her rank as a "Doctor of the Church," which John Paul II awarded her two years ago.

The American Catholic authorities couldn't satisfy all the requests that came pouring in. More than a thousand parishes, monasteries, and sanctuaries had called for the relics' visit....

Thérèse is also a modern saint. Her American admirers dedicated an Internet site to her, using her nickname, "The Little Flower."[132]

Fifteen thousand people came to venerate the relics for three days in Washington: "We didn't expect that," Fr. Kieran Cavanaugh, a Carmelite, declared. The church was still full at 9:15 p.m. There were 4,500 and 4,000 people at the Masses in the Basilica of the National Shrine of the Immaculate Conception on Thursday and Friday. Then the "Thérèse-mobile" left for Baltimore.

There were already 5,000 people in the National Shrine of the Little Flower in Royal Oak in the Archdiocese of Detroit at 5:30 a.m. There were 14,000 of them at noon. It was estimated that there was a crowd of 75,000 people at the end of the day. People came on foot, by car, or by bus, despite the cold.

We closed the doors of the shrine at 9:30 p.m. on Wednesday, November 3. Fifty thousand people had approached the reliquary, but 25,000 of them couldn't go in. All of this amazed the clergy. They expected 20,000 people at the most.

[132] Jérôme Godefroy, *Le Point*, October 15, 1999.

Fr. William Easton, the chaplain, had a feeling that November 3 would be exceptional when he was awakened at 3:00 a.m. by a noise.

"I heard a noise," he said. "I got up and got dressed to go out. I saw a whole line of people there who were saying the Rosary at 3:00 a.m.! The line was getting longer and longer, and very soon, it reached all the way to the back doors." The crowd went beyond all the expectations of the priest. "So when have we seen a saint on the front page of the newspapers and on all the news stations?" he asked the 3,500 faithful who participated in the 8:30 Mass.[133]

The reliquary visited the Carmel of Terre Haute on November 4. The Carmelites wrote this testimony:

Sally Davies, a recently married young woman, came to visit the Carmel of Terre Haute a few weeks before the arrival of St. Thérèse's reliquary. Sally asked the extern sisters who welcomed her to pray for her because she had discovered a tumor and was very worried. She explained that she had never come into this Carmel before because she belonged to another parish in the city. The sister told her to put all her trust in God, assured her of the prayers of all the Carmelites, and added that, fortunately, Thérèse was going to visit that Carmel. She encouraged Sally to try to come and participate in one of the Masses that would be celebrated on November 4 in the Church of St. Benedict.

The relics arrived in the church around 5:00 a.m. (All the Carmelites and a beautiful crowd were there to welcome them.) The bishop celebrated Mass at 11:00 a.m., and a

[133] Olivier Pascal-Mousselard, *Télerama*, November 3, 1999.

thousand of the faithful attended it. They were packed into the church. After Mass, they approached the reliquary in a continual stream to touch it and entrust their intentions. A Carmelite sister helped two little altar servers approach the reliquary when she perceived Sally putting her hand on it and asking Thérèse to have mercy on her. Both of them silently prayed together for a few minutes. They then exchanged a few words, during which Sally introduced her mother to the sister, while promising to visit soon after she saw the doctor.

Two weeks later, a radiant Sally rang the Carmel's doorbell. She'd just seen her doctor, and the tumor had disappeared! Sally had become another person. She was utterly glowing! She told the sister that when she returned to her car after Mass, her mother asked her what kind of perfume she was wearing. Sally replied that she wasn't wearing any perfume that day, but she also perceived the smell of roses. It was so strong that it clung to her clothes!

Sally and her family participated in a Mass of Thanksgiving in the monastery on Christmas morning.

Simple witness accounts like this reflect the atmosphere and feelings of those who converged from everywhere to join Thérèse:

Thousands of people gathered together in the Sioux City convent on a magnificent Sunday in November to see the remains of a very beloved Catholic saint.

"St. Thérèse, we welcome you to our Diocese of Sioux City," Bishop Daniel DiNardo said at the monastery's door, while an escort accompanied the reliquary into the packed chapel. "You traveled around the world — to France, Belgium, Luxembourg, Germany, Italy, Brazil, the Netherlands, Russia, Kazakhstan, and Argentina. Now you're coming to us."

The bishop added: "We thank God for having sent her to our country at the threshold of the new millennium."

Bishop DiNardo and the other Catholic Church leaders celebrated the welcoming Mass outdoors on Sunday, and hundreds of people knelt on the grassy hillside's to the south of the monastery, while praying and singing in communion with the others who were packed in the little chapel.

Don Stevens, Sioux City's former postmaster, his wife, Mary, and Gary and Joyce Aguirre, who are also from Sioux City, escorted the relics in Saint Louis. The Stevenses left Saint Louis around 8:30 p.m. on Saturday to reach Sioux City around 4:45 a.m. on Sunday. They drove the car that was specially equipped to transport the reliquary across the United States. The Aguirre family followed them in their own car.

"Experiencing such an event is a unique opportunity in life," Don Stevens declared. "Faith is still experienced in this country." Mary Stevens added: "I think St. Thérèse is a great example of what God asks each of us. He doesn't ask us to succeed but only to be faithful."

Buses of pilgrims from Iowa, Minnesota, Nebraska, and South Dakota traveled to the monastery.

Linda Olson, from Andover, Minnesota, told us that a pilgrim coach that transported Catholics from three parishes left the Twin Cities area around 5:00 a.m. on Sunday. People prayed, read passages from St. Thérèse's writings, and recited the Rosary during the trip.

"I didn't know much about her," Linda explained to us. "I wanted to come because she's a saint who was coming here, and I didn't have to go all the way to Europe [to see her]."

Other groups arrived in buses that parked in the Hillcrest Center's parking lot, near Highway 75 and Glenn Avenue.

Some city buses shuttled to the monastery. Hundreds of people walked from the Morningside neighborhoods where they were parked — sometimes more than a mile away!"

Joe Frisbie, the police chief who watched over the traffic, estimated that more than three thousand people came to the monastery in the early afternoon. Hundreds of others continued to arrive afterward.

Paul Zimmerman, from Westphalia, Iowa, came with his wife and four children. Some of his friends also came. "We weren't sure we'd come, but when my wife and I got up this morning, we felt that God wanted us to be here. I hope we can go in and see the relics," he concluded, looking at the hundreds of people who were patiently waiting in line. . . .

Some members of the Intercessors of the Lamb, a contemplative community from Omaha, were among the religious who made the trip. "We have a great devotion to St. Thérèse, and we want to pray in front of her relics," explained Mary Madeline, who was wearing a white habit lined with bright green. "We pray for the gift of contemplative prayer for the world. God is putting this wish in our hearts." Sr. Mary Clare added: "I think that being here is a once-in-a-lifetime opportunity."

Fr. Thomas McDermott might have traveled farther than anybody else to see the relics. He came from Nigeria. He was born in Wayne, Nebraska, and is the Dominicans' provincial in Nigeria and Ghana. He has been a Dominican missionary in Africa for sixteen years. He wanted to come and pray to St. Thérèse for his sick mother. . . .

"It's a very rare blessing to have the relics here," Dr. George Spellman of Sioux City noted. "Little Thérèse has spread love all over the world, and now she's here." His wife, Carol, held a copy of the saint's autobiography and recommended it to all those who wanted to learn more about God's love.

Trang Vo, from Sioux City, told us: "We came today because we wanted to see a saint's body. There are many handicapped people here who are praying for their health or for the forgiveness of their sins."

Msgr. Lawrence Soens, the former bishop of Sioux City, concelebrated the Mass with Msgr. DiNardo and Msgr. Daniel Sheehan, the former archbishop of Omaha. Msgr. Soens said he wasn't surprised by the success. "It's an opportunity for many people to renew the strength of their faith. They recognize that St. Thérèse is near the Lord and intercedes for them."

Dr. Ken Roach, a veterinarian from Sioux City, explained that he saw the relics in their historical context. "[Thérèse] holds such an important place in the Church's history.... This is an unusual opportunity to be in a saint's presence. It's really unbelievable to have her here in Sioux City." "There certainly are saints on earth today, except we don't recognize them yet."[134]

It's estimated that twenty thousand people came to Sioux City from neighboring states on these days.

Ten thousand pilgrims rushed to the Carmel in Des Plaines, Illinois, on Sunday, November 14, according to the police's estimation. "This is reinvigorating my faith to see so many people. I've never seen this," confided Sgt. Michael Krueger. Mrs. Wosneski confirmed: "Some incredible things are occurring with these relics.[135]

[134] Lym Zerrsching, *Journal* staff writer, November 8, 1999.

[135] *Chicago Tribune*, November 14, 1999.

A reporter in Miami, Florida, described the arrival at the airport. The reliquary descended from a jet:

> She's known as "the Little Flower." But her influence on the Catholics in southern Florida was anything but little.
>
> This could be seen on the faces of the tens of thousands of people who gathered in four churches in southern Florida. It could be seen in the trembling hands of an elderly man who was being driven in his wheelchair to the reliquary to touch it and pray. It could be seen in the attitude of the schoolchildren who were bowing their heads with their eyes closed, silently praying on their knees, and putting their hands on the reliquary. It could be seen in the attitude of the muscular employees from the airport's warehouses. They were humbly bowing their heads, placing their calloused hands on the reliquary, and praying with their lips.
>
> It could be seen in the tears of about twenty Catholics who were touched by this earthly connection with someone who could hear their supplications from Heaven and intercede for a loved one or help alleviate the world's suffering.
>
> It could be seen on the radiant faces of the nine Carmelite sisters who were standing on the Miami International Airport's tarmac amid the wind when the French saint's relics arrived.
>
> "The relics make Thérèse's presence real and very close to us," said Sr. Marisa Ducote, principal of St. Thomas the Apostle School. "This helps the children understand that the saints are real. It helps them to know St. Thérèse and deepen their love for and devotion to her. We've spoken to the children a lot, and it has been beautiful to see how they have reacted. Thérèse is becoming real in their lives. The saints' reason for being is to be our heavenly friends. They are friends who help us to know

and love God better. The children really understand this. It's an experience I'll never forget."

Carolina Ribar, a student and part of an honor guard at the entrance to St. Thomas Church, was holding a picture of St. Thérèse. When we asked what all that this meant to her, she responded: "I think it's a privilege to have [Thérèse's] relics in our school. She has personally helped me to become closer to God. Look at all these miracles she has obtained since she has been in Heaven!"

Thirteen-year-old Jasmine Cuesta had yellow and orange roses in her hand. She said, "[Thérèse] said she wanted to be a missionary and come to us. Well, this is what she's doing today. This means she's helping everyone get closer to God and be there to pray to her. Many children were excited by this idea."

Thousands of others went to other places in southern Florida where the relics were welcomed. These included the Church of the Little Flower in Coral Gables, the Church of the Little Flower in Hollywood, Our Lady of Mount Carmel in North Dade, and St. Jude's in Boca Raton.

Mercy San Miguel, the mother of two boys who were enrolled in St. Thomas School, was waiting for the relics behind the yellow cord. Why did she come? "St. Thérèse died very young, and she followed the very simple little way that makes daily life special. We can also do this. We may not be able to experience the life of the martyrs, but we can build our lives on the basis of a daily routine that's offered to God."

The reliquary was magnificent but heavy, and those who carried it obviously found it to be physically strenuous. One of them, Luis Rodriguez, told us: "At one point, I started feeling the weight, and my hands began to hurt. I then thought about [Thérèse's] suffering when she had tuberculosis, and I offered her my pain. That's what allowed me to continue carrying the reliquary in a procession all around the garden."[136]

Mass was celebrated outdoors with 4,500 of the faithful in attendance on November 21.

It's estimated that sixty thousand of the faithful went to St. Jude Catholic Church in Boca Raton, Florida, in three days. This went beyond all of the organizers' expectations.

More than twenty thousand people went to the cathedral. Bishop Edward O'Donnell pointed out that Mother Teresa of Calcutta, who came to speak in 1986, attracted only fifteen thousand listeners. "This is a unique experience for our diocese and the whole state," declared Mother Mary John Billeaud. Despite the rain, some people came from Texas, Tennessee, Florida, and Louisiana.

The Carmelites of Lafayette had prepared this unusual event for six months. Ten thousand people came to Santa Fe, New Mexico, on Thursday, December 16.

Up to eighteen thousand visitors in Reno, Nevada — both Catholic and non-Catholic — swamped the church in two days. "The visit was phenomenal and fabulous. Every other superlative can be used," F. X. Mullen reported in the *Reno Gazette Journal* (January 18, 2000).

A journalist in Shoreline, Washington, expressed this appreciation in the Carmel of St. Joseph: "There are no words to describe this. We'll never see such a thing again."[137] Ten thousand people gathered around the cathedral.

The American journey's last stage was in Honolulu on January 27 and 28, 2000, after the trip to the Salt Lake City Cathedral, where fifteen hundred people attended Mass. Thérèse went to the Philippines and landed in Manila from there.

[136] Robert O'Steen, *Florida Catholic,* December 2, 1999.

[137] *Catholic Northwest Progress,* January 27, 2000.

Fr. Donald Kinney, the organizing committee's director, would pass the baton to Msgr. Ramón Arguëlles, a Filipino bishop and administrator of the Military Ordinariate, who would escort the reliquary. The United States Conference of Catholic Bishops thought the flight's cost was too high, but a Japanese woman came forward and offered to pay for the trip. She was profusely thanked and told: "You're a very generous Catholic" — to which she responded: "But I'm not Catholic. I love St. Thérèse, and I'm paying for her trip."

Fr. Kinney, who had followed the relics' travels, made an assessment at the airport in front of the press. "We in North America are practical. So we need to talk numbers." He would speak more as a pastor later.

Here's the first assessment:

> The reliquary made 130 stops in 117 days and crossed 25 of the 50 states![138] It traveled on 4 domestic airlines. The car that was used for the rest of the trip was nicknamed the "Thérèse-mobile." It traveled almost 13,000 miles — that is to say, more than three times the distance from the East Coast to the West Coast!
>
> It's estimated that 1,083,000 people came out to see the reliquary between October 5, 1999, and January 28, 2000.

People had never seen such crowds in many cathedrals and churches. The cathedral in Buffalo, New York, experienced the most important gathering of the faithful in all of its history.

Likewise, never had anyone recalled such an assembly in the Diocese of Sioux City. Never had such a crowd been seen in the cathedral in Philadelphia since the International Eucharistic Congress in 1976. All of the diocesan bishops participated in the event, with the exception of the western bishops, who had gathered for their annual retreat

[138] This is the final number. We offered projections before.

one week in January. The American cardinals were also present, except for two who were absent for health reasons.

Fifty-one dioceses out of two hundred were visited.

A man from Honolulu told me twice: "My father died seven years ago. I've finally accepted it here, with St. Thérèse's relics."

I heard seven or eight cases of miraculous cures of serious illnesses during St. Thérèse's visits. Of course, we'll have to study these cases very attentively and objectively.

It seemed that it wasn't even necessary to visit the relics in order to be healed. The Carmelite sisters of Eugene, Oregon, told me that one of their friends, who had suffered from ringing in her ears for ten years, hadn't been able to come to the celebrations on January 19 and 20. But she had, nevertheless, asked to be healed through St. Thérèse's intercession and was healed the very next day!

Many mentally and physically disabled people — even some who were in wheelchairs that were equipped with respirators — and a lot of elderly people, who had been devoted to St. Thérèse for many years had asked their children and grandchildren to drive them near their friend. The organizers very lovingly reserved the first places for them in line during the celebrations. They even organized celebrations that were especially for them. Their presence and prayer helped us recall the peace Jesus gives us (see John 14:27), which we so powerfully felt from one city to the next.

Americans aren't used to waiting patiently in line, yet we could see them waiting for three hours at times in city after city, without complaining. We often saw thousands of people standing, and the organizers never heard a single complaint!

Fr. Paul Tongas, the pastor of St. Mary of the Hills in Boylston, Massachusetts, greeted the reliquary in his parish for only a few hours on October 25. Since that day, he has given out pictures of St. Thérèse to help the faithful grow closer to Christ. He spoke to me about a couple who had been drawn into satanic rituals and desecrations of the Eucharist and had recently found their way back to the Church. They now have a very prominent portrait of Thérèse in their home.

> Thérèse's faithful people are from every ethnic origin. One of the most important communities is made up of Vietnamese people. Eleven buses of Vietnamese people from the same parish went to Alhambra, California, on December 30. It was touching to see many of them crying in front of the reliquary. They had suffered a lot and had gone to pray to the saint who had dreamed of going to their country. It's still not possible for the relics to be received in Vietnam. But this will certainly happen in coming years.
>
> It's hard to fathom the incredible organization and immense amount of work required to greet several thousand people for one or two days in a single place. This young girl, who didn't want to bother anyone, mobilized hundreds and hundreds of volunteers for her trip to the United States!
>
> It wasn't unusual to see fifty volunteers mobilized for an hour or five hundred for several days in a parish. A serious preparation had first been required. The volunteers had to be informed about St. Thérèse and her life and message so that they could evangelize through her.
>
> The weather was great. Hurricane Irene threatened New York in the middle of October, but "Hurricane Thérèse" was stronger, and it didn't rain at all! It always rains in the winter in Seattle, but it didn't rain during the four days that Thérèse was visiting it (January 21–23). We were somewhat afraid of the road that leads from the Georgetown Carmel to the Carmel of Reno, which was across the Sierra Nevada's high mountains. Almost two feet of snow had fallen the day before the trip,

but the road was cleared by morning, and the Thérèse-mobile could drive its precious load on schedule.

The media's coverage of the event from one end of the United States to the other amazed us, but we didn't have much experience or many contacts in this country. It was really surprising to see television cameras and journalists from day one. They were able to report fairly accurately on the event's religious character. There were five television crews even in the small town of Seaside, California, on January 11. The same thing occurred in Salt Lake City, an area that's dominated by Mormons.

The last festivity was the farewell Mass, which was celebrated by Bishop Francis X. DiLorenzo at Star of the Sea Church in Honolulu on January 28. Television stations also filmed Bishop DiLorenzo from Hawaii and Bishop Argüelles from the Philippines. One of them rebroadcast the program five times!

We were also lucky to benefit from the options that computers offered us. Our Internet site allowed visitors to know the precise itinerary by country and around the world. We're very thankful for the volunteers from Seattle, Washington, and Darien, Illinois, who were in charge of answering our 800 number. The phones often rang from morning until night![139]

Fr. Kinney was to give a lecture titled "Thérèse in the United States, Who Exceeds Our Expectations and Inspires Us With Great Desires"

[139] Excerpt from *Thérèse de Lisieux* 799 (April 2000). See *A Shower of Roses for the USA*, which is an appreciation for the extraordinary visit of St. Thérèse's relics in our country from October 5, 1999, to January 29, 2000. This was collected by Karen Eliason and edited by Fr. Donald Kinney, O.C.D. (2000).

during the symposium "Thérèse and the New Evangelization" in Lisieux in September 2001. Alas, the New York tragedy on September 11 prevented this from occurring. But *Vie Thérèsienne* published the text.

Here are a few lines from a Carmelite prioress:

> We've worked to organize this project for five years. The responses were positive but didn't indicate much interest. What a difference when we were flooded — almost overwhelmed! — by requests to receive Thérèse a few weeks before the reliquary's arrival. After the relics left, those who had been the most lukewarm about receiving them were often the most touched and thankful. . . .
>
> The frequent question we heard two years ago: "What if nobody comes?" was quickly changed into "What are we going to do with this crowd?"
>
> Thousands of people in our city were touched, but the biggest change that I witnessed was the behavior of the bishops and priests. I noted that Thérèse's visit really did something to help them grow in their faith. . . . They became aware that people in our materialistic world had a deep faith. This included not only elderly people and women but also people from all walks of life. The priests had been "magnetized" and "captivated." When I thanked them for having come, they replied: "Oh, Mother, don't thank us. We have to thank you." I apologized for being unable to invite them to lunch after a noon Mass on the last day. They replied: "Mother, you have more than nourished us with St. Thérèse!" I think the happiness of the bishops and priests was my greatest gift from Thérèse's visit, and it still is.

Two years after Thérèse's visit in my country, I can personally say that hardly a week passes by without my hearing about someone whose life was changed by Thérèse's arrival. Here

> are two examples: I know a young man named Justin in the Mount Angel Seminary in Oregon, who decided to become Catholic during Thérèse's visit. He's now started his studies. A few months ago, I met a young married couple who met each other during the relics' tour in Seattle.
>
> Many Carmels (of men and women — including those in our province) in my survey already had postulants and novices who were influenced in their vocation by the relics' tour.

The prioress of the Carmelites of Salt Lake City replied:

> During the tour of St. Thérèse's relics in Salt Lake City, the media, television stations, and newspapers outdid themselves to make the great event of the relics' presence known to the public. Everyone knew about it. It was the biggest news on the city's television and radio stations and in the newspapers. This had a huge impact in attracting big crowds to our monastery and cathedral. Since then, we've been able to note to what extent the prejudice that existed against Catholics fifteen years ago in Utah has collapsed. People feel more comfortable and freer in talking with us — especially about their religious thoughts — in doctors' waiting rooms, for example.

The Carmelites of the Most Sacred Heart of Los Angeles in Duarte, California, replied: "We're continuing to meet people who are speaking about their meeting with Thérèse. They have noticed that their return to the sacraments has been bearing lasting fruit."

These same Carmelites opened a perpetual adoration chapel for patients and their families in their Santa Teresita Hospital.

Almost two years after Thérèse's visit, many Carmelite convents noticed that more people attended Mass. Fr. Timothy Johnson, O.C.D., is the pastor of St. Jude Catholic Church in Boca Raton, Florida (where sixty thousand people came to pray with Thérèse). He wrote that their bishop, Msgr. Anthony O'Connell, had been so impressed by St. Thérèse's visit that he wanted the next parish in his diocese to be named St. Thérèse. He kept his word. This new parish's blessing took place in October 2001.

These were some of the consequences of Thérèse's tour in the United States. Fr. Kinney is a former Methodist who converted to Catholicism after reading *Story of a Soul* in 1980. He became a Carmelite, and he expressed his appreciation for the relics' visit in the book *Shower of Roses for the USA*. He could easily have published a second volume.

A plane carrying the reliquary left Honolulu for Manila on January 29, 2000. The great adventure continued, and Thérèse made another giant step forward. She arrived in Asia to discover the Philippines and China (Taiwan and Hong Kong).

Philippines (January 30–April 28, 2000)

On July 12, 1998, during its seventy-seventh General Assembly, the Bishops' Conference of the Philippines unanimously approved the proposal of requesting the relics of St. Thérèse of the Child Jesus in their country. This journey's great organizer was Bishop Ramón Arguëlles, who was appointed by the bishops' conference, presided over by Jaime Sin.

The country is made up of seven thousand islands. Therefore, the reliquary would travel in a plane, a helicopter, and a boat. The army and the police would be in Thérèse's service along the journey for transportation and security purposes in this country, in which about 80 percent of the people are Catholic. There were Muslims in the south, and some of them were in armed opposition to Manila's regime at times. We recalled the hostages held on the island of Jolo. And bandits sometimes got mixed up in the armed political opposition.

There was an enthusiastic and popular reception in the Manila Cathedral and at the Shrine of Our Lady of Mount Carmel. On February 1, the relics visited the prison in Muntinlupa, where 12,000 inmates were held. Eight thousand occupied the high-security area, and 959 of them were sentenced to death.

An exhibition of pictures of Thérèse had prepared her arrival. A helicopter that was flown by the prison's chaplain, Fr. Roberto A. Olaguer, rained roses on the prison at 6:00 a.m. and did it two more times — at noon and at 6:00 p.m. for the departure.

Forty inmates sang in a choir during the Mass. Others offered an image of Thérèse that was engraved on wood.[140]

Unfortunately, the reliquary, which was too large, couldn't go into Building 1, the one in which those who were sentenced to death were held. The prisoners were allowed to go out into the yard in groups of three to venerate the relics. They prayed, along with the priests, to ask for the abolition of the death penalty.

In fact, the president granted a momentary suspension of the executions on March 25 — shortly after this visit from Thérèse. The first beneficiaries were eighteen convicts who were to be executed by injection. The death penalty in the Philippines had been abolished by President Cory Aquino in 1987 and then reintroduced in 1993. The Philippines' bishops led an incessant campaign to abolish it. Seven who were sentenced to death were executed by injection in 1999.

A little later, President Estrada, to everyone's surprise, decided to commute all life sentences in prison and to release the political prisoners in mid-December 2000.

This decision obviously had a great impact in the whole country — chiefly among the convicts, who exulted. Fr. Olaguer, their chaplain, declared: "They attributed this miracle to St. Thérèse's intercession." During the relics' visit, the media, which was far from sympathetic to Catholics, joined in the prayer of those who were sentenced to death. This journey of the relics may have some political consequences.[141]

[140] It can be seen in Lisieux in the International Center of Pastoral Outreach.

[141] One of those who was sentenced to death, twenty-six-year-old Dexter C. Tagle, wrote a letter to Cardinal Sin. He told him about his connections with St. Thérèse and his joy in seeing her in this prison. He hoped something good would come out of this for everyone.

Thérèse's tour was, of course, everywhere linked to the Great Jubilee in 2000. She was greeted as the millennium saint in this vast country. It's the only really Catholic country in Asia, and it had become a missionary nation.

On February 2, 2000, there was a youth rally (50 percent of the population is under fifty years old) in the Manila Cathedral Although he was very sick, Cardinal Sin celebrated Mass. He also presided over the farewell Mass at the Villarmor Air Base on April 28. He had received the relics in his residence in Manila on April 19 and had spent a long time in front of the reliquary in his office there.

Again, it's not possible to follow this Theresian journey in detail. Forty-seven dioceses would be seen. But there were the same diverse crowds in the cities and villages that lined up everywhere to venerate the reliquary. There were the same banners: "*Mabuhay*" ("welcome" in Tagalog), the same posters, images, spoken prayers, dances ... These were seen in the 106 places where the relics stopped, day and night. Only the pictures and videos can give us a small idea of what these gatherings were like.

For example, up to fifty thousand people came from all around when the relics' visit was announced in the little parish of Santa Teresina, which had five thousand residents. It was about seventy-five miles south of Manila. The mayor had some lamps installed all along the road to illuminate the entire village.[142]

This debate on the death penalty that has lasted for many years in the Philippines is one of the important points of the Catholic Church's struggle. After President Estrada's deposition, the new president, Gloria Macapagal Arroyo, who came to power in January 2001, announced a moratorium on capital punishment. She suspended it on October 1, 2002 (the feast of St. Thérèse).

[142] Thérèse was very well known in the Philippines at the beginning of the twentieth century, thanks to the missionaries.

Graces and favors were granted, as they were everywhere else, and we know about only a tiny portion of them.

Violeta Garcia, from Makati, who was married to Norberto, was told by her doctor that she couldn't have any children, but she became pregnant a month after her prayer near the reliquary.

A seventy-year-old woman told Bishop Arguëlles that she had attended church only a few times in her life but that she felt compelled to enter the San Pedro Cathedral in Davao City to find faith there. "Thérèse prompted me," she said.

A couple in Zamboanga City who were on the verge of separating came to pray to Thérèse in the church, and the grace of reconciliation touched them.

A lady in Dagupan City told Bishop Arguëlles that her father's doctor thought that he was terminally ill. He reached the reliquary, was healed, and resumed his work.[143]

We were struck by the following event: The helicopter that was carrying the relics was always being escorted by a smaller police or army helicopter. One of these army helicopters, an Air Force AN MG helicopter that was headed toward Cebu, crashed in the Manila Memorial Park in Liloan on March 9. The three occupants not only didn't die, but they weren't even wounded. The pilot, Lt. Primitivo Dispo Jr., noted that a piece of his rotor's assembly had fallen. He was accompanied by Rodelio Gabriel and first-class pilot Gerry Fernandez. The authorities ordered an investigation but didn't hesitate to attribute this "miracle" to St. Thérèse.[144]

To conclude with the Philippines, let's allow Msgr. Ramon Arguëlles to speak. He followed the relics everywhere in Asia and mentioned one of the consequences of Thérèse's arrival in his country:

[143] Our archives have many testimonies of healings that were confirmed by the medical profession.

[144] *Freeman* (October 13, 2000).

The impact of the tour of Thérèse's relics in the Philippines was obviously the spread of her doctrine. From the start of the preparations for their arrival and while they were crossing the Philippines in every direction, we were more and more certain that this extraordinary grace of the Great Jubilee was not supposed to remain sterile or useless. The Holy Father's firm hope that Thérèse would become the spiritual guide and model of men and women — especially of young people in the third millennium — had to be fulfilled. The Millennium Saint Foundation (MSFI), which was formed by Carmelite groups and friends, continues to function. But this time, the goal is to spread Thérèse's doctrine in all countries and everywhere. The Filipinos, already trained in the knowledge of the little way, will be able to aid in this endeavor. Small prayer groups . . . are being organized under the MSFI's sponsorship.

The former church that was dedicated to Thérèse, which received her relics and was the last place she visited before returning to France, must be renewed to become the national pilgrimage site in her honor. This has to become a Theresian apostolate center to propagate the story of her life and doctrine. The church is near our country's most modern future international airport, which will open in 2003. St. Thérèse will welcome all travelers in their Asian homeland. All missionary Filipinos will be sent out into the world by the Patroness of the Missions to preach the good news there via her presence and her teaching. This pilgrimage site will have a secondary patroness, Our Lady of the Nations. The Virgin Mary and Thérèse are both loved by Filipinos. They are going to accompany the missionaries of the third millennium to announce the good news of hope to Asia and all other nations.[145]

[145] *Vie thérésienne*, no. 167 (2002): 20–21.

China: Taiwan (April 6–14, 2000)

It was not surprising for Thérèse's relics to linger in the Philippines.

But then, once again, an astonishing adventure started. Even though the island of Taiwan is politically separated from the huge country of China, Thérèse, nevertheless, arrived in China!

She was accompanied by a Filipino delegation, which included Bishop Arguëlles. The relics landed at 4:00 p.m. at the Chiang Kai-shek International Airport[146] on April 16, 2000.

The Diocese of Chiayi received the relics in St. John's Cathedral after various stops. Msgr. Peter Lin Chen-chung offered flowers and incense and bowed three times, a greeting reserved for high-ranking people. The cathedral was too small for all the visitors, but an outside tent sheltered the faithful, with TV screens set up so that they could follow the celebration.

Cardinal Paul Shan greeted the reliquary in Zuoying in the church that was dedicated to Thérèse. Msgr. Matthew Kia, the archbishop emeritus, joyfully received Thérèse in the Church of the Immaculate Conception in Taipei. This Theresian had often gone on pilgrimage to Lisieux and once presided over the August 15 feast.

[146] Now called the Taoyuan International Airport.

The visit on this island of 20,900,000 residents was relatively brief. There were twelve stages, including five monasteries.

The reliquary flew to mainland China after a national Mass that Bishop Bosco Lin presided over on April 14. We knew it was hostile to Taiwan, which rejected communism.

Hong Kong (April 14–19, 2000)

Thérèse in mainland China! Even though Hong Kong (which the British returned to China in 1997), with its six million residents, maintains a special status, the reliquary stayed in China for five days. This was short, but it was a formidable symbol.

How can we not recall the connection of Sr. Thérèse of the Child Jesus with this huge continent through her friendship with the young missionary Adolphe Roulland (1870–1934)? He had announced the gospel in eastern Sichuan as early as 1896.

We know what correspondence they exchanged after the first Mass that this priest from the Paris Foreign Missions Society celebrated in the Carmel of Lisieux on July 3, 1896. Sr. Thérèse sent him six very important letters in which she assured him that she would help his mission through prayer and sacrifice. She had pinned the map of Sichuan on the wall in the place where she worked to help her follow her "brother's" missions.[147] This was near the end of her life. Tuberculosis had consumed her. Throughout our time among Hong Kong's Chinese Catholics, we recalled this friendship and Thérèse's prayer for China.

[147] Thérèse of Lisieux, *Lettres à mes frères prêtres* [Letters to my brother priests] (Paris, Éditions du Cerf, 2003).

China's political situation has certainly led to a most complex religious situation for Christians. How many times during the celebrations did people say that they wished that one day the reliquary would go farther? It was impossible now.

The enthusiasm in Hong Kong was stronger for it, although it was more restrained and less demonstrative than in the Philippines. It can be estimated that there are 250,000 Catholics in fifty-two parishes without priests.

The stay's briefness limited the celebrations. The reliquary moved in a "Thérèse-mobile" that carried the Jubilee 2000 logo and a sign in Chinese and English that read, "The tour of St. Thérèse's relics in Hong Kong."

We left in a procession behind the car that was going to St. Teresa's Church in the Kowloon district on Saturday, April 15. The Hong Kong site's view was both splendid and overwhelming. The buildings were very tall. Everything was modern and state-of-the-art. The residents experienced the stress of a life that was focused on financial and economic problems. This city was once one of the world economy's strongholds.

Cardinal John Baptist Wu Cheng-chung, the bishop of Hong Kong, did the honors. He was surrounded by many priests, including some French missionaries.

Fr. Edward Yu gave a lecture in Chinese. People then rushed toward the relics. There was also a beautiful exhibition about Thérèse and a bookstore with Chinese and English books.

The next day, there was a celebration and veneration in the Cathedral of the Immaculate Conception. Here again, various lectures about Thérèse's life and spirituality were given throughout the day.

On Monday, the reliquary arrived at the Carmel in Stanley via a very picturesque coastal cliff road. Thirteen Chinese Carmelites were praying in the monastery. Their chaplain was American. A few of them came in parish groups. The Carmelites were eager for details about Thérèse's relics and her influence in the world.

It was already time to go back to Manila on Wednesday, April 19. The reliquary was waiting in the lounge reserved for heads of state at the Hong Kong International Airport before being put on board the Air Philippines' Boeing 747.

A missionary offered these thoughts at the end of this very important tour:

> This year, of course, is marked by the Jubilee, which touches us in a special way since the diocese has designated us as one of the pilgrimage's nine parishes for the Holy Year. Nonetheless, our church, which is in the heart of the city, doesn't attract a lot of pilgrims. They prefer more remote places, which allow for a deeper pilgrimage undertaking. On the other hand, the arrival of St. Thérèse of Lisieux's relics was a great parish and diocesan event that attracted almost ten thousand pilgrims. We were advised to receive them for a few days. We gladly accepted them, without measuring the size of the task, especially as this coincided with Palm Sunday and the start of Holy Week (a naturally busy period in parishes!). I, as a young French vicar and friend of the Carmel, was naturally associated with the event's preparation and was in charge of the liturgies. This was a good opportunity to dive back into little Thérèse's writings with pleasure. It was a high point for the parish on two levels. It was an opportunity to get to know our holy patron and her spiritual teachings. Their simplicity and depth are especially beneficial to Hong Kong's residents. But it was also an opportunity to unify the parish around a great event, for which all the people really gave the best of themselves (sometimes until late at night). They unreservedly collaborated with one

another. Thus, the arrival of St. Thérèse's relics was more efficient than the different activities, reflections, and reforms that were started in recent years to improve harmony in the parish community.

Return to the Philippines and the Departure (April 19–28, 2000)

The reliquary would spend Holy Week in Manila again. This time it was in the Mother of Life catechetical center.[148] It was magnificently decorated. The chapel wasn't big enough. A "green cathedral" would welcome the thousands of believers from the surrounding area. People were already waiting patiently in line when the doors were opened as early as 6:00 a.m. I was informed that the Philippine Army's head general was there in civilian clothes along with his whole family.

The violent evening storms forced us to shelter the reliquary in the church, and we had to insist that the faithful agree to leave at midnight. The priests heard confessions throughout these days.

In Manila, a megalopolis of thirteen million residents, where rich buildings and slums coexist, we could see huge signs connected to ads for Coca-Cola and McDonald's with the picture of Thérèse and this text: "Remember the visit of the Pilgrim Relics of St. Thérèse of the Child Jesus in the Philippines, 1/30–4/28/2000." The media made everyone aware of this event.

[148] Foundation of Notre-Dame de Vie, a secular institute that was set up in the Philippines in 1954.

The last days in the Philippines would occur in Infanta and Antipolo on the west coast, which faces the Pacific Ocean.

We left in two helicopters. The bigger one transported the relics. The region where we landed was much poorer. But the reception at the Infanta Stadium was very colorful and enthusiastic. The Protestant mayor delivered a welcoming speech. Then there was a procession, in which people rushed toward the packed and well-decorated church. Traditional and modern dances followed one another on the premises and even in the sanctuary, for they were part of the liturgy.

There would be a visit to the St. Thérèse Parish in Dipaculao and a stopover in the Infanta Carmel, which, though well hidden in the expansive vegetation, was overrun by all the neighbors.

The relics would leave Asia on Friday, April 28, 2000, after a journey that had lasted three months. They would head back from the Philippines' military airport. They were exposed and venerated in a silent place one last time. Laypeople, nuns, and soldiers who worked in the airport came. Superior officers, soldiers, and servicewomen knelt in silence. In the same silent way, the relics were placed in the box, which was filled with some of the region's flowers. It was loaded into the hold of an Airbus A340. It would arrive at the Charles de Gaulle Airport in Paris after a flight of fifteen hours and forty minutes.

The Carmelites of Lisieux welcomed their sister and the Philippine delegation around 10:00 a.m. A Mass in the chapel would bring some Parisian Filipinos together in the afternoon. They wanted to escort the reliquary to Lisieux and to greet the tireless Bishop Arguëlles, who had accompanied Thérèse during all these months — even in Taiwan and Hong Kong.

> The millennial saint's visit reinforced the beginning of a missionary age in Asia. This continent is proud of its religious and cultural values, such as the love of silence and contemplation,

harmony, nonviolence, and compassion for everyone. . . . The Church has the deepest respect for these great ancient traditions. The challenge for the Church in the Philippines and Asia is immense; the task is huge. But our young Doctor is offering her way of confidence and love, which the Church can use "for a sincere dialogue with the disciples of these great traditions." Thérèse's little way will allow the Church to communicate the gospel to the Asian soul. . . .

The Asian synod took place from April 18 to May 14, 1998. It became clear on the following June 10 that Thérèse's relics would come to this huge part of the world at the beginning of the great Jubilee Year. Was this a coincidence or a marvelous part of the divine plan? The good news would again be announced in Asia, where everything started. Our guide for the third millennium had a role to play in this new Pentecost. Her Asian missionary adventure had just begun. We're certain that she's with the Church in this thrust of the third millennium's evangelization.[149]

[149] See *Vie thérésienne*, no. 167 (2002): 21–23.

Italy Again (May 4–December 26, 2000)

We noted the relics' popularity in Italy in 1997. But this country wasn't satisfied with such a brief visit. Eighty Italian dioceses asked to host the relics for seven months. Let's not forget that we were still in the Jubilee Year 2000, which siphoned off millions of pilgrims to Rome.

The first step (May 5–11) was the meeting of two eminently popular saints: the French Carmelite saint in Anthony of Padua's home! This young pilgrim had rapidly gone through Padua on November 11, 1887: "After Venice, we went on to Padua where we venerated the tongue of St. Anthony."[150] Crowds venerated Thérèse's relics in this huge basilica on May 11, 2000.

The recent suburban church that was dedicated to Thérèse couldn't be forgotten. The weekly diocesan magazine *La Diffesa del Popolo* published twenty thousand copies of a book about Thérèse. There were several concerts, debates, conferences, celebrations, and a night of prayer, and at the Carmel of Monselice, the Carmelite Fr. Antonio Sangalli, a passionate Theresian, gave three talks.

The relics visited Rimini from May 11 to 15. San Giustina's pastor, whom we already met here, was insatiable. He had requested the

[150] St. Thérèse of Lisieux, Manuscript A, 59 v, in *Story of a Soul,* 128.

reliquary for the third time. He himself said that "Thérèse fell in love with his parish."

Twenty-five to thirty thousand people came from various Italian regions in four days — even when they knew the relics would still pass by their own regions.

Of course the Sanctuary of Loreto wanted to receive the saint's human remains (May 15–22), for we knew how joyful and emotional she was when she went on a pilgrimage there on November 13, 1887. She described these intense moments:

> I was indeed happy to be on my way to Loreto. I am not at all surprised the Blessed Virgin chose this spot to transport her blessed house, for here, peace, poverty, and joy reign supreme; everything is primitive and simple. The women have preserved their graceful Italian dress and have not, as in other cities, adopted the *Paris fashions*. Loreto really charmed me! And what shall I say about the Holy House? Ah! How deep was my emotion when I found myself under the same roof as the Holy Family, contemplating the walls upon which Jesus cast His sacred glance, treading the ground bedewed with the sweat of St. Joseph, under this roof where Mary had carried Jesus in her arms, in which the angel had appeared to the Blessed Virgin. I placed my rosary in the little bowl of the Child Jesus. What ravishing memories!
>
> Our greatest consolation was to receive *Jesus Himself* in His *house* and to be His living temple in the very place He had honored with His presence. As is the custom in Italy, the Blessed Sacrament is reserved on only one altar in the churches, and here alone can one receive Holy Communion. This altar was in the Basilica itself where the Holy House is to be found, enclosed like a precious diamond in a white marble casket. This didn't satisfy Céline and me! It was in the *diamond* and

> not in the *casket* that we wanted to receive Holy Communion. Papa with his customary gentleness did like all the rest, but Céline and I went in search of a priest who had accompanied us everywhere and who was just then preparing Mass in the Santa Casa by special privilege. He asked for *two small hosts* which he laid alongside the large one on the paten and you can well understand, dear Mother, the joy we *both* experienced at receiving Communion in that blessed house![151]

The bishop of Loreto took the initiative in leading the reliquary in this Santa Casa where Thérèse had received Holy Communion 113 years before.

Fr. Nicola Mattia bore witness to what happened in the Cathedral of Termoli (May 23–25):

> Many priests made themselves available for Confession at any time, and there were never enough of them. Five priests had a hard time distributing Communion during the two Masses. Despite the great number, the atmosphere always remained prayerful, meditative, and silent. When it was time to leave, the young people gathered together around the relics and didn't want to let them go! We, along with a lot of parishioners, accompanied them to the next destination, which was 466 miles from Termoli! Their departure left a big gap!

The relics' visit to Gallipoli (May 26–29), specifically to the Carmel there, was a historic event. Thérèse had gone there on the night of January 16, 1910, during an apparition to Maria Carmela of the Sacred Heart. This was one of those most amazing "physical" miracles that were part of her official Process of Beatification.

[151] Manuscript A, 59v to 60r in *Story of a Soul,* 128–129.

These poor Carmelites no longer had any resources. They didn't even have money to buy bread. One night, Thérèse appeared to the prioress, Mother Maria Carmela, and led her to a box in which there were 500 lire.

One year after the "miracle," the bishop of Nardo, Msgr. Nicola Gianattasio, who wanted to celebrate the anniversary (and undoubtedly do a test), asked to have a sealed envelope containing a 500-lire bill put in the convent's collection box. He himself came to take the sealed envelope on January 16, 1911, and he had Mother Maria Carmela open it. People noted that four bills had been added to the 500-lire bill. There were two hundred-lire bills and two fifty-lire bills![152]

This miracle made a big splash and remained in the city's annals. Also, Thérèse's return mobilized crowds — and not only from Gallipoli. We saw pilgrims who had come from Sardinia. Dean Rosaria Palese Tondo, who was born seven years after the miracle, wanted to come to the Church of St. Thérèse. The city's mayor and the new bishop, Msgr. Domenico Caliandro, welcomed St. Thérèse. This was his first visit to Gallipoli.

At the suggestion of Mr. Francesco Di Pilla, a college literature professor, a symposium on the theme "Thérèse of Lisieux and the Joy of Loving" had been scheduled (June 6–8) in Perugia, Italy, a university city. Some eminent Theresians spoke. These included the Carmelite fathers Jean Sleiman, Antonio Sicari, Jesús Castellano, François-Marie Léthel, and others. Two exhibitions, a concert, and a play were added. Three thousand people visited the shrine.

Let's not forget Pompei (June 8–14) — which Thérèse visited on November 22, 1887 — Acerenza (June 27–July 2), and Fiesole (July 2–8).

On July 21, a Tuscan Catholic cultural center organized a meeting on this theme: "Thérèse of Lisieux and Georgia La Pira, God's pilgrims."

[152] See the Ordinary Process, 96–103.

Severino Dianich, a theologian, published an article in *Toscana Oggi* during Thérèse's visit in Tuscany. He expressed his perplexity about this event "that distracted from the Faith." Several people wrote letters in response, which disputed his isolated point of view. Fr. Alessandro Andreini, who had replied to him, testified: "The passage was and continues to be a blessing for our local church. Our bishop has talked about this subject as a true 'popular mission.'"

When we were in Pisa (July 9–12), we recalled Thérèse's visit there on November 26 and 27, 1887. A plaque on the Place de la Gare, which was destroyed during the war, had recalled that visit.

Among the churches, cathedrals, and monasteries we stopped at was the convent of the Sisters of St. Joseph in the Aosta Valley. Thérèse miraculously healed a novice, Sr. Raffaella Corgnier, there in 1916. She later became a novice mistress and superior general. At the end of the vigil around the reliquary, Mother Leonia read the official report on the healing.

The relics also went to San Giovanni Rotundo, the famous sanctuary of St. Padre Pio, who was beatified by John Paul II on May 2, 1999, and was canonized in 2002.

From August 13 to 18, the relics revisited Rome and, in particular, the Vatican's small contemplative Mater Ecclesiae Monastery, founded by John Paul II. Luckily, the contemplative order that was there at the time (a different contemplative order would occupy the monastery every five years) was the Carmelites, who came from different countries. They prayed for the world and the pope's intentions in the heart of the Vatican.

Msgr. Giovanni Battista Re, the representative of the secretary of state and Msgr. Nguyen Van Thuan, president of the Pontifical Council of Justice and Peace,[153] among others, came to concelebrate there.

[153] Msgr. Van Thuan died in 2002.

Msgr. Van Thuan confided that Thérèse had healed him of tuberculosis before he spent thirteen years in a Vietnamese prison. A young Japanese nun came to tell the Carmelites: "She, little Thérèse, led me from Buddhism to the Catholic Church and then to religious life. She irresistibly attracted me."

From there, the reliquary went to several places in Rome to honor different requests. It was greeted there by Swiss guards each time.

The priests in Piedmont, in Terme (August 18–29), for example, noticed that many of the faithful had found their way back to the sacrament of Reconciliation.

The reliquary stopped at the Great Bernard Monastery. A young man named Louis Martin was thinking for a while about entering that monastery in September 1843.

The Italian journey continued as the reliquary crossed the strait to travel across Sicily (November 13–December 15, 2000). It went to about fifty cities and into three prisons. Cardinal Salvatore De Giorgi and Mayor Leoluca Orlando received the relics in the Palermo Cathedral.

The next day, the cathedral in Cefalù — a picturesque city at the edge of the sea — with its splendid mosaics, welcomed it. After going to the famous Monreale Cathedral, the reliquary returned to Palermo, where the Pagliarelli Prison's inmates had asked to have the relics return for a second visit.

The relics left again in a ferry on December 15, with a stopover in Calabria before reaching Rome.

All the bishops participated in the relics' travels in their diocese during these thirty-two days in Silicy. As we had done everywhere, we were able to see some Theresian exhibitions and listen to lectures and concerts (among others, Sylvie Buisset, from the Community of the Beatitudes, who has sung Thérèse's poetry around the world). More than six thousand copies of *Story of a Soul* were sold.

This is how the great journey across Italy, which lasted seven months, ended in the Jubilee Year. Thérèse hadn't stayed in any country except Brazil for so long. But hadn't she made a very crucial one-month pilgrimage in November 1887, which proved to be extremely informative for that fifteen-year-old girl in the nineteenth century? "I understood my *vocation* in *Italy* and that's not going too far in search of such useful knowledge."[154]

[154] Manuscript A, 56r, in *Story of a Soul*, 122.

Mexico (January 16–March 31, 2001)

"Una flor del Cielo visita nuestra tierra"[155]

The reliquary would cross the Atlantic Ocean once again to visit a country that had experienced a virulent anti-religious wave from 1924 to 1928. Pope Pius XI had entrusted Mexico to St. Thérèse after her canonization. But times had changed, and "Teresita" was going to receive an enthusiastic reception that was worthy of the exuberant spontaneity of this population of more than ninety-five million.

The anticipated journey was impressive yet again. It covered the whole country, from the north to the south, in thirty-eight stages. It went from Mexico City (13.6 million residents) to Merida, while passing through Guadalajara and Acapulco.

Msgr. Luis Morales Reyes, president of the Episcopal Conference of Mexico, had asked as early as October 13, 1998, that the reliquary come to Mexico; at that time, the reliquary was in Brazil. Many other Mexican bishops very much favored this. But there were a lot of requests from other countries, and people had to register in turn and be patient, and that is what was done.

[155] "A flower from Heaven is visiting our land." This was a phrase that Mexico adopted for the relics' arrival.

The program was put in place in February 2000, and fourteen bishops asked to receive the relics. By November, thirty-five had asked.

The Mexico City International Airport was wildly excited about the arrival of the plane that was bringing "Teresita" on Tuesday, January 16. A press conference took place in the official lounge with Msgr. Abelardo Alvarado Alcántara, the episcopate's secretary-general, and various religious and civil authorities. He read a message from John Paul II to the Mexican people.

Fireworks exploded when the relics arrived in the cathedral. The first news in Lisieux was enthusiastic and set the tone: "Mexico City is full of joy and love for Thérèse. It's incredible to witness all the people who have come from all over. Television and radio have covered the whole event."

A Theresian exhibition circulated in the country, and people waited in long lines to see it. The organizers said that "people's responses went over our heads". They added, "We're delighted about the Mexican people's response to this visit. It's an enormous blessing for our country to receive the relics."

After a Mass celebrated by Cardinal Norberto Rivera Carrera on January 17, Thérèse visited Mexico's biggest prison. This occurred after the inmates had listened to a lecture on her life and spirituality. Thérèse would visit twelve prisons in the country.

The crowd was huge in the Church of La Esperanza de María en la Resurrección del Señor, south of Mexico City. Four hundred novices in the city's religious congregations came to venerate their Carmelite sister. It would be the seminarians' turn the next day.

The relics stayed in the cathedral until Saturday, January 20. Thousands of people waited there to approach the reliquary. Five thousand people still hadn't been able to enter the church when it was time for the relics to leave the Diocese of Ecatepec. Then the government granted special permission for the reliquary to tour the great Zócalo

Square in front of a silent, praying guard of honor, under a shower of roses.

The visit to the hospital was especially impressive. Many of the patients there had crutches or were in wheelchairs. They came to touch the shrine and to pray.

Thérèse's trip during these seventy-five days covered 13,670 miles and attracted about fifteen million Mexicans.

Let's proceed to some reflections and conclusions as well as reports published in Mexico about the important events. And let us not forget the splendid pictures by Don Ramon, the tour's official photographer. He had long worked for the presidents of Mexico, but he declared this the most beautiful of all his missions. He was a member of the Mexican delegation of eight people who brought the relics back to Lisieux on March 31, 2001. One airline company offered all the international and national tickets to Thérèse and the delegation.

Mr. Roberto O'Farrill, a knight of Malta and the father of three children, was in charge of Radio Malta, which covered the whole trip and had prepared for it for six months. He came to give thanks. He told us that in October 1997, when Thérèse became a Doctor, he had gone to Rome for Radio Malta in order to contact Vatican Radio. He entered St. John Lateran's Archbasilica "by chance" and discovered that St. Thérèse of Lisieux's relics were there. He felt impelled to go to the reliquary and ask for a great blessing through Thérèse's intercession. His son Robie, when he was a year old (he's now seventeen), fell from several floors and sustained a brain injury that caused him to suffer ten to fifteen seizures per day. Roberto prayed for his son's healing. He stayed in Rome for eight days for his work. When he returned to Mexico, his wife told him that Robie had had no convulsions for a week. The healing was confirmed in 2001 and lasted for years, to the doctors' amazement. When the relics arrived in Mexico City, we understood why Robie wanted to be one of the carriers of the relics that his father had seen in Rome.

Mexico's president, Vincente Fox (the first Catholic president after several decades of persecutions against the Church), offered his own guard to escort Thérèse.

All the places where the relics stopped — cathedrals, churches, and stadiums — were too small to accommodate the crowds. Twenty thousand people swamped the stadium in Culiacán. There were twenty-one thousand in Mexico City for the farewell celebration on March 31.

Roads were blocked, and there was a shortage of roses in the florist shops in several cities. This disappointed people who couldn't even see the reliquary.

The atmosphere was festive, typical of Mexico. A journalist said, "In the Diocese of Jalisco — but also in others — we heard everything at once. This included drums and trumpets, brass bands, parish church bells, police patrol sirens, ambulances, fire trucks, the priest's voice on the sound system, and a multitude that was shouting: 'Viva! Viva!' The people raised candles with one hand and roses with the other."

Nonetheless, there were no incidents or accidents anywhere. Msgr. Luis Barrera Flores, the secretary of the Episcopal Conference of Mexico, followed the whole trip. He told us later in Lisieux that he had been impressed to see people of all ages and conditions along the roads at 2:00 a.m., when it was five degrees below zero. There were sick people who wanted at least to see the "Thérèse-mobile" go by. You had to wait six hours to reach the reliquary in Saltillo.

Selena was a paralyzed thirteen-year-old who approached the reliquary in a wheelchair in Veracruz (Diocese of Orizaba). After having touched it, she said: "I want to walk." She got up. We supported her. She walked![156]

[156] See the picture in *Thérèse de Lisieux,* no. 813 (July–August 2001): 21. See other pictures in the pilgrimage of Lisieux's archives.

> A man in a hospital was in intensive care, with electrodes connected to a heart monitor. Suddenly, the monitor flat-lined. The man's heart had stopped beating.... But his family, who knew that St. Thérèse's relics would arrive the following week, prayed this prayer: "Teresita, we trust you. You must do something *right away* because next week it will be too late!" They went back home to fetch a portrait of the saint and came back with it to pray near the man. Ninety minutes had gone by. The beating heart's outline started registering again on the cardioscope's screen.[157]

At the end of the journey, Msgr. Luis Morales Reyes emphasized that Thérèse was the bearer of an important message of peace in a changing society. "It's interesting," he said, "to note that God is giving us this gift in the middle of winter. It's social as well as physical. Thérèse is arriving like a spring rose." John Paul II's message, which was sent for the occasion, was along the same lines. This major time of prayer would be an occasion "for promoting the true values of a just and fraternal society." It was an opportunity to refocus on the essential.

In San Luis, the same bishop said: "We all want to approach something that speaks to us about the supernatural — about that which is beyond daily material experiences. What we experienced here conveyed the hunger for God that John Paul II spoke of. The new millennium's world will be a religious world — a world of searching for God — of searching for the supernatural in the noble sense of the word."

Many bishops reminded the people that the new millennium's first urgent need was for holiness. A big headline in Zacatecas read: "Thérèse, the Doctor of Urgent Needs"!

[157] *Thérèse de Lisieux*, no. 813.

Ireland (April–July, 2001)

"A Hurricane in Ireland"

So many people had never come to venerate St. Thérèse of Lisieux's remains. We estimated that 60 percent of the population were involved — that is to say, around three million people. This obviously goes beyond Catholics alone. How could we be amazed, considering that it was Ireland?

For many years, Fr. J. Linus Ryan, a Carmelite, went on a pilgrimage with groups of Irish people to each Theresian celebration in Lisieux. They were often accompanied by Cardinal Daly, who presided over the feasts in 2001.

Fr. Ryan wrote to Fr. Zambelli on March 11, 1999. He said that "the Irish Catholic Bishops' Conference had unanimously decided to request a tour of the relics in their country." Msgr. Comiskey was designated as the committee's chief organizer, and Fr. Ryan would be a co-coordinator.

We knew what special care the Irish pilgrims who were devotees of Thérèse took to welcome the Little Flower into their homes. This was the first time this had happened for the reliquary. This time, it was leaving on a cruise from Cherbourg to Rosslare on the Irish Ferries' *Normandy.*

A delegation that Fr. Ryan brought came to see the relics in Lisieux on Saturday, April 14, 2001. It was in a "Thérèse-mobile" that was connected by satellite to Ireland and was driven by Sgt. Major Pat Sweeney, copilots Liam O'Keefe and Jimmy Doyle, Peter Byrne of Donegal, and Jean-Michel Jeslin, a French policeman.

We did a live radio show on the street with Irish listeners who asked us questions.

The *Normandy* raised the anchor at 6:00 p.m. An honor guard, made up of officers and the team, escorted the reliquary, which remained in a specially prepared room. The 736 passengers and team members came to venerate the relics until 11:00 p.m. The head of the liner's security guarded them all night. Captain T. Sansfield had planned everything. Fr. Ryan and Fr. Flanagan celebrated Mass in a packed auditorium.

Msgr. Comiskey greeted Thérèse at St. Patrick Church in Rosslare, on the island's southeastern tip. The first surprise was that 3,000 people flocked to the place — not including the people on the streets. Around 12,000 people, who weren't necessarily regular churchgoers, came and went by the reliquary in St. Aidan's Cathedral in Enniscorthy. This is how it was in the seventy-four locations where the reliquary would stop during the seventy-eight-day tour. We hesitate to list dull statistics, but how can we not mention the 80,000 people who crossed the threshold of St. Mary's Cathedral in Kilkenny, or the 70,000 in the Church of the Nativity of the Carmelite convent in Dublin, or the 80,000 who came to the Cathedral of the Assumption in Carlow?

Cardinal Desmond Connell, archbishop of Dublin, greeted Thérèse in St. Mary's Cathedral. Various parishes ensured that they would pray all night long. Three Masses were celebrated on Tuesday, May 1. The crowd reached a record in two days — 110,000 people!

The reliquary went into a prison again on May 4. It wasn't easy because we had to dismantle a porch and a window in order for it to enter the chapel. Fifty-five inmates visited the chapel. One of them said:

"It's a once-in-a-lifetime opportunity." A Mass for the prison staff and their families gathered 3,000 people together that night.

A peak was reached on May 11 and 12 in Kildare in White Abbey, where the Carmelite fathers have lived for eight hundred years and where Fr. Ryan was living. The soccer team carried the reliquary, and 100,000 people came in three days.

The pastor of St. Joseph's Church on Berkeley Road declared: "This day is undoubtedly the most historic day our parish has experienced. It's a day of graces and blessings that we'll never forget."

The sacristan who had worked there for forty-five years affirmed, "I've never seen anything like this. It has exceeded all our expectations."

The influx of crowds continued until May 23. The Church of St. James asked for the relics to visit Cooley, an area that had been disturbed by an outbreak of foot and mouth disease. This unplanned stop delayed the very symbolic passage over the border between the Republic of Ireland and Northern Ireland on the fortieth day of our travels. The reception beyond this border occurred in the Newry Cathedral of St. Patrick and St. Colman.

The enthusiasm of the crowds of these regions that had suffered many deadly conflicts for more than thirty years was even more pronounced. Twenty-five to thirty thousand people flocked to the Passionist fathers' home in the Holy Cross Retreat Center in Ayrdoyne in only twenty-four hours on May 29. A witness reported: "We saw the proof of people's real thirst for God. Something special was happening. The young, the elderly, the sick, the disabled, practicing Catholics as well as those who weren't practicing, whom we never thought we'd see there, all came and were captivated. Thérèse's presence was very noticeable."[158]

We found the same atmosphere in St. Eugene's Cathedral in Derry, which is historically connected to so many deaths and tragic events.

[158] *Thérèse de Lisieux*, no. 816, 12.

The traffic was interrupted in the area because of the crowd. Many of them stayed outside in the rain.

Msgr. D. Grealy, rector of the basilica in Knock, an international Marian shrine, noted: "This is the biggest crowd we've seen in Knock aside from the pope's visit in 1979. More than a hundred thousand people crossed the basilica's threshold these last two days."[159]

Fr. Tom Hayes, the Diocese of Cork's spokesman, estimated that eighty thousand people approached the reliquary in twenty-four hours. He didn't say he was surprised by this extraordinary influx. "Thérèse has been a part of the Irish people's popular consciousness for a long time. The story of her life is very close to many people's lives today."

Priests heard hours of confessions.

To end this extraordinary Irish journey, the reliquary took a helicopter to the island of Lough Derg. This was also the first time a helicopter had landed on the island. It had been sanctified by hundreds of years of prayer, rooted as it was in Celtic tradition and in history.

The reliquary left on Sunday, July 1, in the presence of Fr. Linus Ryan, the nuncio, and the thousands of volunteers who had organized this one-of-a-kind journey. Ireland had largely beaten all the records of attendance and enthusiasm. Until this day, it's the only country that has published two books of testimonies, including one by Don Mullan, a famous journalist, with the collaboration of the National Organizing Committee of St. Thérèse's relics in Ireland: *A Gift of Roses: Memories of the Visit to Ireland of St. Thérèse.*[160] Don Mullan interviewed about a hundred extremely diverse people to highlight Thérèse's action on people's minds, hearts, and bodies.

Let's listen to a few testimonies.

[159] Ibid., 15.

[160] Wolfhound Press, 2001.

Josephine Kealy, from Dublin, suffered from backaches and couldn't find any relief, despite all the care doctors gave her. She went to pray near the reliquary in the Hampton Convent and asked Thérèse to relieve her. She returned and had a strong personal prayer experience. Her pain went away and for several weeks, she was able to resume all her activities, including gardening. She thanks St. Thérèse every day.

Kitty Hennessy, from Dublin, had a cyst on her finger for two years. The doctor at Beaumont Hospital decided to operate. Kitty went to Mass on Clarendon Street on May 10 and touched the reliquary. During Mass the next day, she noticed that her finger had become normal again. The operation wasn't needed.

When Daire Whelan, from Dublin, learned about the arrival of St. Thérèse's relics, he thought it was "grotesque, macabre, terrifying, and sickening. I couldn't believe it when I read the program." He wondered who in his right mind would go to see the bones of a nun who died in the nineteenth century. But curiosity prevailed, and he went to take a look with his mother. He experienced his "road to Damascus" while waiting in line to approach the reliquary in an atmosphere of fervent prayer.

After three months of being immobilized in her bed, Joan Rigney, from Louth, couldn't walk. She had diabetes. She said she was healed around 10:30 p.m. on Sunday, after having a vision of St. Thérèse "in a corner of the room near the wardrobe." She then wanted to pray near the reliquary at Our Lady of Lourdes, so she got up and starting walking by herself without any pain. She could hardly believe it, after so many years of suffering. She said: "I'm still shocked, and my whole family is as well."

We could add to these testimonies of healing, conversion, and inner renewal. Let's listen instead to some thoughts after Thérèse's tour in Ireland.

> Fr. J. McEvoy:
>
> The fact that a very ordinary and unknown, so to speak, young French girl became one of the world's most beloved saints is a phenomenon that I can't humanly explain and a powerful sign of God's blessings. Thérèse wanted to redefine the meaning of holiness. It was often too pious, formal, or inaccessible. But she chose to remain simple and offered each small gesture to acknowledge God's love. The meaning of Thérèse's visit to our country must not be underestimated because we need to touch Thérèse. We must connect with her just as the woman [in the Gospel] wanted to touch Jesus' clothing. We are privileged and honored. This day is a blessed day for all of us.[161]

Fr. Ryan confided this to Don Mullan in a long interview entitled "Those Moments Will Never Be Forgotten":

> My special work as a co-coordinator of the travels gave me a perspective that was surely unique. I read all of the diocesan reports, and I saw that there were common denominators. There was this one, among others: "Think big — it will be even bigger than you think." There was another one: "Be ready for confessions. There will be a lot of significant ones." Thérèse brought peace and an atmosphere of charity everywhere she went.
>
> The abundance of prayer nights in Ireland, which favored working people, was undoubtedly distinctive. Entire families came. It's uncommon to see families — a mother, a father, and children — arriving at church at 11:00 p.m. or midnight. The churches remained open all night long.

[161] *Thérèse de Lisieux,* no. 814, 23.

"When you look at these eighty days, what do you feel?" Mullan asked Fr. Ryan.

> A lot of gratitude. When you see lines that are hundreds of meters long, you give thanks because it's successful. I never doubted that God's hand and Thérèse's hand could touch people's hearts. There's no human explanation for these people's behavior, which is so magnificent in so many ways.
>
> The cynical critics remained silent. Isn't it extraordinary, in light of the media's current hostility toward religion, that they were neutral throughout this time and positive in so many cases? It was astounding that the three national television networks that everyone watches were favorable. I saw Thérèse's hand in all of this.
>
> The Lord prepared everything, and I think something happened. I believe that the Church in Ireland will never be the same. It will leave a mark. This was amazing for eighty days. The newspaper *Sunday Business Post* spoke of the "biggest gathering of the Irish people in the history of this country."
>
> These days were the most important ones in my life.
>
> Let's add that with the problems of violence in our country, the English newspaper the *Times* estimated that it was extraordinary that during the nine days when the reliquary went through Northern Ireland, there wasn't the slightest incident.

Msgr. Comiskey[162] reported the response of a young girl to the question she was asked on a television program: "What did the tour of St. Thérèse's relics mean for you?" "Very simply, it changed my life." The bishop commented: "There was certainly no hysteria or superstition in that — simply a conversion."

[162] See *A Gift of Roses*, 33–47.

In closing, he wondered: "We must try asking this question and answering it: 'Why did the largest number of Irish people in this country's entire history come to venerate St. Thérèse's relics in more than one hundred places in each of our island's dioceses? What did they come to see? What did they find? Did they discover what they came to look for in the churches every Sunday?' We must consider the answer carefully. We must not let such a beautiful opportunity go by."[163]

[163] Ibid., 237.

Bosnia-Herzegovina (July 13–23, 2001)

In a Martyred Country

The unexpected keeps popping up with Thérèse. A letter from a priest in Bosnia-Herzegovina arrived in Lisieux on November 28, 2000: "We're living in the ruins of war. The interethnic conflict is continuing in people's minds. We're in a state of no war rather than that of a lasting peace.... This is why I thought of St. Thérèse of the Child Jesus. I'm convinced that if these relics come to Bosnia, there will be a miracle."

After various exchanges, Cardinal Vinko Puljić wrote to Fr. Zambelli from Sarajevo on February 6, 2001:

> You know about the dramatic situation we've experienced here in Bosnia-Herzegovina.... The work of peace hasn't been fully implemented yet. This is why — with the bishops of Bosnia-Herzegovina and in their name — I allow myself to ask you if it would be possible to have the little Carmelite saint's relics come here so that the peace in people's hearts can finally see the light of day. We remain convinced that St. Thérèse of the Child Jesus and the Holy Face will do a lot to help achieve a lasting peace in our country.

Thanks to a "French witness" who kept a log of the fourteen stations of this tour, we could follow the reliquary's itinerary in this country, which has been a land of suffering.

The plane coming from Paris landed in Sarajevo late at night on Friday, July 13. After a few administrative customs hassles, which was usual in formerly communist countries, the relics were received by Msgr. Mato Zovkić, the Archdiocese of Sarajevo's vicar-general, and some nuns, military chaplains, and French soldiers from the Stabilisation Force in Bosnia and Herzegovina.

The first stop was the Carmel of Sarajevo, which had been bombarded and destroyed by the Serbians from the start of the war. The Carmelites returned there only in September 2000.

The reception in Žepče, in central Bosnia, the next day was triumphal. Ten priests who came from neighboring parishes (including many that had been ruined) concelebrated with two thousand of the faithful — including some who were outside — that is to say, almost all the Catholics in that city. Five priests heard confessions nonstop.

On Sunday, July 15, there was a stopover in Zenica, where there was a lot of unemployment. The Muslim influence was strong there.

The police escorted the reliquary in oppressive heat as we crossed dangerous areas to reach Jacje. Cardinal Puljić concelebrated Mass there for two thousand people, including some who wore the country's traditional costumes. The Mass was held in a temporary wooden church. (The Serbs had destroyed the original church.) We had never seen so many people — even for the Franciscan feasts of St. Anthony and St. Francis. Some of them couldn't enter the church.

The reliquary left Our Lady of Mount Carmel on July 16 and crossed the Republic of Serbia's border. The police took over and escorted the relics to Banja Luka. They were greeted by Bishop Franjo Komarica, who preceded them to the church in Presnače that is dedicated to the saint. Catholic had been martyred there in May. Mass was celebrated in the midst of the church's ruins. There were only thirty members left in the parish. But there were more than a hundred praying to Thérèse during the night.

After having crossed a region of violent battles — there were ruins everywhere — the relics arrived at St. Thérèse Church in Bistrica Uskoplje. Muslim fanatics had bombarded and desecrated that church. The enthusiasm of the crowd, which had come from far away, became poignant. There was an explosion of joy and then a lot of silence. Confessions were heard all night long.

Herzegovina was geographically very different from Bosnia. Duviro, Ledinac, Studenci, Stolac, Buna, and Mostar were our stops.

The reliquary was quite well surrounded when it returned to the Franciscan Seminary, the Church of the Holy Trinity, and Sacred Heart Cathedral in Sarajevo on July 21. The French ambassador was there, along with some French, Italian, German, and Spanish soldiers and their chaplains.

The relics left the Church of Sts. Cyril and Methodius to the sound of muezzins very early the next morning, Monday, July 23. This was another amazing ten-day journey in an extremely difficult historical context. Everything went well, and there were no incidents. People who had suffered a lot were comforted.

Our witness concluded:

> The necessary material reconstructions aren't enough. If the wounds are also "moral" or "spiritual," you need the same amount of investment to heal them. The tour of St. Thérèse's relics is an example of this moral and spiritual investment. It's difficult to heal the soul's wounds with international agreements; it must be done through conversions of the heart and a country's moral "reconstruction." Moreover, we can only note the immense "success" of the relics' travels — the joys,

the crying, the simplest people's contentment, the roses, and the endless lines of the faithful who rushed to kiss the relics. What is there to see? What can we understand in this movement of crowds? We must be blind or in bad faith not to see a crowd movement in this "adventure." The few Catholics who haven't been exterminated or haven't emigrated went to see the relics! As for the others — those who don't have faith, hope, or charity — these relics are only a "pile of bones." There are piles of bones everywhere in Bosnia. They are mass graves that are "discovered" and exploited in order to revive interethnic hatreds — with predetermined choices. They are the sad testimony of the recent conflict's absurdity.

Bosnia's faithful, like all Catholics, think that "St. Thérèse's mortal remains" deserve to be venerated and are a source of inestimable grace. St. Thérèse's "remains" visited them, since [these people] couldn't go to Lisieux. Therefore, St. Thérèse of the Child Jesus went to Bosnia. Since little Thérèse "spends her heaven in doing good upon the earth," it's certain that she did this in Bosnia and that she's not done doing it in this martyred land.[164]

[164] *Thérèse de Lisieux,* no. 817 (December 2001).

Diocese of Bayeux and Lisieux in Honfleur (August 12–15, 2001)

Louis Martin and his three daughters Léonie, Céline, and Thérèse went on a pilgrimage to Our Lady of Grace in Honfleur in July 1887. It's a charming little port on the English Channel. Two Gosselin ladies in this spiritual hotspot (how many sailors came here to pray before going to the New World?) had prayed on August 15, 1838, for a Carmel to open its doors in Lisieux. This occurred on March 15, 1838, and Thérèse Martin entered that Carmel on April 9, 1888.

One hundred fourteen years later, Fr. Olivier Ruffray, pastor of Notre-Dame de l'Estuaire, received the reliquary from August 12 to 15, 2001.

It arrived by sea aboard the *Little Bambino* trawler, which came from the Port of Trouville-sur-Mer. The entrance into Honfleur was triumphal. Tourists from many countries increased the crowd of believers.

The reliquary, which was then drawn by a solid Percheron, climbed the coast that led to the small Chapel of Our Lady of Grace. We could celebrate and pray only on the vast wooded esplanade outside.

We felt like having a restful break after having traveled so many thousands of miles. As Fr. Ruffray said: "Thérèse, you are here at home."

Canada (September 16–December 17, 2001)

Meeting Christ . . . with Thérèse of Lisieux[165]

Close connections had been created between St. Thérèse of Lisieux and this huge country. When she was twelve years old, Thérèse drew a "physical map of North America." Her "spiritual director," Fr. Almire Pichon (1843–1919), a Jesuit, left her in 1888 to go preach in this country, where he led 1,015 retreats. The two exchanged correspondence which, alas, has been lost.[166] And *Story of a Soul* spread very quickly into Canada. Conversions and healing miracles were highlighted in 1901, 1908, 1910, and 1911. Some of them appeared in the Process of Beatification.

Sister Marie of the Incarnation, an Ursuline sister from Trois-Rivières who was of French origin, contacted Mother Agnès of Jesus in Lisieux in 1899 and tirelessly worked to make Thérèse known in Canada. There are a lot of chapels, churches, sanctuaries, and hospitals in Canada that are dedicated to St. Thérèse. Missionaries such as Msgr. Charlebois, Msgr. Turquetil, and Msgr. Fallaize spread the devotion

[165] This was the logo that the Church in Canada chose.

[166] Fr. Pichon destroyed all of Thérèse's letters — perhaps seventy or more. Thérèse kept the Jesuit's rare letters.

to Thérèse into the great Canadian North. The proposal to Pius XI to declare her the Patroness of the Missions would come from Canada and would come to fruition in 1927.

The Canadian Conference of Catholic Bishops, in turn, requested the relics. The program was led by a National Committee that was presided over by Jacques Binet, along with Sr. Jeannine Sauriol, O.C.D.; Sr. Barbara O'Reilly, C.U.D.; Joséphine Greatti Duhamel; and Gérald Baril. Jacques Gauthier, a theological writer, played a major role in it. He accompanied the reliquary to Quebec for one month and gave many lectures.

The program was substantial. It was spread out over three months and included 118 stages in 49 dioceses, but requests came from parishes, religious communities, hospitals, prisons, and schools at the last minute.

The reliquary went from Vancouver and Victoria to Montreal — from one ocean to the other. It wasn't afraid of traveling through the Great North.

Rather than listing the 118 places — Toronto, Ottawa, Sherbrooke, Trois-Rivières, Halifax, and so forth — it would be better to go straight to the National Committee's summary.

> The twin towers in New York collapsed on September 11, 2001. The world was astonished! The reliquary was stopped at the Charles de Gaulle Airport for thirty-six hours for security purposes. Could it leave for North America?
>
> Yes, it would be in Vancouver on Sunday, September 16 — barely two hours before the start of the planned celebrations.
>
> The confidence in the future was strong from the start. Fifty thousand people came to see the reliquary. On the whole, we evaluated that nearly two million people traveled to Canada. There was a lot of media support. Thérèse was on the front pages of all the Canadian daily newspapers. There was no irony

or derision in the commentaries about the event, and that was astonishing for a press that's so critical of Catholicism.

The Thérèse-mobile, which was often driven by Gérald Baril, traveled more than twelve thousand miles. The relics flew seven times. They crossed the Great White North and Labrador aboard a helicopter from November 29 to December 2. Gérald Baril followed this whole air trip.

The helicopter left from Sept-Îles, where six thousand people out of a population of twenty-four thousand had greeted Thérèse on the previous day. Jacques Gauthier gave an important interview to the *Globe and Mail* that would have an impact even in Boston and London. Msgr. Douglas Crosby, bishop of Labrador City–Schefferville, absolutely wanted the relics to go there, where Thérèse is the patroness, but the distance was enormous, and the costs were considerable. Thanks to the generosity of Mr. Craig Dobbin, owner of CHC Helicopter, which included 320 planes, an A-Star was made available to Thérèse free of charge.

Don McKnight, the helicopter's pilot, who had more than thirty years of experience, was amazed by a rather unusual rear wind that made him arrive early at every stage throughout the flight.

This was the case for Lourdes-de-Blanc-Sablon. Almost the whole population — eight hundred people — was in Our Lady of Lourdes Church. Thirty people had come to Newfoundland by boat. The church in Blanc-Sablon was dedicated to Thérèse. Many of the villagers (there were only four hundred of them) took turns near the reliquary in the evening.

We went through the same rear wind to reach Black Tickle. The temperature was five degrees Fahrenheit. There were two hundred residents, who were among the diocese's poorest persons. Sr. Mona, who led the Sunday prayer, usually saw only fifteen of the faithful. There were more than a hundred of them on that day. They were squished into the small chapel, and more of them returned in the afternoon.

Then we left for Goose Bay. Let's give the floor to Gérald Baril here:

> A few moments before taking off, the pilot contacted Goose Bay's control tower to inquire about the meteorological conditions. He was informed that a violent snowstorm had struck halfway and that it might be better to delay the trip until tomorrow. The pilot nonetheless decided to take off, even if he had to turn around. We approached the stormy strip after an hour of flying. The heavy clouds let us foresee the worst. We undoubtedly would have turned back if we hadn't seen a wide passage that separated the clouds into two compact blocks. Don McKnight smiled at me incredulously and said to me: "Thérèse surely had something to do with this, right?" As was the case with the Red Sea, we could thus pass through the storm without any problem, and we reached Goose Bay at the appointed time.[167]

Msgr. Crosby waited for Thérèse in Labrador City. There was a new means of transportation for the reliquary there. To get to Wabush, it slid over the snow on a sled pulled by eight dogs.

A woman from these desert regions said: "I would never, in my craziest dreams, have imagined that Thérèse would come here."

I experienced a much more modest week in Quebec in the company of the relics.

I was struck by the extraordinary influx of people in the famous St. Joseph Oratory in Montreal. Fr. Aumont, the rector, estimated that there were thirty thousand pilgrims. People waited in line there to go to Confession as well. A highlight was the side-by-side meeting of the

[167] *Thérèse de Lisieux,* no. 820, 16.

reliquary and the tomb of Blessed Brother André[168] (1845–1937), without whom there would be no St. Joseph Oratory.

Ottawa's cathedral was full by 1:00 p.m., but two thousand people waited in line outside in the cold at dusk. Once again, we hadn't thought that so many people would come. We had them enter in groups of thirty. The priests noted that they didn't know all those people.

The Lebanese Maronites in Ottawa learned too late that the relics were in the city. They requested to have the reliquary for one night. We went there and arrived under a flowery triumphal arch, with some of Thérèse's words in Arabic and English. A few Lebanese people had come from all over with their families. The church was packed, as was the crypt. We could follow the Mass on a big screen there.

We returned to fetch the reliquary the next day. Many people had spent the night in prayer.[169]

The St. René-Goupil parish and its archbishop, Msgr. René Ébacher, greeted Thérèse. From there, it went into the Hull Prison, where the inmates, who had been prepared by their chaplain, venerated Thérèse. We, along with Msgr. Ébacher, spoke with them, and a Quebec television network interviewed some of them.

The National Organizing Committee was in the best position to provide pastoral guidance about the Canadian journey:

> Everywhere where the reliquary was received, whether it was in the most populated centers, such as Vancouver, Edmonton, Winnipeg, Toronto, Montreal, Quebec, and Halifax, or in the most isolated regions, such as the St. Theresa Point First Nation community, in the Diocese of Keewatin-Le Pas, and the Montagnais village of La Romaine, or in the Diocese of

[168] Brother André Bessette was canonized in 2010.

[169] This happened in September 2002.

Labrador City–Schefferville, we could attend meditative and enthusiastic celebrations that were very fruitful. The welcoming and farewell celebrations, as well as the solemn Masses that the diocesan bishop presided over, were particularly moving. The different local organizations developed simple and significant liturgies that touched the hearts of people of all ages, conditions, and races. The special edition of *Living with Christ* (Novalis), in collaboration with the national committee, helped these organizations to do this.

The reliquary's visit was also a unifying event everywhere. Young people and older ones prayed together in a beautiful spirit of simplicity, along with those who weren't practicing Catholics and people from different religious denominations. They united with members of the Catholic Church to venerate the mortal remains of little Thérèse, whose message of love, confidence, and an unspeakable hope in God's merciful love undeniably called out to the public at large. The local organizers had an easy time recruiting volunteers to fill the numerous tasks that were needed for the relics' visit. We could, in many places, count between 150 and 200 volunteers, who all had the same feeling of collaborating in an exceptional event.

Young people weren't forgotten in this ecclesiastical pan-Canadian project. A dozen dioceses organized a time for prayer and activities for them. Thérèse Martin is undoubtedly a witness of God who connects with young people. The presence of ecstatic love, which was almost excessive in Thérèse's life — the love of God and the love of neighbor — particularly hits young people. The relics' tour, in this context, turned out to be a leading preliminary event for World Youth Day 2002 in Toronto. Most dioceses made sheets of paper available to visitors so they could write down requests and reasons for giving thanks. These sheets have been used quite a bit. It was touching to see people taking the time to fill them out in order to put them in the basket or the case that was very respectfully placed near the reliquary. Some people were visibly moved. Several of them then went to one of the many confessors. Moreover, the confessional booths didn't "let up" all throughout the relics' travels across Canada. The resort to the sacrament of mercy was one of the special blessings that Thérèse granted during her passage among us.

It was not a coincidence that the Youth Cross of World Youth Day and St. Thérèse of Lisieux's relics traveled across Canada at the same time during the fall of 2001. Both pilgrimages were specially connected with World Youth Day 2002, which was an extraordinarily faith-filled pilgrimage for thousands of young people across the world. Through her faith, this young French-speaking saint, whom Pope John Paul II named one of the nine young patron saints for World Youth Day 2002 in Canada, took advantage of her visit to remind us that we must have a deep faith and must abandon ourselves to the Lord's grace and love.

We need Thérèse, a Doctor of God's mercy, because she lived in a world similar to the one we're living in now. It's a scientific and technological world in which many people don't believe in God or don't accept the message of Jesus, the Lord of the universe.

Thérèse is speaking to us here and now in this particular moment of history. She must have encountered the same challenges that the young people of today have to face.

We need Thérèse to care for us and to show us her little way of love and grace. The Church, in entrusting her with the role of Doctor of the Church and honoring her with this title,

> reminds us to sit at the feet of this amazing young woman and reread the pages of the Gospel in order to be renewed by its light and become the salt of the earth and the light of the world.

The tour of St. Thérèse's reliquary has made it possible to see the spiritual thirst of many people in Canada. None of them would say that this was more about a thirst for the supernatural. But the silence, the atmosphere of prayer, the great respect for actions that were taken, the joy of the faithful, the conversions, and the diversity of the people who were present were all signs that bore witness to an authentic experience of the Christian faith. As one of the diocesan officials emphasized very well: "The relics' tour must not be perceived as being *the expression of popular faith*, but rather *as the popular expression of faith*." This tour opened up a free expression of people's devotion. They were able to venerate the relics at their convenience, pray in silence — while kneeling, standing, or sitting — offer a rose, light a candle, march in a procession, recite the Rosary, sing or pray in a choir, read the Word of God, celebrate Mass, and so forth.

As the visit's theme indicated, people came as part of a pilgrimage "to meet Christ... with Thérèse of Lisieux." The visitors came — individually or in groups — from different places and various backgrounds. They gathered in the same place. Some were drawn by their attachment to Thérèse. Others were driven by curiosity. All or almost all of them were motivated by the desire to pray. In this regard, a stranger said to a diocesan official, "You should organize more pilgrimages like this one."

Jacques Gauthier, the Canadian theologian who wrote four books about St. Thérèse of the Child Jesus and gave many lectures as part of the passage of the relics across Quebec, emphasized:

> Thérèse restored the Church to ordinary people. She created a space of freedom and celebration that was manifested during liturgical celebrations, conferences, entertainment events, and

prayer nights. People need tangible elements to feed their faith and to be able to express it. Thérèse's relics acted as a catalyst. They aroused the expression of faith among people — a faith that some people thought was practically extinct but is still very much alive. They also allowed people to express their faith outside of the sacraments and the usual places, where the ritual doesn't always allow people to be spontaneous and sentimental.

We must not be amazed at the considerable number of favors and healings of all kinds that were brought to the National Committee's attention in such an enthusiastic whirlwind. Thérèse, of course, really attracts people, but it's her message that truly speaks to them. It's a message that's a very pure and faithful echo of the gospel.

The relics' tour, on the ecclesiastical and pastoral levels, clearly proved that the Catholic Church in Canada can still mobilize around a project that connects with people's experiences and embodies the Faith. It has been done with the authentic testimony of a holy life in union with God. This tour led more than one pastor to question pastoral practices that are at times abstract and too intellectual.

It's appropriate to wonder, after the reliquary's tour, what actions will be taken and what paths will be used to continue to feed the devotion of the faithful and what spaces will be developed to allow them to express their faith outside established rituals. Without taking away the value of the sacraments, the Eucharist in particular, we must recognize that pastoral care is often unilaterally sacramental — especially the Eucharist.

Diocesan officials made various suggestions. Here are some of them:

- to create other events that offer many possibilities to express one's faith
- to place the veneration of the saints in the context of the whole Faith, to review the reality of the communion of saints, to present witnesses of the Faith such as Thérèse of Lisieux (in fact, who talks to us about God better than the saints?)
- to be more aware of the appeal of this pilgrimage
- to pay attention to the gospel's essential message: the love of God (a message of which Thérèse was an exceptional witness)
- to revisit certain devotional practices that we've let fall away without asking what they brought to the popular expression and transmission of the Christian faith (pilgrim statues, statues in churches, novenas, Vespers, various processions, benedictions, and so on)
- to explore new paths of devotion and animated prayer
- to restore the sacrament of Confession, which so many people received during the relics' tours
- to promote St. Thérèse's spirituality — since her witness knows how to touch people's hearts in general

There will be so much to say, analyze, interpret, and gauge after the visit among us of the relics of St. Thérèse of the Child Jesus and the Holy Face.

As an organizing committee, we thank the Lord for letting us collaborate in this beautiful and rich ecclesiastical experience and for letting us be the privileged witnesses of the work the Lord has accomplished with Thérèse's support. We thank the Canadian Conference of Catholic Bishops for trusting us with the organization's tour on the national level. St. Thérèse wanted to be a missionary in the whole world. More than one century after her death, we have to recognize that Thérèse is fulfilling this wish because she has been traveling across the world since 1994. During her too-brief stay in Canada, we've been given the opportunity to note that Thérèse is a leading witness of the new evangelization, which was promoted by Pope John Paul II, and is an instrument of the Holy Spirit for the Church today.

Australia (February 1–April 30, 2000)

A Ninety-Day Pilgrimage of Blessings

The passage from Canada to Australia through Lisieux was one of the reliquary's longest trips.

At first, we were surprised by the Australian bishops' request. We knew very little about that huge country that's so far away, except through a few superficial clichés.

The request of the Australian Catholic Bishops' Conference was officially made in February 2000.

Australia is a country of 7.7 million square miles and has 18.3 million residents. An organizing committee that was led by Mrs. Jean Cornish carefully prepared this new journey for six months. A tour was planned in twenty-one dioceses with sixty-three stops, including sixteen cathedrals, thirty-three parishes, and eleven Carmels. The airline company Quantas paid for all the international and national trips.

Once again, it would be dull to talk in detail about what happened in Perth, Melbourne, Canberra, Sydney, Brisbane, and so on. The success was the same as we had noticed in all the preceding countries.

The media covered the event very well. The press ran the headlines "The Relics of a Spiritual Giant Are Arriving Here," "The World's

Greatest Show," and "The Extraordinary Life and Writings of a Young French Nun Occupied the Minds and Hearts of Thousands of Australians over the Last Three Months." Some witnesses drew conclusions from the pilgrimage and ran this as a title: "Relics — an Opening of the Heart?"

It's estimated that more than five hundred thousand Australians approached the reliquary.

> We saw huge lines that were waiting to access the relics in many places — around eight hundred people per hour. There were smaller groups of pilgrims in other places who sometimes prayed near the reliquary for several hours.
>
> What attracted so many people to come from other dioceses and states to take part in this pilgrimage? Many of them wanted to participate in this unique historical event — unlikely to happen again! — that aroused the interest of millions of people across the world in twenty-seven countries.
>
> Others wanted to contact a very beloved saint — a deep desire they had had for a long time. She had been their guide for living "the little way." Many came with requests and needs that were in their hearts and also on paper. They asked for Thérèse's intercession and help for "a shower of roses" in their lives. Several people appreciated this "upside down" pilgrimage. The object of their veneration came to them instead of their going to Europe or the Holy Land. It became possible for Australians to go on a pilgrimage in their own cities for the first time. This was a common experience for many Europeans, but it was never seen here.
>
> It was an opportunity for Catholics, many of whom don't have English roots, to express their devotion to the most popular of modern saints and venerate the relics in a concrete way. Australian Catholics communed with the sacred through

touch and through gestures without fearing of being ridiculed and with the Church's encouragement. They threw roses on the reliquary to express their love, gratitude, and respect for the wisdom of a "little person" like them.

For some, the relics' arrival was, above all, an opportunity to satisfy their curiosity about all this excitement. A few went back confirmed in their skepticism, whereas others, who didn't expect anything, returned with a deep personal feeling of God's grace and love.

The moments of conversion were precious. Many people deeply experienced God's love in the relics' presence. Pilgrims often celebrated this love by taking advantage of the opportunity to receive the sacrament of Reconciliation. Miracles are possible. We saw them in many people's return to the Church's sacramental life after long absences.

Members of other Christian churches and sometimes other religions came to recognize the Carmelite's deep simplicity and extraordinary holiness. This sums up a whole people's ardent desire to live fully in the service of God's love throughout their lives.

The celebration of Mass and other liturgies attracted huge crowds and was a strong and vibrant expression of the faith.

Thousands of pilgrims were offered the opportunity to discover the Carmelite tradition's prayer and liturgy. The Carmelites opened their doors and their hearts to them. For the first time, these pilgrims discovered the strength of this hidden prayer that supports the Church in the modern world. Through their intercession, these Carmelites supported the local churches in their evangelical mission.

Was this event first welcomed by traditionalists and those who love devotions and who thought that the Church ignores and even despises their need for such encounters? No. Our experience in the Archdiocese of Brisbane suggested that the pilgrims came from various backgrounds within the Church. They arrived with their faith to recognize the gift of holiness.

Our celebrations often seem sterile, cerebral, and insensitive to many Catholics. We must "open windows to Heaven." If we sincerely want to nourish the faith and spirituality of different cultures, we have to promote the pilgrimage's importance. It's only then that faith-filled hearts will have opportunities to encounter "the stranger on the road to Emmaus."

The pilgrimage of St. Thérèse of Lisieux's relics has given us this opening of the heart. This was hard to accept for some people. For others, it was a breath of life and a deep spiritual encounter with God's mysteries through the young Carmelite's extraordinary life and holiness. She speaks powerfully to people who are trying to experience love in their lives today. This pilgrimage promoted a model of spirituality in the minds and hope in the hearts of many Australians who shared a very strong experience. May we discover several other openings of the heart starting with our Catholic tradition's riches. (Mike Humphrys and Fr. Anthony Randazzo)

The February 19, 2002, issue of the *Sunday Morning Herald* ran this headline: "St. Thérèse's Relics Are the Greatest Success Seen in Australia Since Pope John Paul II's Arrival."

The February 17, 2002, issue of the Archdiocese of Sydney's *Catholic Weekly* emphasized that the pilgrimage of Thérèse's relics attracted thousands of Catholics and non-Catholics (for example, forty thousand in the Diocese of Perth in the first week).

Fr. Greg Homeming, a Carmelite, followed the reliquary everywhere. He indicated that the priests who were available for the crowd of pilgrims were sometimes happy to get two hours of sleep. He noted that many people who were sitting in the church suddenly got up to go to Confession. Some of them hadn't done so for ten, twenty, or thirty years.

Let's end with three very different testimonies, among so many others:

> I'm thinking of the thousands of people who faithfully came forward to touch St. Thérèse's reliquary. These were people from all social statuses with different attitudes and expectations. There were the hands of innocent children who were pleading for protection, the hands of mothers who were sharing their joys and difficulties or confiding the load that was weighing down on their hearts, the hands of men who were anxious because of their work or relations with others, the hands of nuns and priests who were aware of their flaws and praying to find inspiration and strength for their mission, the hands of sick people who were preoccupied by their health and perhaps wanted to experience Thérèse's abandonment to God's will, and the hands of young people who were torn between doubt and enthusiasm and looked to the young saint as a model to guide them. There were so many expressions of faith! The act of physical touch isn't what counted. It was well beyond that. This was an opportunity to establish a personal contact and share the burdens of human hearts. From there, we could confront our situations with a renewed spiritual energy and be confident about following a better path in our search to do God's will. Following Your will, Lord — that's where our peace is.[170]

[170] Msgr. Francesco Canalini, papal nuncio in Australia, homily on Palm Sunday, March 24, 2002, in the Carmel of Canberra.

I was in dangerous missions in the British Air Force for many years. St. Thérèse has always been the saint I prayed to. I asked her to watch over me and keep me alive. When I found out she was coming here, I had to go see her and thank her, and here I am. I'm happy now.[171]

When my children told me for the first time that they were searching for volunteers to "guard" St. Thérèse of Lisieux's relics in the parish's church, I asked, first of all: "Volunteer? For whom? From where?" I'd never heard about her. But I offered my help, as a good father should do, and they said yes. As time went by, I saw everything that had been implemented, and I started to doubt. Wasn't all that going to have very little to show for? Then I received a very detailed message with the date and time of my service, the name of the person whom I'd relieve, and some instructions. Here again, I began to doubt. Wasn't this a bit too much? When D-day arrived, I had to be realistic — that I hadn't understood anything. I don't know exactly how many hundreds of people can stand in Morley's church, but I know that it's a lot. I thought that if all these people suddenly wanted to rush toward the reliquary, I wouldn't be able to do much. But I didn't have to worry. I was touched by the enthusiasm of these people who were so respectful and full of love for St. Thérèse. I thank my children and am grateful to them for such an experience.[172]

[171] An Englishman, seventy years old, living in Australia.
[172] Ken Pether.

French Polynesia (May 4–August 20, 2002)

Maeva Teretia peata![173]

The reliquary would not soon return to mainland France. It went directly to Tahiti from Australia. This time, Thérèse approached the Pacific Ocean's immense stretches and its strings of marvelous islands that are spread out over an area far greater than Europe. This is a landscape of dreams. There are volcanic islands emerging in seas with various shades of blue, lagoons with green coral, luxurious vegetation, flowers with vivid colors, and summer temperatures. In this place, transportation for the reliquary entailed boats, helicopters, and planes.

It all started with a letter of September 12, 1999, that was written by a resident of the Island of Raiatea. She was a great friend of St. Thérèse who had subscribed for a long time to the *Thérèse de Lisieux* magazine and who passionately followed the relics' trips across the world. She noticed one of Thérèse's phrases and concluded: "We are on the most remote isles."[174] She added: "But will our request be taken

[173] "Welcome, St. Thérèse!" in Tahitian.

[174] "I would want to preach the Gospel on all the five continents simultaneously and even to the most remote isles." Manuscript B, 3r, in *Story of a Soul*, 193.

into account, for we are a grain of sand on the globe." She ended with an act of trust: "If Thérèse wants it, then God wants it, and I have a lot of confidence in her."

Mrs. Maeva Reid was right. Her wishes were granted beyond her desires. There was a request that came from the Episcopal Conference of the Pacific in February 2000. Melbourne, New Caledonia, Vanuatu, Wallis and Futuna, and the Marquesas Islands were the petitioners.

The preparations were put in place with a steering committee. To get to know Thérèse better, Fr. Patrick Lemoine,[175] a chaplain in Lisieux, would go on site for two months to help raise awareness and make preparations (conferences, exhibitions, prayer vigils, novenas, and so forth).

We joyfully discovered that as a schoolgirl, Thérèse had drawn a map of the Pacific Ocean region and Australia. Thus, as a child, she had become interested in these very distant islands!

How could she have imagined the future?

Everything accelerated. Msgr. Michel-Marie Calvet, the archbishop of Nouméa and president of the Episcopal Conference of the Pacific, would meet the relics in Sydney to bring them to the Tontouta Airport in Nouméa.

The program was huge. The reception was in the Cathedral of St. Joseph. There was a transition to the prison in the Valley des Colons, and to Montravel, Rivière Salée, Mont Doré (St. Thérèse Chapel), Dombeya (St. Pierre Chanel Chapel), La Foa, Moindon, Bourail, Paita, and Tomo. (The residents had called out to St. Thérèse here while facing an attack of leprosy in 1931.) Then, after the tour in Wallis and Futuna on May 14 and 17, we left for Polynesia, accompanied by Fr. Tahiri Tiaoao, vicar-general of the Diocese of Papeete.

175 Author, composer, and interpreter, especially of St. Thérèse of Lisieux's poems (cassettes and CDs).

Msgr. Calvet would write on September 12, 2002:

> The tour of St. Thérèse of Lisieux's relics in the Diocese of Nouméa in May 2002 was a continuation of the high point that expressed and revived New Caledonia's spiritual vitality during these last few years. First of all, in 1993 and 1994, there were preparations and celebrations of the 150th anniversary of the first Mass in New Caledonia. Then there was the great Jubilee 2000. . . .
>
> St. Thérèse, the Patroness of Missions of the Universal Church, thus joined St. Peter Chanel, the first martyr of the Pacific Ocean region's distant islands. He died in Futuna on April 28, 1841. St. Thérèse continued to illuminate our paths in the third millennium. She is the one whom Pope John Paul II — at the request of many episcopal conferences, including ours, the Episcopal Conference of the Pacific (CEPAC) — had declared to be a Doctor of the Church because of the reliability of her spiritual teaching.
>
> Thérèse guides us to the Lord Jesus Christ, along with Mary, according to the words of Pope John Paul II in his letter *Ecclesia in Oceania,* to follow His path, proclaim His truth, and experience His life. We noticed that the relics' arrival closely followed John Paul II's text *Ecclesia in Oceania* (November 22, 2001), which recalls the work of the first missionaries and stresses the need for a new evangelization. Thérèse took her part in it in her own way.

Msgr. Hubert Coppenrath, archbishop of Papeete in Tahiti, greeted the relics on May 18. They passed through at least twenty parishes and spent a night in each of them. The archbishop testified that the churches weren't empty. The impact was quite strong. There were people who had stopped going to church, some strangers, and also Protestants,

Mormons, Seventh-day Adventists, self-righteous people, and others in the crowds that went beyond the faithful parishioners.

On June 10, we left for the Leeward Islands — Huahine, Bora-Bora, Taha'a, and Raiatea. After a passing through Mo'orea, we left again for Rangiroa, Fakarava, Makemo, Hao, Mangareva, Tubuai, and returned to Tahiti — that is to say, nearly twenty-five hundred miles.

From there, we visited the Marquesas Islands, which are about nine hundred miles from Tahiti. Then we visited Taiohae, Ua Pou, and Hiva Oa. Some delegations from Ua Huka, Fatu Hiva, and Tahuata went to the islands that Thérèse would go to, for some of the reliquary's movements were now physically impossible. It didn't go in small planes.

These "most remote isles" gave Thérèse a triumphant reception. For example, the newspaper in Raiatea reported: "There were thousands of people. For three days (June 14–16), the sacred island reserved an ecumenical triumphant welcome for St. Thérèse's relics. There was such a crowd that on Sunday, the *Meherio II* had to leave for Mo'orea seven hours late!" These Meherio boats circulated from one island to another and came to the edge of the beach. One door opened up, and the Thérèse-mobile descended to the sound of local instruments ("*pahu pu, toer, mave et orero*").[176]

In fact, the pastor of the Church of Saint-André testified: "We've never seen so many of the faithful in the church." This island of fifteen thousand residents had never seen the rallying of such a crowd "even for President Giscard d'Estaing's" arrival, a witness said. Fr. Zambelli had been at these gatherings and had preached Thérèse's doctrine there.

Msgr. Coppenrath concluded: "Thérèse now has an important place in our lives."

He expressed the following in the August 25, 2002, issue of *Le Semeur tahitien*, a special issue about St. Thérèse:

[176] *Pahu*: drum; *vivo*: nasal flutes; *pu*: shells, conches.

> After the last Mass in Maria no te Hau on Saturday, August 3, the relics of St. Thérèse of the Child Jesus left Papeete to reach Guam and then Lisieux. They had stayed in Polynesia for two and a half months, including two months in Papeete's only diocese (4,660 miles).
>
> Their arrival had been prepared for since October 1, 2001, and Thérèse didn't disappoint us. She visited thirty-two out of eighty-two parishes in our diocese. She filled the churches and attracted not only practicing Catholics but also those who had fallen away from the Church, not to mention Christians from other denominations. Groups followed one another to the reliquary night and day. Thérèse healed not only bodies but hearts in particular. She reconciled enemies and brought people back to God. The number of communicants doubled during her passage. They went from thirty-five thousand every two weeks to thirty-five thousand per week.
>
> The most important thing remains to be done. After the effervescence and exaltation, we must now ensure the permanence of the blessings that have been received and must organize Thérèse's aftermath to this end. Above all, this is about placing ourselves in her school of thought and becoming her disciples and committing ourselves, in turn, to the "little way," which led her to become very holy. We must read her writings — mainly the little masterpiece that Manuscript B represents — and soak up her spiritual doctrine.

The same newspaper gave us some really diverse testimonies — unexplained healings, answers to questions, the consolation of those who were distressed or worried, spiritual conversions, reconciliations, radical changes in behavior, and so on. These haven't all been verified. Many of them won't be known or will be limited to the family circle.

Guam (August 5–16, 2002)

Having learned about this vast trip, Msgr. Anthony Sablan Apuron, archbishop of Agana, in Guam,[177] asked to receive the relics on the Northern Mariana Islands (an American territory) because it had a long Catholic tradition and St. Thérèse was very much loved there. People with vocations to the priesthood and religious life go to the Carmel there from all over the Pacific Ocean's regions. "This visit would be a great blessing," Msgr. Apuron wrote. Fr. Zambelli responded in a letter that this would be possible. The dates just had to be coordinated with the region's bishops. Organizing a tour like this in a place made up of hundreds of islands is no bed of roses! But once again, everything came to fruition. And we must pay tribute to those volunteers who had invested themselves in this adventure.

The reliquary made a dozen stops on a small island of 135,000 residents, including St. Dominic's Hospital in Barrigada Heights and the Mangilao Prison.

The August 11, 2002, issue of the *Pacific Voice*, the Diocese of Agana's Catholic newspaper, talked about the conversion of Jeannette

[177] Guam, which was occupied by the Japanese from 1941 to 1944, is a strong American military base.

Alejos, a Canadian residing in Hong Kong who visited the relics in Guam. She told us:

> Shakespeare, Jane Austen, the Brontë sisters — these were the idols I still adored two years ago. One day, a nun from Hong Kong who knew about my love of literature lent me *Story of a Soul*. What could I find that would be interesting in the insignificant story of a little Catholic girl? A saint. Mercy! More of these fables in which only miracles, stigmata, and martyrdom are talked about!
>
> I very indifferently opened the book. To my astonishment, I found only simple little daily events — Thérèse traveling with her father or doing the laundry. What? No mortifications? How did this antihero become a saint? It seemed to me that I could do the same thing! Wait — that's true! Even I could do it!
>
> These were the simple words of a soul who was touched by a love greater than Romeo and Juliet's love! There was a passion that even Shakespeare couldn't have described — and that my soul had never suspected. The more she wrote that she was delighted to be Jesus' little flower, the more my life seemed to me to be a sterile desert. I was hungry and thirsty. It was then that a friend invited me to Guam to go on a "small tour." The procession had started when I arrived. There were elderly women who were all dressed up, babies who were sleeping in strollers, and Knights of Columbus who were adorned in feathers. I felt quite excited in spite of myself.
>
> The procession arrived and little St. Thérèse along with it, in the midst of flowers. She invited my very small soul to go into the church for the first time. Once I was inside, I finally found myself face-to-face with the mysterious source of her deep happiness. He was there — Love, who was humbly attached to

> a cruel Cross. You can imagine that this "small tour" became a long trip and a formidable spiritual voyage. Only Thérèse could choose the small island of Guam to teach me about the Catholic Faith's great mysteries.

Jeannette is now preparing to be baptized.

The visit to the Mangilao Prison had been added to the program. The cathedral's rector said to the inmates: "We haven't forgotten you."

The August 18, 2002, issue of the *Pacific Daily News* reported this:

> The prisoners in Mangilao's penitential center were invited to approach St. Thérèse's reliquary. Among them were R. M., fifty-one years old, who was serving the ninth year of his fifteen years of imprisonment for murder. After having prayed near the reliquary, he went to sit in the back of the chapel and reflected on the mercy that he was looking for: "I want to change my life. I don't know what happened on the night that I killed that man. I didn't even know him. I was dead drunk. When I heard that the saint was coming, I was happy. I prayed to be forgiven, and I promised God that I would change."

Lebanon (September 1–November 17, 2002)

A dual request came to Lisieux from this country of 4,105 square miles and with a population of three million residents who had suffered terribly from a long war. Many had emigrated. The Mariamite fathers wished to receive the relics at their St. Thérèse of Lisieux monastery in Shaïlé, which was celebrating its seventy-fifth anniversary. His Eminence Cardinal Nasrallah-Pierre Sfeir, patriarch of Antioch and of the whole East, willingly agreed to this in a letter of April 21, 2001.

The Carmelite fathers from Lebanon and Egypt also wanted this visit. Msgr. Paul Dahdah, a Carmelite, the apostolic vicar and the ordinary of the premises for the Mediterranean people in Lebanon, then made the request "for Libya and the neighboring regions" in a letter of May 11, 2001.

After being made aware of this, the Assembly of Catholic Patriarchs and Bishops of Lebanon, during its thirty-fifth ordinary session, held in Bkerké from December 10 to 15, 2001, named a national welcoming committee for St. Thérèse of Lisieux's relics.

The journey's program, which would last seventy-seven days, was important. But when the committee met on October 7, it was bombarded with requests from all over. They would try to respond to them.

One of the solutions would be to venerate the relics day and night without any rest.

Many Muslim villagers in southern Lebanon along the border with Israel would ask for Thérèse to stop in their homes. She was a holy woman of God and a blessing from God. The same was true for the Druzes. This would be one of the characteristics of the passage to Lebanon — the significant number of Muslims who approached the relics with their families.

Those of other rites — the Maronites, the Greek Catholics, the Syrians, and the Armenians — would come to celebrate Mass in the relics' presence. There would also be meetings with Orthodox Armenians and Syrians in Kousba, Amioun, Kfaraakka, Zahlé, and Shaïlé.

There was an ecumenical gathering of Christian Maronites, Greek Catholics, Orthodox Christians, and Evangelicals in Kfarshima. A tent with a vast podium for the celebrations was set up in the Mariamite Maronite monastery, dedicated to St. Thérèse of Lisieux. The reliquary stayed there for fifteen days. People had to wait in line from morning to night — even while the prayer that was being led by various groups, and the choirs, dances, and Masses were taking place. These followed one another from 6:00 a.m. to 1:00 a.m.

The relics spent the night in the small chapel and left again each morning in a procession to the tent. Families came from everywhere on Sunday, and the adjacent streets and alleys were crowded with cars. I met and interviewed nine-year-old Sebastian M. from Klayaa in the presence of his Maronite family in this monastery on October 5. He had suffered from earaches and hearing loss since he was five years old and had seen several doctors, but they were not able to help him. He was in front of the television on September 1, the day the relics arrived in Beirut. His grandmother told him to pray to this saint for healing, and he did, although he didn't know Thérèse. That evening, fluid began to drain out of his ears. He could hear! He told me he saw Thérèse in his room and that they had spoken to each other. His testimony, which has been recorded, would be examined by the Maronite monks.[178]

The relics visited the Carmel of the Theotokos in Harissa, which receives many vocations, from October 21 to 24. This Carmel is famous for its magnificent icons. I could see the famous icon of Thérèse in the midst of the Doctors. In a long, enthusiastic report, the sisters told us about what they had experienced. They had been inundated by a huge crowd and helped by several volunteers, many of whom were young. The church, which was too small to accommodate the pilgrims, would stay open all night long.

The Carmel's chronicle ends like this:

> Something rose in the Lebanese people's hearts. Thérèse's reception wasn't folklore or hysteria. We could see that very clearly. They weren't devotions of older people either.... No, Lebanon was going through a crucial moment in its history.... It wasn't hysteria. It was the cry of Christian people who felt threatened and abandoned to themselves.... They yearned for, as our Holy Father the pope had requested, a message of love and understanding between Christians and Muslims in what is most beautiful.

The relics' visit was a popular success from their arrival in the Beirut Airport on September 1. Msgr. Bernard Lagoutte, the pilgrimage of Lisieux's new rector, would be its witness for ten days. The commercial television station LBCI covered the arrival at length and provided a summary of the relics' journey every evening during the seventy-seven days of the visit.[179] Nobody in the Middle East could ignore Thérèse's

[178] A nun, a sister of Msgr. Tanios El Khoury, the Maronite bishop in Sidon, testified to these facts.

[179] An LBCI team came to Lisieux to film the Theresian sites and to produce reports, videos, and so forth.

presence, as it was spreading in Syria, Iraq, Jordan, and Egypt. Télé Lumière, NBN, and other networks also broadcast this news, as did the radio stations Voix de la Charité (Voice of Charity), Liban Libre (Free Lebanon), and others.

The Parliamentary Assembly of the Francophonie was going to meet that year in Lebanon with President Jacques Chirac and delegations from fifty-five countries. The three thousand people who were assembled were also aware of Thérèse's presence in that country.

The economic impact was quite significant in four areas: the restaurant industry, florists (they had to supply themselves with roses from Jordan and Syria), fireworks merchants (the Lebanese people are very fond of using them to express their joy), and the print shops. The latter couldn't satisfy the requests for booklets, posters in all formats, pictures, streamers, banners, and so forth. These were everywhere. They bore quotations from Thérèse in Arabic and French and decorated homes, shops, and streets.

The memory of Thérèse's tour would continue to be inscribed. People baptized streets with her name in Hadath-Beirut and Fiayadé as well as in squares in Ballouneh, Kaukaba, Mtolleh, and Ain El Delb. A school was dedicated to her in Beiteddine and sanctuaries in Bkassine, Tebnine, and Damour. Commemorative plaques were unveiled in Zouk Mosbeh and elsewhere. Book booths were very well supplied. We found an edition of Thérèse's complete works in Arabic.

The September 2, 2002, issue of *L'Orient le Jour* emphasized that the faith and enthusiasm that Thérèse stirred up hadn't been seen since John Paul II's visit in 1997 and ran this headline: "Extraordinary Popular Reception."

On November 16, the reliquary went into the prison in Roumieh, which has five thousand inmates. The patriarch Cardinal Sfeir — whose moral authority was undisputed — celebrated Mass outside in the night, in the presence of President Émile Lahoud, Prime Minister Rafic Hariri, and the minister of the interior. Some prisoners, dressed in white, served at Mass. But we could admit only five hundred of them because all of them couldn't fit in the inner courtyard. There were Muslims among them who had asked to attend. One journalist commented, "Thanks to the little saint, some inmates became aware that the rest of the world hadn't forgotten them."

At the end of these seventy-seven days that saw so many people approaching Thérèse, Msgr. Paul Dahdah, Msgr. Jean Sleiman, who came from Baghdad, and Fr. M. Farha celebrated a solemn Mass in Our Lady of Lebanon, with about seven thousand people in attendance. Emotions were strong.

It was time to leave. But the reliquary didn't return to Lisieux. A new destination awaited it: Iraq. The Lebanese crowd burst into a long applause after learning this.

The Mariamite Fr. Fadi Abou Chebl, the relics' official transporter, summarized his rich experience in accompanying the reliquary daily across the whole region of cedar trees (4,350 miles). Like many, he noted that Lebanon was going through a very difficult stage. All the Lebanese people, and Christians in particular, were suffering from despair, mediocre economic conditions, an oppressive political situation, and unemployment. Many young people were leaving or wanted to leave the country.

Thérèse's arrival was like the good Lord's gaze on our pain and suffering. Lebanon had experienced the coming of this spouse of Christ and sensed that holiness is the source of true happiness.

Christians and Muslims found each other side by side near Thérèse in many places. People waited for the reliquary for more than four hours in Kfar Remen, a Shiite region. Those who carried the reliquary paused between the mosque and the El Husseiniya courtyard to signify the need for common life.

The residents in Kahlouniyeh, a Druze village, venerated the relics at 3:00 a.m. Together, we sang: "How do we get to Heaven without loving? Love the world as God loves you."

Thérèse accompanied the Lebanese people in their joys and sorrows in the cities and villages. She forgot no one. She touched men and women, big people and small ones, the rich and the poor. She was present at infant Baptisms, at more than ten marriages, at monastic professions, at ordinations, at three burials, and among prisoners in Roumieh. She visited young people who were suffering from alcoholism. She went to five public and private hospitals for the Em El Nour organization.

The children and young people came together to honor her by singing. One meeting of young people brought together sixteen hundred of them.

Some famous male and female singers sang Thérèse's poetry in Arabic and songs in her honor.

We estimated that 1.5 million Lebanese people visited the reliquary.

Iraq (November 20–December 26, 2002)

Egypt's Catholic bishops had requested that the relics come to their country.[180] At the same time, Msgr. Jean Sleiman, a Lebanese Carmelite who became the archbishop of Baghdad of the Latin people in November 2000, and his brother bishops ardently wished that Thérèse's relics could come to Iraq. Msgr. Sleiman contacted Lisieux on February 25, 2002: "Iraq needs Thérèse."

We needed to find possible time slots in this internationally difficult situation. But once again, the difficulties were ironed out. Egypt's bishops withdrew their request on July 24. The scheduled dates did not suit them. Msgr. Sleiman stepped into the breach and undertook all the official procedures for the visit. He planned to come himself to greet the reliquary, which rode in a car to Beirut through Syria.

But Joseph Rouphaël, the "JR" airline company's director, offered to fly the plane carrying the reliquary from Beirut to Baghdad. There were around twenty seats for the guides, including Msgr. Sleiman,

[180] We know the importance, for instance, of the Carmelite church in Shubrā. It's dedicated to Thérèse of Lisieux, and many Muslims go to venerate her there. They have benefited from several miracles of healing. Construction was initiated in 1932 and finished in 1942.

Msgr. Tanios El Khoury — the Maronite bishop of Sidon — and some Carmelite and Mariamite fathers. Roundtrip airline connections between Lebanon and Iraq are no longer common. A special flight called "Thérèse One" was organized for Thérèse.

Iraq occupies 167,568 square miles and has a population of 21 million residents. About a million of those residents are Christians. This includes 80 percent who are Catholic or Orthodox Chaldeans, with seventeen Catholic bishops, five of whom are in Baghdad. The difficult situation has caused many Christians to emigrate.

It had not been predicted that the relics would arrive at Baghdad Airport the same day as the disarmament inspectors who were delegated by the UN — Wednesday, November 20. Because of that, world television networks were on the premises and filmed the event.

It must be said that in France, the travels of Thérèse's relics into twenty-four countries since 1994 had hardly, up until now, attracted the attention of the media — including the Catholic media. But suddenly Thérèse arrived in Iraq! All eyes were set on Baghdad. People waited for the inspectors, and she was the one who landed! Journalist Patrick Poivre d'Arvor commented on the images on the eight o'clock TF1 news. The reliquary was carried under Saddam Hussein's portrait in the middle of a reverential crowd of about three hundred people.

Fr. Ghadir, an Iraqi Carmelite, declared: "We're really expecting her to help us be more peaceful. We're going to pray to her a lot in order for peace to reign here and for the embargo to be lifted."

We visited the Latin Cathedral of St. Joseph in Baghdad, where Thérèse was greeted as a messenger of peace. The Mass united the apostolic nuncio, Msgr. Fernando Filoni, the French and Polish ambassadors, and the leader of the United Nations Development Program. Msgr. Sleiman saw a sign of the times in this visit, which was to help those who had lost hope to become more hopeful.

The Muslim colonel who provided security declared: "It's a wedding feast!"

The prayers were oriented toward peace and all Christians joined forces in praying for peace.

Nobody could ignore that St. Thérèse's relics were in Iraq. The newspapers spread the word to the television stations — each in its own way: *Ouest-France*, the *Tablet*, the *Catholic Herald*, *France Catholique*, the *Michigan Catholic*, the *Washington Post*, and the *Canard enchaîné* (December 11, 2002) which ran the headline "Catholic Baghdad." The Associated Press got involved in this. LBCI, which had followed Thérèse in Lebanon every day for seventy-seven days, made a long report on the arrival in Baghdad. The famous Lebanese newspaper *An-Nahar*, whose correspondent was in the private jet, published a long article on the same subject.

The relics were venerated in twenty-eight Baghdad churches and chapels; two main churches in Basra, to the south; four churches in Mosul, to the north; and fifteen villages in the province of Nineveh. All the rites wanted to welcome Thérèse and pray to her.

The relics were in the Syrian Catholic Church in Basra (1.5 million residents) on November 23 after they arrived in the Carmelite church.[181] We also saw Catholic and Orthodox Syrians, Catholic and Orthodox Armenians, some Assyrians, and various Evangelicals visit the reliquary — not counting non-Christians. Churches everywhere stayed open at night for prayer vigils. A new Jordanian parish priest greeted Thérèse in the Melkite Greek Catholic Church.

The trip in the north reached its peak in Qaraqosh (a Christian city with a Syrian Catholic majority of twenty-five thousand residents). The

[181] The French Carmelites have been on a mission in Iraq since the seventeenth century. But they left Basra several years ago. Their church in Baghdad was harmed by the coalition's bombings in March 2003.

bishop had declared Thérèse to be a "citizen" and the third patron of this city that boasts the Immaculate Conception and St. Behnam, an Eastern martyr, as protectors. In a highly symbolic gesture, a woman offered Thérèse a woven shawl similar to the ones traditionally worn by Christians in the area. It was unfolded during the public jubilation and is now in Lisieux.

Msgr. Atamian, the Armenian Catholic patriarchal vicar, celebrated Mass in the Armenian cathedral on the 28th. Mass was celebrated on the 29th and 30th among Baghdad's Syrian Catholics. The numbers of visitors remained high. People also listened to lectures, watched films about Thérèse, and prayed in silence.

After passing through the interreligious major seminary, the reliquary visited the "Daughters of Mary, the Mother of Hope" kindergarten. Because of the shrine's width, the front door had to be dismantled and the frames had to be sawed! Then there was a meeting with Mother Teresa's community, who take care of handicapped children, and a stop at Baghdad's main hospital.

Christmas celebrated with Thérèse at the Latin Cathedral of St. Joseph in Baghdad. The reliquary would return to Lisieux on December 26, 2002.

At the end of these thirty-seven days, Msgr. Emmanuel-Karim Delly, auxiliary bishop of the Chaldeans' Babylon Patriarchate, stressed that Thérèse's arrival

> fostered a great religious enthusiasm in Iraq's Christian community. It was an event that awakened our courage in this difficult time in our history. Iraq's Christian community very devotedly responded to this blessing. The churches were filled with faithful people. The parishes insisted that the competent authorities would ensure that the relics would be worthily welcomed, if only for a day. Thus, we experienced a moment

of spiritual relaxation. We prayed, in particular, for peace, while the whole Iraqi church organized its day of fasting and prayer for this intention.

Msgr. Jean Sleiman wrote: "Thérèse, a Word of God for Iraq":

Many Iraqis shared their sufferings with St. Thérèse. It was obvious that, to them, the relics weren't merely an object to be venerated. They signified the presence of a loved one and a trustworthy person you could share everything with and entrust everything to.

The faithful, from the north to the south, who were serious but quickly became serene, poured the pangs in their own hearts into Thérèse's heart.

It was striking to see so many young people among the crowds who prayed to St. Thérèse in Iraq. They seemed to be charmed by the young contemplative woman and were available for the preparations. There were a lot of them at the celebrations, and they always wanted to know more. These were young people who often helped to carry the reliquary. They organized the programs and ensured that the atmosphere was orderly and secure. They also sang, kept watch, danced, and worked. The pastor in one of Baghdad's parishes was opposed to receiving the relics, as he would be away at the time. The young people of the parish arranged to have them during their pastor's absence; this was done in agreement with the pastor's replacement. But the pastor gave in to his young parishioners' desire and changed his plans so he could be there.

We can say for certain that Thérèse evangelized the young people in Iraq in a special way, not only because she died when she was young but because she had managed to become extremely wise in her short life. The young people in Iraq wonder about the present, which is dominated by threats and shortages. They had been feeling deprived in the face of a future that's more than uncertain, and they discovered the wisdom of love and youthful hope in the young Carmelite. The teacher teaches them that their Christian identity lets them confront every situation. She shows them how uncertainties and suffering can be transfigured by love and how the precarious and fleeting moment can be inhabited by eternity. Thérèse reveals to them in concrete terms that their love for a homeland that's humiliated today and resists the wear and tear of these bad times through their fidelity to their Christian vocations renews the presence of Christ Himself and enables it to take root.

Thérèse wanted to console the women who were grieving over the tragic disappearance of beloved husbands or children and suffering over the sicknesses caused by wars and other misfortunes. But she spoke, above all, to the many young people in Iraq's churches who couldn't easily find a life companion because of the tragic imbalance between young men and young women. This was caused by armed conflicts and emigration. Thérèse offered them her spiritual motherhood as a model to give meaning to their lives. She encouraged them to find their place in the Church.

The world thought this trip to Iraq was very interesting. News about the relics was sent via e-mail to 117 sites in North America where the relics had been. Prayer vigils for peace were organized. These sites were apprised of the peace vigils that were being organized. E-mails from Ireland, the United States, Canada, Mexico, French Polynesia, Argentina, Luxembourg, and Switzerland came to Lisieux. A huge world prayer chain for peace was created. France's Christian radio stations and the KTO network broadcast the news.

Indian Ocean in Réunion (January 11–February 14, 2003)

The transition between the Middle East and the Indian Ocean was to be brief. The traveling reliquary stayed only a few days in Lisieux after returning from Iraq. The Episcopal Conference of the Indian Ocean (Réunion, Mauritius, Seychelles, and Madagascar), which is under the chairmanship of Msgr. Gilbert Aubry, who is from Réunion, had asked for the relics for several months.

It took a long time to reach this island, which has 720,000 residents and is in the middle of the ocean. It's beyond the Atlantic and Pacific Oceans and has beautiful seascapes and mountainous landscapes.

Msgr. Bernard Lagoutte, the pilgrimage's rector, would accompany the reliquary for the first few days. Fr. Louis Yon, Lisieux's chaplain, had stayed to prepare for Thérèse's arrival.

Msgr. Aubry welcomed Thérèse at the Gillot Airport[182] on Sunday, January 12, 2003, with these words:

> Thérèse Martin, Thérèse of the Child Jesus and the Holy Face, as the bishop of Réunion, I'm happy to greet you in our

[182] Now called Roland Garros Airport.

diocese and our island. Yes, welcome to our place! Our place is also your place.

You know us better than we know ourselves. You know we're children of this earth and the whole world. Originally, we learned to write our history on this desert island together. This was done through violence and slavery, emancipation, abolition, and the release of our strength to be reconciled and to love.

Yes, we know it, and you know it better than we do. We're white, black, and yellow. We're made up of all colors. We're a rainbow people, and the same blood flows in our veins. It's the blood of the life that comes from God and makes us brothers and sisters of Jesus Christ.

Thérèse of the Child Jesus and the Holy Face — we belong to the same family. You know us and love us. We'll tell you about our joys and sorrow, family tragedies, economic worries, and concerns about war and peace in the world. We'll tell you about the secrets that we don't express. You'll gather the smiles and tears on our faces to offer them to the Father of all mercies. We'll tell you about our hearts, and that will get us closer to you, to God, and to each other. Your holiness will help us grow in holiness. Help us put the power of love into our daily actions, and make our island a sacrament of peace in the heart of humanity for the share that's ours. May glory be given to the Father, the Son, and the Holy Spirit forever and ever through you and with us.

Parish facilitation groups made preparations everywhere. A sixty-eight-page pilgrim's booklet titled *Follow Christ with Thérèse* was written to provide information, prayers, and songs for community singing. The island's grand tour could start.

The relics visited the Avirons Carmel, on the Indian Ocean (January 13 and 14). We can imagine the Carmelites' joy in receiving their sister, who was surrounded by shimmering colors in a very intense heat.

Then we went to L'Étang-Salé, Le Tampon, the Holy Land, the Plaine des Cafres ... Let's stop there because we'd have to cite ever place — about thirty stops. I should also mention the visit to the Prison du Port's inmates on February 1.

We can give only a few newsflashes. Crowds came to churches in the East — St. Anne, St. Rose, St. Benedict, and St. Andre. Almost two thousand of the faithful walked to Beaulieu in Bethlehem in stifling heat.

The island is made up of high mountains and impressive coves. (The Snow Peak is 1.9 miles high!) The reliquary could go to the top of Mafate only by helicopter. A round of helicopters was organized so that the 180 people from Mafate could come to La Nouvelle. A woman named Claudine said: "I would never have been able to go to Lisieux, France. So when the Church was good enough to bring [the reliquary] here, I couldn't miss it." Someone else said: "The reliquary will never return to Mafate but will forever remain in our hearts." Many people came from far away.

There were some very lively discussions in the letters from readers of Réunion's newspapers. On January 16, 2003, *Le Quotidien* ran this headline: "Relics: Fetishism." One Protestant offered his extremely negative point of view on the cult of relics. Some readers responded with what they saw and experienced with the crowds from Réunion.

This was an opportunity to look differently at the communion of saints, the mystery of death and resurrection, and the meaning of the body and its destiny.

Msgr. Gilbert Aubry wrote a brief article on "The Body and the Person: Life Eternal":

The Ramses II mummy came to Paris to spruce itself up. It was greeted with the honors that are due to a head of state. Why? The ashes of Victor Schoelcher, Jean Moulin, and Alexandre Dumas were brought to the Panthéon in Paris. This was obviously not about worshipping the dust of their decomposed bodies. It was about honoring these great figures of the nation who were presented as examples to imitate in such-and-such a field. People said that "they were entering the Panthéon." Why?

There's a basic connection between the body and the person. The body is the visible expression of the substance of the person who brings the substance to life and escapes it as a spiritual being. To venerate the ashes of someone or his remains is to acknowledge that this person's influence doesn't end with death. He could have done something exemplary — in space and in time — thanks to his physical body that was animated by a spiritual breath. Everyone then reflects on the meaning of his own life.

When the Church venerates the saints' relics, it's not about "locking oneself up" in a spiritual hall of fame. In faith, we proclaim that these people are more alive than we are in our earthly condition. Our relationship to the saints who proceeded us can be reinforced through the veneration of their relics. This is already the case with the deceased in our own families. Likewise, the saints who maintain a unique relationship with what was the substance of their bodies on earth can then pay particular attention to our requests in the presence of their relics.

This dual relationship of the living with the dead and the dead with the living grows in the communion of saints around Jesus Christ and in Him who gathers us together in the life of

> God our Father. Human life is much more concentrated in the Spirit's breath than in what appears to our eyes of flesh. It's eternal. Life doesn't stop with death. We have only one and the same life, now and after death. It's experienced in a different way after the passage "on the other shore" of life. Now, it's through the power of love that we're called to succeed in our eternal life. Such is Thérèse of Lisieux's message (January 8, 2003).

We're stopping our report here, but Thérèse's journey was to continue in the Indian Ocean — to Madagascar and Mauritius.

Then there would be another visit in Italy from May 3 to June 9, 2003 — to Venice, Terni, Monza, Bergamo, Treviso, Brescia, Trento, Trieste ...

The reliquary would go to Malta from July 20 to August 7. It would cross Spain in the last three months of 2003. This is where Thérèse would connect with her mother, St. Teresa of Jesus (of Ávila), and her father, St. John of the Cross.

A new adventure would start in 2004. Thérèse was going to Africa, the fifth continent. Benin would be the first country she'd visit, from January 15 to April 15.

God only knows what will be next and how much time this earthly journey will last. The requests for the reliquary continue to arrive in Lisieux. They are now being extended to 2005.

So far, St. Thérèse's words are being put to the test now that she has visited twenty-seven countries in four continents:

She was shown a photograph of Joan of Arc in her prison.[183] "The saints also encourage me in my prison. They tell me: As long as you are

[183] This is her own picture that her Sr. Geneviève (her own sister, Céline Martin) took when Thérèse played the role of Joan of Arc in the play she had composed.

in chains, you cannot fulfill your mission. But later, after your death, it will be the time of your works and conquests."[184]

Whether she's called "little Thérèse," "the Little Flower," "Teresinha," or "Teresita," depending on the country, she continues to keep her promises.

To be continued . . .

[184] St. Thérèse of Lisieux, *Yellow Notebook,* August 10, 4, 144.

Some Pastoral Questions

Pastoral discernment is needed to sustain and support popular piety and, if necessary, to purify and correct the religious sense which underlies these devotions so that the faithful may advance in knowledge of the mystery of Christ (cf. John Paul II, CT 54). At its core the piety of the people is a storehouse of values that offers answers of Christian wisdom to the great questions of life.

—CCC 1676

The holy Patroness of the missions is from your region—from Lisieux. Thérèse of the Child Jesus and the Holy Face has made her missionary fervor shine in the world. Her spiritual teaching, which is radiantly simple, continues to touch the faithful from all conditions and cultures.

—John Paul II to the French bishops in the apostolic region of the West, Ad limina visit, February 1992

Having reported on these events, which, so far, have covered about twenty-seven countries, it seems possible and desirable to emphasize a few consistent patterns. These are all the more interesting as they can be found in very different people, civilizations, and societies, as we've already seen.

I'm going to try to gather these consistent patterns, which nobody could have imagined, in order to ask some pastoral questions about "popular devotion" at the beginning of the twenty-first century.

We could think that, in what is called "postmodernity," the human mind, which is saturated with rationalism, will soon be freed of all beliefs, superstition, and magic in an era of widespread secularization that has the most specialized techniques and technology.

At the end of the nineteenth century, our grandfathers already hoped that if they drove out obscurantism, progress would bring permanent peace and happiness to humanity. It would be founded upon reason.

So today, sects of all kinds are abounding in the world, and they are making their followers swallow the most extraordinary stories. These followers include engineers, doctors, and lawyers. It's as if these people, who are highly rational in their jobs, lose all common sense by discovering a certain "spiritual world" in the New Age style.[185]

We know that thousands of "fortune-tellers," "gurus," "sorcerers," and "therapists" of all kinds are found everywhere. They are well off and promise healings, wealth, joy, and happiness. The most serious newspapers and weekly magazines carry pages of advertising for these charlatans.

Moreover, a Catholic priest pointed this out in a rather provocative catchphrase: "Our churches are empty. Our chapels are full." Luckily, this isn't totally accurate, but it's worth thinking about this observation.

[185] See Pontifical Council for Culture and Pontifical Council for Interreligious Dialogue, *Jesus Christ, the Bearer of the Water of Life: A Christian Reflection on the "New Age"* (February 3, 2003), https://www.vatican.va/roman_curia/pontifical_councils/interelg/documents/rc_pc_interelg_doc_20030203_new-age_en.html.

Whereas, in a church, the main altar — the altar of the Eucharistic sacrifice — focuses on Christ, the side chapels are often dedicated to saints. It's possible that some people prefer to talk to the saints rather than to God.

The fact remains that all these saints surround Christ and live only with Him and for Him. Therefore, we must evangelize about this Faith and these popular beliefs and devotions without scorning them, looking down on them, rejecting them, or condemning them. In this brief context, I've assembled the consistent patterns of the travels of St. Thérèse's relics in the world in order to list them and draw a few pastoral insights from them. I want to do this without forgetting that, in part 3, I cited some significant summaries from episcopal conferences of bishops, priests, lay organizations, journalists, and so forth.

The first observation is about the crowds. After all, the relics' arrival in any country, diocese, or sanctuary could have attracted hardly anybody. Yet in nine years and in so many countries, the turnout was never low. Of course, in the heart of Siberia, fewer than 1 percent of Catholics came, but we couldn't hope for crowds in that region.

This phenomenon was often noted. *Before* the relics' arrival, there was a certain skepticism, a fear of failure, and the fateful phrase "Nobody will come."

Afterward, people were astonished at the crowds, which surpassed all expectations. The preceding anxious phrase was transformed into "There are too many people. What will we do?"

We've given some rough figures about each country. At the moment, the total number of people who have traveled to see the reliquary exceeds several dozen million.

What struck the bishops, priests, volunteer witnesses, and others everywhere?

Thérèse attracted Catholics who don't usually come to church or who no longer do so.

I recall the astonishment of a priest from Arlon, Belgium, who told me, while the relics stopped in his church on a weekday: "There are more people here than at Christmas!"

Likewise, the rector of St. Joseph Oratory in Montreal, Canada, noted that the crowd equaled or even surpassed the one that came for the feast of St. André Bessette.

People among these crowds returned to the Faith, rediscovered prayer, and attended services, including Mass.

Here's a major factor. We noticed that people really wanted to receive the sacrament of Reconciliation. We know that Reconciliation has been one of the sacraments most affected by the crisis of faith. Yet people in the Netherlands, Canada, France, and the United States rushed to find confessors, who themselves were amazed by the request. They listened to penitents who hadn't gone to Confession in ten, twenty, thirty, or even sixty years!

What does this mean? We know, for example, that there were longs lines for Confession in pilgrimage sites in the provinces (Lourdes, Lisieux, La Salette, Ars), in Paris (Saint-Louis d'Antin, Notre-Dame, Our Lady of Victories, the rue du Bac), and so forth.

We were surprised to note the extent of the response when people were invited to go to Confession.[186] And let's recall the thousands of young people who went to Confession during the various World Youth Days in Paris, Rome, and Toronto. In these responses, shouldn't we see a call to foster the sacrament of Reconciliation with new acts of faith?[187]

Speaking of the sacraments, let's not forget that Anointing of the Sick was widely offered in the relics' presence in various countries and that

[186] Eleven hundred people were drawn to a day of the sacrament of Reconciliation in the Diocese of Luçon. Forty-seven priests heard nine hundred confessions.

[187] See John Paul II, *Letter to Priests* (Holy Thursday 2002).

thousands of Masses were celebrated. But we must also remember all that was done during those years to facilitate prayer and personal devotions:

- the personal veneration of the relics, silent personal prayer, and the recitation of the Rosary
- prayer vigils and prayer throughout the night
- teenage processions and the processions of the relics
- visits to prison (at least twenty-five in ten countries)
- visits to the sick, the disabled, and the mentally ill in hospitals and clinics

Wherever people prepared for the relics' arrival (via booklets, journals, posters, pictures, songs, plays, concerts, exhibitions, conferences, novenas, meditations, and so forth), the fruits of the relics' visit were all the more numerous. We must stress the importance of the teachings that were given on these occasions. These included the homilies of bishops and priests, and the conferences of Theresian specialists who traveled across the country or were invited to other countries. Almost all the subjects in Thérèse's doctrinal teachings were covered: the Trinity, Christology, ecclesiology, Mariology, the missions, unbelief, the Eucharist, contemplative prayer, fraternal and communal life, suffering, sickness, the end times, the family, theological virtues, Thérèse and the priests, the little way, the Offering to Merciful Love, the commentaries and writings, and so on.

We often found booths that presented her works in the country's language, Theresian books, and pictures, along with exhibitions on her life and message. This was a unique opportunity to read *Story of a Soul* and discover the doctrinal and spiritual richness of Thérèse's poetry. A certain number, which were translated, were set to music and sung by soloists, choirs, and orchestras.

I also want to emphasize the profound influence of the photographs that her sister Céline took. Seen on posters or pictures, Thérèse's face truly "speaks." From this look, some people wondered: "Who is this person looking at me like this?" This visual observation inspired some to discover Thérèse in depth and to read her writings.

The crowds' attitude also really struck the witnesses and observers. We feared — at least in certain countries — some ugly demonstrations, stampedes, and mishaps.

But what we experienced, of course, were many processions with shimmering colors, accompanied by music, the release of balloons, fireworks, shouts of joy, showers of roses from planes and helicopters, and more. We found this in Brazil, the Philippines, the Pacific Ocean region, Lebanon, and other places. During the veneration of the relics in churches, cathedrals, chapels, and sanctuaries, there was calmness, enthusiasm, patience, silent prayer, and the presence of children, the sick, and the disabled. Nobody observed any mishaps, stampedes, hysterical scenes, or even accidents that would have had serious consequences.[188] This serenity over ten years and over thousands of miles in the presence of millions of people is worth noting.

Only God can know what's going on in the lives and especially in the hearts of the people of all ages and social conditions and from so many countries who came to see Thérèse. We noted some physical healings, conversions, apparitions, and mysterious fragrances.[189] All this must be discerned with serious investigations, under the bishops' watchful eyes. But everything that happens in people's hearts — the intimate blessings, the spiritual favors, the vocations that have emerged and will mature in only a few years, and the blessings of reconciliation and unity — all this is private. That's the way it is. Let's respect "the King's secrets" (see Tob. 12:7).

[188] I noted a helicopter crash with no casualties in the Philippines and a grenade that was launched into the crowd that didn't explode.

[189] These scents of flowers have been one of Thérèse's specialties since 1898.

The most important thing is obviously the discovery or deepening of Jesus' merciful love, which Thérèse reveals in her own way. It's the evangelical path that Christ traces — the revelation of God's love for everyone.

This is Thérèse's mission, which she indicated before she died: "My mission is about to begin, my mission of making God loved as I love Him, of giving my little way to souls."[190] Here's the main point; everything else is subordinate to it. The miracle leads to spiritual conversions. We've given a few examples in part 1.

But the consequences of the relics' visit in a country aren't limited to "devotion" in the Pauline sense — that is to say, for the good of the city. We also noticed some "political" consequences. We saw communities that are usually separated gather together around Thérèse — Inuits and white people in the great Canadian North, Catholics and Protestants in Ireland, Christians and Muslims in Lebanon and Iraq, rivals in Bosnia-Herzegovina, Catholics and Orthodox people in Russia, Evangelicals and Catholics in the Pacific Ocean region, and so forth.

The relics' presence encouraged an understanding that led to hope in countries that were suffering and were eager for peace.

In the context of a good-natured mockery of "popular devotion," a Canadian journalist ran this headline: "A Flash in the Pan?" This was possible in some places. But we've noted that what has stayed in the depths of people's hearts can't be counted by any statistics or sociological investigation.

Moreover, we didn't see any media campaigns that were taking advantage of this event to criticize "Catholic obscurantism." On the contrary, many television networks and newspapers commonly came together with positive commentaries — even enthusiastic ones.

[190] St. Thérèse of Lisieux, *Yellow Notebook,* July 17, 102.

"A flash in the pan?" No, not when St. Thérèse chapels and churches were built or restored after her visit. And not when squares, streets, and hospices were dedicated to her, when a foundation was created in the Philippines to build her a sanctuary and study her spirituality, and when Theresian prayer groups and study groups gathered in her name to know her better. Let's not forget about the impact after her tour: the pilgrimages in Lisieux to thank her and discover the places where she had lived.

I myself have evolved regarding this issue of "popular religion." While I was a student at the Sorbonne in the 1950s and was happily discovering academic treasures, I could only look arrogantly at elderly ladies reciting their Rosary and smile condescendingly at the "good people" who lit candles in front of St. Thérèse's statue. I was not interested in going into the Carmel in Lisieux while I was spending my vacation in that city. I knew Thérèse only through her syrupy statues.

These were youthful sins. The priestly experience of a lifetime teaches you to look differently at the lame, the blind, the lepers rushing over to Jesus of Nazareth in order to be healed, the widow offering all she had in the Temple's treasury, the hemorrhaging woman who dared to touch the hem of the Master's robe, the Syrophoenician woman who looked for the crumbs that were falling from the table, some Jews, and the actions of Nicodemus, Zacchaeus, and others.

I've seen crowds coming to Lisieux for more than fifteen years. I no longer sneer. We, of course, have to "evangelize about popular piety," but at the same time, we must let ourselves be evangelized by the poor. They know a lot about life, suffering, death, prayer, and God.

Now, from this experience, I think I know what "popular piety" is. It's the religion of the people of God, as the Second Vatican Council defines it.

The people of God are made up of a variety of those who are baptized. They include children, adults, the elderly, the sick and the healthy, the poor and the rich, the illiterate and the intellectual, manual laborers, technicians, priests, and laypeople — in short, everyone.

The people of God include the Parisian cab driver who didn't make me pay for my trip because he subscribed to *Thérèse de Lisieux*. They also include the man carrying an attaché case who kneeled in front of the reliquary in Paris's Holy Trinity Church every morning around 7:30. I asked the pastor if he knew him: "Yes," he replied. "He's a professor at the Sorbonne. He prays every day for his daughter who has leukemia."

The people of God also include Georges, who is HIV positive and suddenly stopped drinking under Thérèse's influence. The people of God also include a Parisian psychoanalyst who told me that when things weren't going well, he lit a candle on St. Thérèse's altar in Our Lady of Victories Church, hoping that nobody would recognize him.

We deplore the decrease in religious practice, the lower attendance in catechism classes, and the drop in men's and women's vocations. But suddenly, crowds came around a saint's reliquary. Bishop Christophe Dufour rallied around the monstrances to honor the local saints in the Diocese of Limoges. These reliquaries, which are seven centuries old, attracted crowds and, therefore, the media. Msgr. Léon Soulier, the diocesan bishop, wrote in a pastoral letter in 1995: "The saints are God's friends.... They are also our friends. They lived with us. They stay close to us. They made the Gospel emerge and grow in our country. They watched over this church."

Msgr. Dufour wrote in his 2002 pastoral letter *All Are Called to Holiness*: "May the veneration of the relics be a time of joy for all those who will be experiencing them. May they motivate the solidarity of all people. May they manifest our common destiny beyond the ruptures that fracture our country."

The Diocese of Limoges is only one example among others. St. Anthony of Padua's relics circulated in 174 Italian cities and in 94 cities in other European and American countries. Eight to ten million pilgrims visited his basilica for the eighth centenary of his birth. One of the many conferences dedicated to him was "To Let Yourself Be Evangelized by Popular Devotion" (February 1995).[191]

Cardinal Frédéric Etsou, the archbishop of Kinshasa and president of the Episcopal Conference of the Democratic Republic of the Congo, had St. Margaret Mary's relics brought over in order to help his people who were afflicted by suffering.[192]

I've never said or written that the cult of relics was going to become a fundamental element of the new evangelization so dear to John Paul II and our Church. I'm simply saying that Christianity is the religion of the Incarnation and of the Word made flesh, and that our whole being must be evangelized, saved, and transfigured. We believe that the resurrection of our bodies will follow Jesus Christ's Resurrection.

I'm saying that the saints are God's family and that the theology of the saints is the path to the experiential knowledge of God and the Holy Trinity and that the communion of saints is an indissoluble link between the heavenly Church and the Church on earth.[193]

I'm saying that the fact that such a "popular" saint who is as all-encompassing as Thérèse of the Child Jesus and the Holy Face would be proclaimed a Doctor is a very strong sign that was given to our world. What is scientific isn't opposed to what is popular. This miracle-worker is both a great theologian and a universal missionary.

Throughout this book, I've provided some texts of episcopal conferences that witnessed the visit of Thérèse's relics in their dioceses. They show that this was a true evangelical mission that bore much fruit.

[191] *Le Messager de saint Antoine*, no. 2 (February 1996).

[192] *Il est vivant*, no. 181.

[193] See Second Vatican Council, Dogmatic Constitution on the Church *Lumen Gentium* (November 21, 1964), no. 51.

Here, I'm adding the text of a French bishop, Msgr. Lucien Fruchaud, of the Diocese of Saint-Brieuc and Tréguier, who clearly and simply told us about his own evolution. The relics were received in his diocese from December 31, 2001, to January 21, 2002.

Thérèse and the Bishop

Frequently reading and meditating on the writings of St. Teresa of Ávila and St. John of the Cross is a deep need and a vital spiritual rejuvenation for me. Thérèse of the Child Jesus led me to these two pillars of Carmelite spirituality. Having read *Story of a Soul,* I tried to understand from what sources Thérèse had drawn to achieve such a relationship with the Lord and such a great love for the Church. I've often thanked Thérèse for having opened for me the pages of *The Way of Perfection* and *The Interior Castle* by Teresa of Ávila and *Ascent of Mount Carmel, Dark Night of the Soul,* and *A Spiritual Canticle of the Soul* by John of the Cross. Just as John the Baptist had invited his disciples to leave him in order to follow Christ after he baptized Jesus in the waters of the Jordan, Thérèse had shown me a path and had faded away before those she had invited me to discover.

She had to become a Doctor in order for me to dive back into her writings and rediscover the depth of her spirituality and the topical nature of her "little way of love." I heard Pope John Paul II proclaim her a Doctor of the Church in St. Peter's Square in Rome on Sunday, October 19, 1997. I was very close to the great reliquary that was lifted up in the midst of a huge bouquet of roses. I sensed that Thérèse had opened a new way for me.

Today, I know that on that day, she affected me more deeply than I could see.

I understood this when some of the diocesan priests offered to have St. Thérèse of the Child Jesus and the Holy Face's great reliquary come to the Diocese of Saint-Brieuc and Tréguier. I felt compelled to refuse this at first for many reasons. How would the diocesan Christians react? Who would take care of all this? We had so many other things to do. How would the media react? Would we be capable of greeting her, listening to her, and allowing ourselves to be converted? But while these questions preoccupied me, I heard the call and understood the hint that Thérèse spoke to me. She had a message to deliver to the whole diocese and to me.

I saw my worries melt like snow in the sun. The dates were easily set, the parishes and reception centers were effortlessly reserved, and the responsibilities were enthusiastically shared. The specific times for different groups — the times for prayer, adoration, celebrations, and conferences — fit into a full program. The twenty-one days that were reserved were too brief to accommodate all that was wished for. The press and the radio and television networks provided an impressive media coverage.

Throughout her diocesan travels, Thérèse knew how to deliver her message to children, young people, laypeople of all ages and conditions, consecrated people, priests, and sick people. Between twenty and twenty-five thousand people came to meet her.

What really happened in the hearts of all these pilgrims? This is the secret of every one of them. It's the mystery of the relationship between man and God. Why did so many men and women come to entrust themselves to Thérèse? Why were they thirsty to hear her message? The subsequent abundant mail bore witness to a path of conversion that many people experienced. They spoke of a truly rediscovered inner peace, a deep renewed faith, an unexpected discovery of the Church, renewed commitments to the service of others, strengthened vocations, and decisive life choices. There were so many other divine blessings that I'm unaware of and will always be unaware of.

Weren't all these men and women of all ages whom I saw coming to meditate around the exposed reliquary, to spend a long time in silence, to listen to lectures, and to gather together to pray — weren't they all searching for wisdom, spirituality, and an intimate union with God? There, they expressed what the world most needs: to find spiritual wells. They felt that Thérèse could connect with crucial questions they bore in themselves through her message. They were waiting for her to open the doors of a gospel that would be a saving path for them. They were living in the midst of a depreciated standard and were assured that she would lead them to a life-giving place.

During the evening of the farewell celebration, she had just brought two thousand people together in the Marian center of Our Lady of Eternal Aid in Querrien in La Prénessaye. I let myself think about this. If I had allowed my doubts and fears to carry me away — if I had said no — I would have impeded the grace that was on many people's paths of conversion.

Today, even more than yesterday, I know that we have to give visible signs to this world and offer reception centers to hear questions about life and death and shed light on people's paths in order to enlighten them. We must take our brothers' and sisters' search for spirituality seriously. We have to open the Gospel's pages in front of them and for them. This is what Thérèse did during her pilgrimage in the diocese.

When the car that was carrying the great reliquary moved away, I saw myself on St. Peter's Square again the day Thérèse became a Doctor and was determined to reread her works. I was unaware that she was leading me on the path of a yes that was a blessing for the diocese.

May this blessing continue its path in everyone's hearts.[194]

I'm emphasizing that we were amazed at this spiritual adventure that unfolded before our eyes and will continue. We can't yet measure its impact. Only the future will tell us.

I think that our Church in France is going through another stage of its history, and nothing will be the same as before. But the gospel is likely to bear fruit there. It could be useful to witness the miracles that God is performing through His saints. Georges Bernanos was right in 1934: "Our Church is the Church of saints."[195]

In the spirit of the *Lettre des évêques aux catholiques de France, Proposer la foi dans la société actuelle* (Letter from the Bishops to French Catholics — offering faith in today's society), (Éditions du Cerf, 1996), we need to respond pastorally to a few questions:

Why this influx of people visiting this saint's relics? What do they expect from the Catholic Church? What do they have to tell us in their diversity? What can we do to listen to them, welcome them, and offer them faith in Jesus Christ, who died and rose from the dead?

To answer these questions practically within the reality of a welcoming and evangelizing pastoral ministry, much work must be done that will require the strength of all the different vocations and ministries.

"Popular religiosity is a starting point for a new evangelization. It contains precious elements of an authentic faith that tries to be purified and interiorized."[196]

[194] *Thérèse de Lisieux* 822 (May 2002): 17–18.

[195] *Jeanne, relapse et sainte* [Joan of Arc, a relapsed heretic and a saint].

[196] Cardinal Pironio, Third General Assembly of the Synod of Bishops, quoted in *La Documentation catholique* 2276 (September 2002): 786.

Paul VI had some strong words in *Evangelii Nuntiandi* (1975). They haven't aged a bit:

> Popular religiosity, of course, certainly has its limits. It is often subject to penetration by many distortions of religion and even superstitions. It frequently remains at the level of forms of worship not involving a true acceptance by faith. It can even lead to the creation of sects and endanger the true ecclesial community.
>
> But if it is well oriented, above all by a pedagogy of evangelization, it is rich in values. It manifests a thirst for God which only the simple and poor can know. It makes people capable of generosity and sacrifice even to the point of heroism, when it is a question of manifesting belief. It involves an acute awareness of profound attributes of God: fatherhood, providence, loving and constant presence. It engenders interior attitudes rarely observed to the same degree elsewhere: patience, the sense of the cross in daily life, detachment, openness to others, devotion. By reason of these aspects, we readily call it "popular piety" that is, religion of the people, rather than religiosity.
>
> Pastoral charity must dictate to all those whom the Lord has placed as leaders of the ecclesial communities the proper attitude in regard to this reality, which is at the same time so rich and so vulnerable. Above all one must be sensitive to it, know how to perceive its interior dimensions and undeniable values, be ready to help it to overcome its risks of deviation. When it is well oriented, this popular religiosity will be more and more for multitudes of our people a true encounter with God in Jesus Christ.[197]

[197] Pope Paul VI, apostolic exhortation *Evangelii Nuntiandi* (December 8, 1975), no. 48.

In many documents, John Paul II enlarged and deepened this path that Paul VI opened up. Here is one example among several others:

> A distinctive feature of America is an intense popular piety, deeply rooted in the various nations. It is found at all levels and in all sectors of society, and it has special importance as a place of encounter with Christ for all those who in poverty of spirit and humility of heart are sincerely searching for God (cf. Mt 11:25). This piety takes many forms: "Pilgrimages to shrines of Christ, of the Blessed Virgin and the Saints, prayer for the souls in purgatory, the use of sacramentals (water, oil, candles ...). These and other forms of popular piety are an opportunity for the faithful to encounter the living Christ." The Synod Fathers stressed the urgency of discovering the true spiritual values present in popular religiosity, so that, enriched by genuine Catholic doctrine, it might lead to a sincere conversion and a practical exercise of charity. If properly guided, popular piety also leads the faithful to a deeper sense of their membership of the Church, increasing the fervor of their attachment and thus offering an effective response to the challenges of today's secularization.[198]

We also know the emphasis this pope placed on the theology of the saints and the importance of their lives and teachings as a theological pillar.

In his apostolic letter *Novo Millenio Ineunte*, which opened up the new millennium, Pope John Paul II reminded people that when they contemplated Christ's suffering face:

> Faced with this mystery, we are greatly helped not only by theological investigation but also by that great heritage which

[198] Pope John Paul II, post-synodal apostolic exhortation *Ecclesia in America* (January 22, 1999), no. 16.

> is *the "lived theology" of the saints.* The saints offer us precious insights which enable us to understand more easily the intuition of faith, thanks to the special enlightenment which some of them have received from the Holy Spirit, or even through their personal experience of those terrible states of trial which the mystical tradition describes as the "dark night."[199]

The case of St. Thérèse of the Child Jesus and the Holy Face deserves our attention because it unites the popular universal devotion with the abundance of graces of all kinds that were granted on the five continents for more than a century. These include her miracles (Thérèse the miracle-worker), her doctrine's rigor, depth, and eminence (Thérèse the Doctor of the Church), and her universal mission that reached everyone (Thérèse the missionary). This has occurred specifically for ten years through her relics' travels.

It's not a coincidence that the bishops ended their letter to the Catholics in France in 1996 in this way:

> The saints are the living witnesses in our history of what God gives to the Church — sometimes in unexpected ways — in order to renew the depth of its faith and the momentum of its mission.
>
> This year, when we're celebrating St. Thérèse of the Child Jesus' centenary, we recognize in the young Carmelite of Lisieux's life and death the relationship that can be established between the depth of faith that's experienced to the end and the participation in the world's Christian mission. For Thérèse

[199] Pope John Paul II, apostolic letter *Novo Millenio Ineunte* (January 6, 2001), no. 27. Right afterward, the pope illustrated this with quotations from two female Doctors of the Church: St. Catherine of Siena and St. Thérèse of Lisieux.

became the "apostle of the apostles" and missionaries' moral support by totally offering herself to the Heavenly Father's merciful Love.

St. Thérèse's astonishing vocation was recognized by another woman from our country: Madeleine Delbrêl, who experienced the struggle of the Christian faith and mission within the working world. She wrote:

> Perhaps Thérèse of Lisieux, the patroness of every mission, was designated to experience a destiny at the beginning of this century when time and actions were greatly reduced, when heroism was indiscernible to those who saw it, and when the mission was limited to a few square meters. This was done in order to teach us that some effectiveness escapes the measurements of a clock, that the visibility of actions doesn't always encompass them, and that bold missions would join extensive ones in the depths of human masses. This is where man's mind questions the world and fluctuates between the mystery of a God who wants him to be small and stripped and the mystery of a world that wants him to be powerful and great.[200]

Thérèse Martin's contemplative and missionary vocation was rooted in this grace that she received in the Cathédrale Saint-Pierre de Lisieux in July 1887. She was a little over fourteen years old. This is how she talked about it:

> One Sunday, looking at a picture of Our Lord on the Cross, I was struck by the blood flowing from one of

[200] *Ville marxiste, terre de mission* [Marxist city, a mission land] (Paris: Éditions du Seuil, 1995), 147–148.

> the divine hands. I felt a great pang of sorrow when thinking this blood was falling to the ground without anyone's hastening to gather it up. I was resolved to remain in spirit at the foot of the Cross and to receive the divine dew. I understood I was then to pour it out upon souls. The cry of Jesus on the Cross sounded continually in my heart: "*I thirst!*" These words ignited within me an unknown and very living fire. I wanted my Beloved to drink and I felt myself consumed with a *thirst for souls.*[201]

When she was at the Carmel eight years later, she echoed this fundamental grace — this basic focus of her life as a Carmelite — in one of her poems, "Jésus, rappelle-toi" (Jesus, remember) (October 21, 1895). She showed that this thirst for love and this missionary fire had only grown:

> Remember the loving moan
> That escaped from your Heart on the cross.
> Ah! Jesus, that moan is impressed in my heart,
> And I share your burning thirst.
> The more I feel myself burning with your divine
> flames,
> The more I thirst to give you souls.
> With love's thirst
> I burn night and day,
> Remember.

Jesus said: "I came to cast fire upon the earth; and would that it were already kindled!" (Luke 12:49). Sr. Thérèse of the Child Jesus and

[201] Manuscript A 45v, in *Story of a Soul*, 99.

the Holy Face kept burning with this flame of love until September 30, 1897. Since she entered eternal life, she hasn't stopped communicating it to the world.

Lisieux, May 13, 2003

Bibliography

With regard to all of St. Thérèse of the Child Jesus and the Holy Face's writings and words, we can refer to:

Thérèse of Lisieux. *La Nouvelle Edition du Centenaire*. 8 vols. Paris: Éditions du Cerf, 1992.

Thérèse of Lisieux, *Oeuvres completes*. Paris: Éditions du Cerf, 1992.

Thérèse the Miracle-Maker

Il est vivant journal. Special edition on Thérèse. 5th ed. 1988.

Marie-Michel. *Nés pour aimer, Thérèse et les jeunes*. Le Sarment-Fayard, 1996.

Archives of the Carmel of Lisieux.

Thérèse the Doctor

Bro, Bernard, O.P. *Le Murmure et l'Ouragon. Une femme de genie*. Paris: Fayard, 1999.

———. *Thérèse de Lisieux, sa famille, son Dieu, son message*. Paris: Fayard, 1996.

Gaucher, Guy. *Une "petite voie" qui conduit au secret de l'existence*. Parole et Silence, 1999.

Huscenot, Jean. *Les Docteurs de l'Eglise*. Médiaspaul, 1997.

St. John Paul II. Apostolic letter *Divini Amoris Scientia* (October 19, 1997).

L'Apport théologique de sainte Thérèse de l'Enfant Jésus, docteur de l'Eglise. Éditions du Carmel, 2000.

Payne, Steven O.C.D. *St. Thérèse of Lisieux: Doctor of the Universal Church.* St. Paul, 2002.

Thérèse de Lisieux journal.

Teresa de Lisieux, Profeta de Dios, Doctora de la Iglesia. Salamanca, 1999.

Thérèse de l'Enfant-Jésus, docteur de l'Amour. Éditions du Carmel, Colloque de Venasque, 1990.

Thérèse et ses théologiens. Saint-Paul–Éditions du Carmel, 1998.

Thérèse au milieu des docteurs. Éditions du Carmel, 1997.

Teresa di Lisieux. Novità et grandezza di un Dottorato. Rome: Teresianum, 2000.

Thérèse the Missionary

Archives of the Pilgrimage of Lisieux.

Haely, Audrey, and Eugene McCaffrey, O.C.D. *St. Thérèse in Ireland: Official Diary of the Irish Visit, April–July 2001.* Columbia, 2001.

"Incroyable Thérèse." *Feu et Lumière* 203 (February 2002): 24–50.

Mullan, Don. *A Gift of Roses, Memories of the Visit to Ireland of St. Thérèse.* Wolfhound Press, 2001.

A Shower of Roses for the USA. Collected by Karen Eliason. Edited by Fr. Donald Kinney O.C.D. St. Thérèse Relics Committee, December 12, 2000.

Thérèse de Lisieux journal, 1994–2003.

On Popular Religion

Congregation for Divine Worship and the Discipline of the Sacraments. *Directory on Popular Piety and the Liturgy* (December 2001).

About the Author

Guy Gaucher was the auxiliary bishop of Bayeux and Lisieux. He has published many books about St. Thérèse of Lisieux, including *The Story of a Life: St. Thérèse of Lisieux*. He directed the critical edition of the complete works of Thérèse, which made it possible for her to become a Doctor.

Sophia Institute

Sophia Institute is a nonprofit institution that seeks to nurture the spiritual, moral, and cultural life of souls and to spread the gospel of Christ in conformity with the authentic teachings of the Roman Catholic Church.

Sophia Institute Press fulfills this mission by offering translations, reprints, and new publications that afford readers a rich source of the enduring wisdom of mankind.

Sophia Institute also operates the popular online resource CatholicExchange.com. *Catholic Exchange* provides world news from a Catholic perspective as well as daily devotionals and articles that will help readers to grow in holiness and live a life consistent with the teachings of the Church.

In 2013, Sophia Institute launched Sophia Institute for Teachers to renew and rebuild Catholic culture through service to Catholic education. With the goal of nurturing the spiritual, moral, and cultural life of souls, and an abiding respect for the role and work of teachers, we strive to provide materials and programs that are at once enlightening to the mind and ennobling to the heart; faithful and complete, as well as useful and practical.

Sophia Institute gratefully recognizes the Solidarity Association for preserving and encouraging the growth of our apostolate over the course of many years. Without their generous and timely support, this book would not be in your hands.

www.SophiaInstitute.com
www.CatholicExchange.com
www.SophiaInstituteforTeachers.org